T0325160

Artificial Intelligence for Healthcare

Healthcare has recently seen numerous exciting applications of artificial intelligence, industrial engineering, and operations research. This book, designed to be accessible to a diverse audience, provides an overview of interdisciplinary research partnerships that leverage AI, IE, and OR to tackle societal and operational problems in healthcare. The topics are drawn from a wide variety of disciplines, ranging from optimizing the location of AEDs for cardiac arrests to data mining for facilitating patient flow through a hospital. These applications highlight how engineering has contributed to medical knowledge, health system operations, and behavioral health. Chapter authors include medical doctors, policy-makers, social scientists, and engineers. In these examples, researchers in public health, medicine, and social science as well as engineers will find a path to start interdisciplinary collaborations in health applications of AI/IE/OR.

SZE-CHUAN SUEN is an Assistant Professor in the Daniel J. Epstein Department of Industrial and Systems Engineering at the University of Southern California. She received her PhD in the department of Management Science and Engineering from Stanford University in 2016. Her research interests include developing applied mathematical models to identify epidemiological trends and evaluating health policies to support informed decision-making. Her work in health policy modeling draws from a variety of techniques, including simulation, dynamic systems modeling, Markov decision processes, cost-effectiveness analysis, and decision analysis. Her previous work has examined the optimal management of tuberculosis, HIV, and chronic diseases.

DAVID SCHEINKER is a Clinical Associate Professor of Pediatrics in the Stanford School of Medicine and the Executive Director of Systems Design and Collaborative Research at the Lucile Packard Children's Hospital Stanford. He is the Founder and Director of SURF Stanford Medicine (surf.stanford.edu), a group that brings together students and faculty from the university with physicians, nurses, and administrators from the hospitals to improve the quality of care using operations research methodology. His research focuses on applications of operations research in healthcare. Previously, he was a Joint Research Fellow at The MIT Sloan School of Management and Massachusetts General Hospital.

EVA ENNS is an Associate Professor in the Division of Health Policy and Management at the University of Minnesota School of Public Health. She received her PhD in Electrical Engineering from Stanford University in 2012 and her dissertation was awarded the Decision Sciences Institute Elwood S. Buffa Doctoral Dissertation Award in 2013. In her research, she applies engineering concepts, including simulation modelling, optimization, cost-effectiveness analysis, and resource allocation, to help inform policies for the prevention and treatment of infectious diseases. Specific application areas include HIV, sexually transmitted infections, antimicrobial resistance, and most recently COVID-19.

Artificial Intelligence for Healthcare

Interdisciplinary Partnerships for Analytics-driven Improvements in a Post-COVID World

Edited by

SZE-CHUAN SUEN
University of Southern California

DAVID SCHEINKER
Stanford University

EVA ENNS
University of Minnesota

CAMBRIDGE
UNIVERSITY PRESS

University Printing House, Cambridge CB2 8BS, United Kingdom

One Liberty Plaza, 20th Floor, New York, NY 10006, USA

477 Williamstown Road, Port Melbourne, VIC 3207, Australia

314–321, 3rd Floor, Plot 3, Splendor Forum, Jasola District Centre, New Delhi – 110025, India

103 Penang Road, #05-06/07, Visioncrest Commercial, Singapore 238467

Cambridge University Press is part of the University of Cambridge.

It furthers the University's mission by disseminating knowledge in the pursuit of education, learning, and research at the highest international levels of excellence.

www.cambridge.org
Information on this title: www.cambridge.org/9781108836739
DOI: 10.1017/9781108872188

© Cambridge University Press 2022

First published 2022

A catalogue record for this publication is available from the British Library.

Library of Congress Cataloging-in-Publication Data
Names: Suen, Sze-chuan, 1987- editor. I Scheinker, David, editor. I Enns, Eva, 1984- editor
Title: Artificial intelligence for healthcare : interdisciplinary partnerships for analytics-driven improvements in a Post-COVID world / edited by Sze-chuan Suen, University of Southern California, David Scheinker, Stanford University, California, Eva Enns, University of Minnesota
Description: Cambridge, United Kingdom ; New York, NY : Cambridge University Press, 2022. I Includes bibliographical references.
Identifiers: LCCN 2021054362 (print) I LCCN 2021054363 (ebook) I ISBN 9781108836739 (hardback) I ISBN 9781108872188 (epub)
Subjects: LCSH: Medical informatics. I Medical care–Data processing. I Artificial intelligence–Medical applications. I BISAC: COMPUTERS / Database Administration & Management
Classification: LCC R858 .A768 2022 (print) I LCC R858 (ebook) I DDC 362.10285–dc23/eng/ 20211202
LC record available at https://lccn.loc.gov/2021054362
LC ebook record available at https://lccn.loc.gov/2021054363

ISBN 978-1-108-83673-9 Hardback

Contents

Contributors

Christine L. Barnett, RTI Health Solutions

Sanjay Basu, Research and development, Waymark

Hamsa Bastani, The Wharton School, University of Pennsylvania

Margaret Brandeau, Department of Management Science and Engineering, Stanford University

Jarrod Call, Graduate School of Social Work, University of Denver

Timothy Chan, Mechanical and Industrial Engineering, University of Toronto

Brian T. Denton, Department of Industrial and Operations Engineering, University of Michigan, Ann Arbor

Tony Duan, Department of Computer Science, Stanford University

Anthony Fulginiti, Graduate School of Social Work, University of Denver

Robert A. Harrington, Department of Medicine, Stanford University

Shuai Huang, Department of Industrial & Systems Engineering, University of Washington – Seattle

Sheldon H. Jacobson, Department of Computer Science, Carle Illinois College of Medicine, University of Illinois at Urbana-Champaign

Janet A. Jokela, University of Illinois College of Medicine at Urbana-Champaign

Shan Liu, Department of Industrial & Systems Engineering, University of Washington–Seattle

Aida Rahmattalabi, Department of Computer Science, University of Southern California

Eric Rice, Suzanne Dworak-Peck School of Social Work, University of Southern California

Fatima Rodriguez, Division of Cardiovascular Medicine and Cardiovascular Institute and Department of Medicine, Stanford University

David Scheinker, Department of Pediatrics, Clinical Excellence Research Center, and Department of Management Science and Engineering, Stanford University

Pengyi Shi, Krannert School of Management, Purdue University

Christopher Sun, Sloan School of Management, Massachusetts Institute of Technology and Healthcare Systems Engineering, Massachusetts General Hospital

Phebe Vayanos, Epstein Department of Industrial and Systems Engineering, Department of Computer Science, Viterbi School of Engineering, University of Southern California

Preface

Sze-chuan Suen, David Scheinker, and Eva Enns

Healthcare has recently seen numerous exciting applications of artificial intelligence (AI), industrial engineering (IE), and operations research (OR). The success of collaborative, interdisciplinary teams of researchers in medicine, engineering, and the social sciences has revealed numerous exciting opportunities. For doctors unfamiliar with engineering and engineers unfamiliar with healthcare, such collaborative opportunities seem inaccessible. This book provides an overview of how researchers form interdisciplinary partnerships that leverage analytics-driven methods in AI, IE, and OR to tackle the most difficult societal and operational problems in healthcare.

Many engineering problems address issues of planning, resource allocation, and data analysis within the context of uncertain environments and repeated decisions – problems that often occur in public health. While engineers have long worked with clinicians to improve medical technology, collaborations between other health researchers and engineers have only just begun to gain traction. This book encompasses engineering models from a wide variety of disciplines (computer science, statistics, operations research, artificial intelligence, industrial engineering, etc.) in a wide array of health topics (public health, healthcare interventions, social and behavioral health, healthcare delivery, hospital operations, etc.)

Artificial Intelligence for Healthcare introduces work at the intersection of health and AI/IE/OR, highlighting how engineering in healthcare has contributed to medical knowledge, health system operations, and behavioral health. This volume provides examples of these types of advances in a way that interested researchers can use to better understand the field or as a path to start interdisciplinary collaborations.

Intended Audience and Content

This book is designed to be of interest to (i) researchers in public health, medicine, computational social science, and related social science fields who are interested in how engineering techniques may open new avenues for exploring social science data and tackling social problems; (ii) researchers in engineering who are interested in health applications of AI/IE/OR; (iii) other researchers interested in both engineering and social science who may be interested in jumping into this area of work.

To ensure the chapters are accessible to a diverse audience, each chapter begins with a brief summary of the health problem addressed and the method used to investigate the problem. These brief descriptions will help orient readers who may not be familiar with the health application or methodology used. In addition, each chapter includes several citations in "Further Reading" after each chapter to introduce interested readers to other works in the field.

While we cannot include work from all fields in healthcare, we do our best to showcase work from diverse areas and backgrounds. We include two main sections in the book – "Personalized Medicine" and "Optimizing Healthcare Systems" – which encompass topics ranging from optimizing the location of AEDs for cardiac arrests to data mining to identify how patients can better flow through a hospital. Authors of these chapters come from a variety of disciplines, including medical doctors, public health researchers, health policymakers, social scientists, and engineering faculty from a collection of universities. The collaborations that motivate these case studies comprise those between hospitals, insurance companies, shelters for homeless youth, outpatient clinics, and schools of medicine, public health, and engineering. We hope that these studies will inspire future collaborations between engineers, social scientists, clinicians, and policy-makers to work to improve the state of health policy and medicine through engineering techniques.

Introduction

1

Artificial Intelligence and Public Health

Opportunities Abound

Sheldon H. Jacobson and Janet A. Jokela

Artificial intelligence (AI) has become the poster child for data science and advanced analytics. Pick up any newspaper or magazine and one finds the promise that AI can bring to solve society's most vexing problems. AI is a critical driver in the next economic revolution as part of the information age expansion, revealing hidden insights and unleashing the power of big data.

Medicine is an attractive target for AI (Maddox et al. 2019). Given the human decision-making element that drives medicine, the potential for AI to enhance diagnosis and treatment protocols is immense. Indeed, any healthcare decision for which there is a plethora of data and which requires human intervention and judgment is a ripe target to benefit from AI.

What exactly constitutes AI? The term "AI" has actually existed for more than 60 years, dating back to 1956 (Bringsjord and Govindarajulu 2018). Since the introduction of the modern computer, researchers have asked whether computers can be designed and programmed to mimic human intelligence, decision making, and reasoning. The classic science fiction movie *2001: A Space Odyssey* portrays HAL as a computer with human decision-making capabilities. Science fiction as such has been inspired by the AI vision, years prior to the actual realization of AI capabilities. More recently, the AlphaZero artificial intelligence program achieved a level of "superhuman performance" in the games of Go, shogi, and chess by reinforcement learning from self-play, an example of the potential power of deep learning (Silver et al. 2018).

At its core, AI is the process by which human decision making and reasoning can be achieved by algorithms programmed on a computer. The advantage of using a computer for such applications is the speed by which they can be executed and the data that can be stored and accessed by such algorithms. Specific types of AI include computer vision (i.e., interpreting images, such as how human sight functions), optimization (i.e., decision making associated with complicated or complex man-made or natural systems), and learning (i.e., using data as input to improve decision making). Several high-profile applications of AI have drawn widespread attention. These include autonomous vehicles (land, water, and air, including drones), high-speed trading of financial products, and consumer marketing. Machine learning is a specific type of AI, whereby algorithms use data to train neural network models so that when such models take in real-time data, they are able to make decisions and use such data to further enhance their learning phase. Deep learning is a more advanced form of machine learning that uses layers of neural networks and massive data sets to achieve a similar objective.

Public health is a ripe area for AI to have an impact, especially in the era of COVID-19 (McCall 2020). AI possesses the potential to provide valuable pandemic-related insights and guidance. For example, efficient and appropriate healthcare system operations to ensure financial stability and enable such systems to fulfill their mission are critical. Smart strategies to estimate and mitigate risk are necessary. The high disparity rates in COVID-19 morbidity and mortality associated with race, ethnicity, and socioeconomic status expose pressing needs for investigation and sustainable solutions. Rising rates of depression, suicide, and mental health concerns present opportunities to appropriately target and deploy innovative solutions, such as telemedicine interventions.

Public health is the science of protecting and improving the health of people and their communities. This work is achieved by promoting healthy lifestyles, researching disease and injury prevention, and detecting, preventing, and responding to infectious diseases (CDC Foundation 2019). At its core, it is concerned with the well-being of a population. The American Public Health Association (APHA) lists 33 targeted topics and issues that they consider within the rubric of public health (American Public Health Association 2019). The Centers for Disease Control and Prevention (CDC) Organizational Chart (Centers for Disease Control and Prevention 2019a, 2019b) partitions public health into one institute (Occupational Health and Safety) and four directorates (Public Health Service and Implementation Science, Public Health Science and Surveillance, Non-infectious Diseases, Infectious Diseases), providing a broader classification that includes the APHA topics and issues. The CDC Strategic Priorities are the following: (1) improve health security at home and around the world; (2) prevent the leading causes of illness, injury, disability, and death; and (3) strengthen public health and healthcare collaboration.

To meet these priorities, the CDC activities include detecting, responding to, and stopping new and emerging health threats; preventing injuries, illnesses, and premature deaths; and discovering new ways to protect and improve the public's health through science and advanced technology. These activities involve tracking the causes and rates of death in a population, as well as surveillance of population health data. Examples of issues that are germane to such public health activities include monitoring infectious diseases (such as seasonal influenza and childhood diseases), obesity, smoking trends, death rates and causes, suicide rates, and drug use (both elicit and legal, including opioids), to name but a few. The emergence of the SARS-CoV2, the virus that causes COVID-19, has projected a bright light on public health data and practices. Surveillance testing and contract tracing, core public health approaches, have drawn attention both in the media and with the general public.

The common thread that permeates public health activities is data, and the tools used to glean information from such data are statistical methods. Given that numerous AI methods require large input data sets, the marriage of public health and AI appears to be a natural fit. Indeed, AI has already been applied to public health problems, though the name AI may not have been explicitly attached to such activities.

1.1 AI Successes in Public Health

Prior to the widespread emphasis on machine learning in AI, numerous data-driven studies were conducted that used optimization models to address public health issues. AI is often demonstrated through the design of an expert system or decision support framework for capturing and enhancing the decision-making process. Operations research, a field that uses models to improve the decision-making process, can be classified within the AI family of methodologies, though it has traditionally not been so formally described.

One public health area that attracted significant attention is broadly designated as pediatric immunization formulary design. Weniger et al. (1998) introduced an optimization model for designing pediatric vaccine formularies based on a variety of cost components, including the price and packaging for the vaccines, and how the vaccine antigens fit into the Recommended Childhood Immunization Schedule (RCIS). This model was then used as the driver in a decision support system for stocking pediatric formularies (Jacobson and Sewell 2008).

Given the complexity of the RCIS, children often fall behind in receiving their vaccines, creating population risk with decreased herd immunity. Engineer et al. (2009) present an optimization framework for designing catch-up schedules for pediatric childhood immunization. The framework is embedded into a decision support system, making it easier for clinicians to assess which vaccines should be administered to a child at any point when they present at a clinic with an incomplete or unknown immunization history.

Population disease screening is another area in which decision support systems have been effectively implemented to enhance the decision-making process. Long and Brandeau (2009) provide an overview of operations research that can be effective in modeling and containing the spread of infectious diseases. Brandeau et al. (1991) outline an analytic decision model for setting intervention screening policies for the human immunodeficiency virus (HIV). Atkinson et al. (2007) outline a strategy for reducing the spread of dengue fever by proposing a model for capturing the growth of the underlying mosquito population. Models as such have important implications that impact the decision-making process for population health. Lee et al. (2006) provide a decision support system to help manage the operation of dispensing clinics in the event of biological threats and infectious disease outbreaks.

1.2 Recent Interest in AI in Public Health

The visibility of both AI and healthcare has been a natural driver for identifying areas of interest for AI in public health. Stead (2018) and Shah (2019) provide thoughtful editorials on the growth of AI in healthcare and its potential to improve clinical care. Hinton (2018) and Naylor (2018) make a similar case for deep learning as a vehicle to improve clinical healthcare practice. Maddox et al. (2019) pose several critical questions that provide indicators for when and how to use AI in healthcare. Beam and Kohane (2018) provide an overview of machine learning and the relationship between data size and the human-to-machine decision-making effort, providing a structured classification for numerous applications in health and industry.

The common thread that permeates such discussions is the proliferation of electronic health records, the vehicle to access enormous amounts of data as inputs for AI algorithms. However, thought-provoking papers as such are not new. Patel et al. (2009) discusses the coming wave of AI applications in medicine, though few recognized the potential for machine learning and deep learning across such a wide swath of healthcare.

Clearly, interest of AI in public health has begun to grow, with applications sprouting up addressing numerous public health issues. The Canadian Institute for Advanced Research (CIFAR) and the Canadian Institutes of Health Research's Institute of Population and Public Health (CIHR-IPPH) co-hosted a workshop in January 2018, "Application of Artificial Intelligence

Approaches to Tackle Public Health Challenges," to bring together public health leaders to summarize the state of AI in public health in Canada, and to identify opportunities where AI may influence public health processes and decision making. The outcome of the workshop provided a roadmap of opportunities for AI in public health in Canada, many of which are applicable in the United States and other countries. Given that the workshop organizers recognized the paucity of such activities to date, the workshop provided a much-needed impetus to begin dialogues between the various stakeholders, as well as initiate the process of introducing and energizing AI applications to address critical public health issues.

AI and epidemiology have a natural connection because of their reliance on data. Thiebault and Thiessard (2018) provide an overview of papers published in the area of public health and epidemiology informatics. The objective of their analysis was to identify the most significant papers published in 2017. Of particular note is that their initial scan using PubMed and Web of Science yielded 843 articles, indicating the substantial interest in the area. Of these papers, one of the two best used an artificial neural network to anonymize patient notes in electronic health records (Demoncourt et al. 2017).

AI has also been proposed to improve health in resource-poor settings (Wahl et al. 2018, Shah 2019). Given the challenges faced in such environments, they explore the types of AI that may be beneficial in such environments, and the types of problems that are most amenable for AI application within a resource-challenged setting.

1.3 AI Opportunities in Public Health

Public health analytics are driven by data. Therefore, statisticians and epidemiologists have found public health a rich domain for analysis. This very surfeit of data makes AI an attractive target for application. The following provides an overview of several public health issues and the opportunities for AI to bring new insights into their understanding and solution.

The COVID-19 pandemic, as a global public health crisis, has disrupted every aspect of society. Given the rapid response and decision making required to meet real-time challenges, AI can support such processes (McCall 2020). Areas that may benefit from AI during the COVID-19 response include the creation and reallocation of resources to respond to the demands of care (such as equipment, personnel, and personal protective equipment); the appropriate allocation of healthcare resources to balance COVID-19 and non-COVID-19 care, including preventive medicine; designing population-based testing strategies that balance costs and societal benefits; reducing morbidity and mortality rates across all sociodemographic strata; and determining the optimal use of telemedicine.

Obesity has become a major worldwide public health challenge. Since the 1960s, the United States has seen a steady increase in the adult (20 years and older) obesity rate, reaching 39.8 percent in 2015–2016, according to the CDC (Hales et al. 2017). Obesity has also become more prevalent in other countries around the globe, making it a global public health epidemic. There is an abundance of data collected and available to root out the causes of obesity. These include patient medical information, societal and economic factors, food sources, and environmental issues. Extensive analysis of such data has provided insights into associations with obesity, yet little knowledge has been gleaned that can be put into practice to reverse population obesity trends. Clearly, the causes of obesity are complex and may not lend themselves to traditional statistical methods. This is where AI may be a useful target of opportunity (Zeevi et al. 2015). Given the abundance of data, coupled with the multiple association vectors that have been observed, machine learning models can be employed to identify hidden connections across multiple factors that may help identify potential drivers for obesity, as well as appropriate population and patient-centric interventions to reverse current obesity trends (Scheinker et al. 2019).

Smoking combustible cigarettes continues to be a public health concern. Numerous studies have demonstrated the detrimental impact of smoking on individual health, including higher rates of cardiovascular disease and numerous types of cancers. Secondhand smoke has also been associated with higher rates of lung cancer. There have been numerous policy changes implemented to limit locations where people are permitted to smoke. The footprint for acceptable smoking locations continues to shrink, with data analysis used to support such policies. Using noncombustible cigarettes, informally termed vaping, represents the new wave of smoking, creating opportunities for data analysis to assess the public health impact of such items (Visweswaran et al. 2020). However, the health problems associated with combustible cigarettes differ from those of non-combustible cigarettes. As such, AI may provide a useful tool to glean public health impacts for such cigarettes and provide insights that can be used to guide policies on their use.

Mass killings have been a persistent plague in society in the United States for the past several decades. Although the rate of mass killings (defined by the FBI as four of more deaths in a single incident) has remained steady for more than a decade (King and Jacobson 2017), the scourge of fear in society due to such events has become a public health challenge. After each such incident, data are collected and analyzed to create a profile of the perpetrators, yet each incident continues to baffle law enforcement officials and policy makers. With over three-quarters of mass killings involving some form of firearm, calls for greater restrictions on gun accessibility and stronger background checks have grown louder but have also been met with resistance by gun advocates who argue for the deterrence value of firearms. Given the visceral reactions on both sides of this issue, AI may provide an avenue to adjudicate this debate, provide a better understanding of unforeseen patterns hidden within the plethora of data, and glean insights into how such events can be prevented or deterred.

Alcoholism and drug addiction (illicit and prescription, including opioids) have been persistent and pernicious public health challenges for several decades. The annual cost to society as a whole has been measured to be over US$500 billion in the United States alone (NIDA 2017). Significant progress has been made to address these issues, including both professional and self-help organizations. More recently the legalization of marijuana has drawn attention and concerns that such a policy will have deleterious effects on society. For these issues, there is a plethora of data available on factors that lead to alcoholism and drug addiction, yet there are no easy answers in eliminating these scourges, or, more realistically, in halting the progression earlier in their destructive cycle. AI may provide an avenue to identify driving factors that could be addressed using traditional treatment plans, or to help to identify new methods that have yet to be deployed, but may be more effective in reducing the negative impact of such diseases on individuals and society as a whole (Mak et al. 2019).

The societal threat of bioterrorism attacks presents major public health challenges. In the event of the intentional release of an airborne pathogen, appropriate preparation and rapid detection and response are the three factors that require attention to minimize the impact during such events. Given the breadth of possible pathogens, and their public health impact, large amounts of data exist to understand what can be done to mitigate their impacts on populations across multiple scenarios (Zaric et al. 2008). Given the extreme nature of such events, traditional methods of response may be challenged because of weaknesses in supply chains and transportation networks. AI may be effective in parsing through such data and providing insights on how public health may optimally prepare for and respond to such events.

1.4 AI Challenges in Public Health

Many of the challenges to using AI in public health apply across other fields. For example, developing domain-specific AI tools often requires a deep knowledge of the domain and a thorough understanding of AI methods, or, more realistically, a collaborative and interdisciplinary environment whereby such individuals can work together. Moreover, given the intense competition for AI skills across numerous fields, public health will need to compete for such talent in such a highly competitive human-capital environment. Such competition in general has driven up the cost of AI talent, possibly taking it out of the reach of many public health settings. As AI becomes even more attractive across a wider swath of societal applications, such competition will only become more intense in the coming years. It is also possible, however, that the COVID-19 pandemic will inspire altruistic AI talent to pursue public health opportunities to tackle this most vexing problem.

Given the need for data in AI algorithms, the issues of privacy become of paramount concern. Electronic health records facilitate the availability of data. However, the Health Insurance Portability and Accountability Act (HIPAA) privacy rule places significant barriers in using such data without prior patient consent. Although HIPAA gives patients control over their health records, it creates a headwind for analysts to use such data (even when anonymized) to drive AI algorithms. A dialogue on such issues with electronic health record designers like EPIC and Cerner is paramount to overcoming such challenges. Possible solutions include requesting patients to release their anonymized data or redesigning electronic health records to allow personal information to be hidden while making anonymized health information accessible for research and analysis. Indeed, AI may be the driving force to revamp HIPAA laws to facilitate such advances.

Along these same lines, AI requires data that may contain inherent biases. Such biases would percolate through any algorithm, resulting in biased decisions. This is particularly critical in issues pertaining to human health, and public health in particular, where decisions can impact the lives and well-being of populations (Obermeyer et al. 2019). Aswani and Olfat (2018) discuss the issue of fairness in AI, and how inherent biases in decision making can be detected and mitigated. Parallel to such issues, Israni and Verghese (2019) discuss not only whether AI can improve healthcare delivery but also whether it can deliver more humanistic medicine. Indeed, the human–computer nexus will be increasingly scrutinized as AI works its way into healthcare systems.

1.5 Summary and Conclusions

Public health problems offer a panacea of opportunities for AI. The enormous amounts of data that are available make it well suited for this domain of application. At the same time, as with any healthcare data analysis, issues of privacy must be addressed to ensure that individuals within a population are appropriately protected. Clearly, the benefits outweigh the risks in using AI for surveillance, assessment, and policy formulation within public health. The greatest challenge may be the will to advance AI and the fortitude to overcome existing barriers so that AI can provide the greatest benefits in public health.

References

American Public Health Association, 2019, Topics and issues. www.apha.org/topics-and-issues.

Aswani, A, Olfat, M., 2018, Designing algorithms to increase fairness in artificial intelligence, *SIAM News*, **51**(10), 1,3.

Atkinson, MP, Su, Z., Alphey, N., et al. 2007, Analyzing the control of mosquito-borne diseases by a dominant lethal genetic system, *Proceedings of the National Academy of Sciences*, **104**(22), 9540–9545.

Beam, A.L., Kohane, A.S., 2018, Big data and machine learning in health care, *JAMA*, **319**(13), 1317–1318

Brandeau, M.L., Lee, H.L., Owens, D.K., Sox, C.H., Wachter, R.M, 1991, A policy model of human immunodeficiency virus screening and intervention, *Interfaces*, **21**(3), 5–25.

Bringsjord, S., Govindarajulu, N.S., 2018, Artificial intelligence. In: *The Stanford Encyclopedia of Philosophy* (Fall 2018 edition), E.N. Zalta (ed.). https://plato.stanford.edu/archives/fall2018/entries/artificial-intelligence.

CDC Foundation, 2019, Public health in action. www.cdcfoundation.org/what-public-health.

Centers for Disease Control and Prevention, 2019a, Organizational chart. www.cdc.gov/about/pdf/organization/cdc-org-chart.pdf.

Centers for Disease Control and Prevention Foundation, 2019b, Who we are/what is public health. www.cdcfoundation.org/what-public-health

Demoncourt, F. Lee, J.Y., Uzuner, O., Szolovits, P., 2017, De-identification of patient notes with recurrent neural networks, *Journal of the American Medical Informatics Association*, **24**, 596–606.

Engineer, F.G., Keskinocak, P., Pickering, L.K., 2009, OR practice – catch-up scheduling for childhood vaccination, *Operations Research*, **57**(6), 1307–1319.

Hales, C.M., Carroll, M.D., Fryar, C.D., Ogden, C.L., 2017, Prevalence of obesity among adults and youth: United States, 2015–2016, NCHS Data Brief, No. 288, October 2017. www.cdc.gov/nchs/data/databriefs/db288.pdf.

Hinton, G., 2018, Deep learning – a technology with the potential to transform health care, *JAMA*, **320**(11), 1101–1102.

Israni S.T., Verghese, A., 2019, Humanizing artificial intelligence, *JAMA*, **321**(1), 29–30

Jacobson, S.H., Sewell, E.C., 2008, A web-based tool for designing vaccine formularies for childhood immunization in the United States, *JAMA*, **15**(5), 611–619.

King, D.M., Jacobson, S.H., 2017, Random acts of violence: examining probabilistic independence of mass killing events in the United States, *Victims and Violence*, **32**(6), 1014–1023.

Lee, E.K., Maheshwary, Mason, J., Glisson, S., 2006, Large-scale dispensing for emergency response to bioterrorism and infectious-disease outbreak, *Interfaces*, **36**(6), 591–607.

Long, E.F., Brandeau, M.L., 2009, OR's next top model: decision models for infectious disease control, *TutORials in Operations Research*, 123–138.

Maddox T.M., Rumsfeld J.S., Payne P.R.O., 2019, Questions for artificial intelligence in health care, *JAMA*, **321**(1), 31–32.

Mak, K.K., Lee, K., Park, C., 2019, Applications of machine learning in addiction studies: a systematic review, *Psychiatry Research*, **275**, 53–60.

McCall, B., 2020, COVID-19 and artificial intelligence: protecting health-care workers and curbing the spread, *The Lancet Digital Health*, **2**(4), e166–e167.

Naylor, C.D., 2018, On the prospects for a (deep) learning health care system, *JAMA*, **320**(11), 1099–1100.

NIDA, 2017, Trends & statistics. www.drugabuse.gov/related-topics/trends-statistics.

Obermeyer, Z., Powers, B., Vogeli, C., Mullainathan, S., 2019, Dissecting racial bias in an algorithm used to manage the health of populations, *Science*, **366**(6464), 447–453.

Patel, V.L., Shortliffe, E.H., Stefanelli, M., et al., 2009, The coming of age of artificial intelligence in medicine, *Artificial Intelligence in Medicine*, **46**(1), 5–17.

Scheinker, D., Valencia, A., Rodriguez, F., 2019, Identification of factors associated with variation in us county-level obesity prevalence rates using epidemiologic vs machine learning models, *JAMA Network Open*, **2**(4), e192884–e192884.

Shah NR., 2019, Healthcare in 2030: will artificial intelligence replace physicians? *Annals Internal Medicine*, **170**, 407–408. doi:10.7326/M19-0344

Silver, D.S., Hubert, T., Schrittwieser, J., et al., 2018, A general reinforcement learning algorithm that masters chess, shogi and go through self play, *Science* **362**, 1140–1144.

Stead W.W., 2018, Clinical implications and challenges of artificial intelligence and deep learning, *JAMA*, **320**(11), 1107–1108.

Thiebout, R., Thiessard, F., 2018, Artificial intelligence in public health and epidemiology, *IMIA Yearbook of Medical Informatics*, **27**(1):207–209.

Visweswaran, S., Colditz, J.B., O'Halloran, P., et al., 2020, Machine learning classifiers for twitter surveillance of vaping: comparative machine learning study, *Journal of Medical Internet Research*, **22**(8), e17478.

Wahl, B., Cossy-Gantner, A., Germann, S., Schwalbe, N.R., 2018, Artificial intelligence (AI) and global health: how can AI contribute to health in resource-poor settings? *BMJ Global Health*, **3**, 1–7.

Weniger, B.G., Chen, R.T., Jacobson, S.H., et al., 1998, Addressing the challenges to immunization practice with an economic algorithm for vaccine selection, *Vaccine*, **16**(19), 1885–1897.

Zaric, G.S., Bravata, D.M., Cleophas Holty, J.E., et al., 2008, Modeling the logistics of response to anthrax bioterrorism, *Medical Decision Making*, **28**(3), 332–350.

Zeevi, D., Korem, T., Zmora, N., et al., 2015, Personalized nutrition by prediction of glycemic responses, *Cell*, **163**(5), 1079–1094.

PART I

Personalized Medicine

2

How AI Can Help Depression Treatment

Designing Patient-Specific Adaptive Interventions

Shan Liu and Shuai Huang

Summary of the Problem

Major depressive disorder, one of the most common mental disorders in the United States, if left untreated in time can lead to disability, reduced quality of life and productivity, and increased risk of death due to comorbid conditions and suicide. Inadequate follow-up care is a major shortcoming in current depression treatment that can lead to poor quality of care and high cost.

Summary of the Solution

Designing artificial intelligence (AI)-assisted technology to better understand the disease trajectory and further develop appropriate strategies for monitoring and treatment of major depression under resource constraints is an important and challenging task. In this chapter, we present seven studies that developed methods for AI-assisted, data-driven decision support systems to aid healthcare professionals. These methods focus on modeling chronic depression's complex disease trajectories, identifying patients at high risk of progression, and recommending adaptive and cost-effective follow-up care. Long-term goals of this research include improving patient health outcomes and facilitating efficient allocation of healthcare providers' limited resources through the use of novel technology.

Summary of Relevance in a Post-COVID World

The economic losses and isolation resulting from non-pharmaceutical interventions deployed to slow the spread of COVID-19 have exacerbated the challenges of mental health and suicide. They have simultaneously increased the risk of in-person counseling and the availability of such appointments. This increased demand and reduced supply for depression treatment make more important than ever the use of technology driven methods to optimize the deployment of counselling resources.

2.1 Chronic Depression as a Significant Public Health Problem

Depression is a complex, dynamic mental disorder characterized by sad mood, loss of interest in activities, weight gain or loss, psychomotor agitation or retardation, fatigue, inappropriate guilt, difficulties concentrating, and recurrent thoughts of death [1]. Depression is diagnosed by five or more of the foregoing symptoms presenting for a continuous period of at least two weeks. It is one of the most common mental disorders in the United States, affecting more than 10% of the population [2]. Undiagnosed depression can lead to disability, reduced quality of life, reduced productivity, and increased risk of death due to comorbid chronic conditions and suicide [3, 4]. Though remarkable progress has been made in reducing the mortality and morbidity burdens for many diseases, including stroke, heart disease, and HIV/AIDS, depression-related morbidity and mortality has been rising in recent decades [5]. Suicide has recently become the number 1 cause of violent death and the 10th leading cause of death in the United States [6, 7]. National and state governments as well as guideline-setting bodies are making efforts to address this urgent problem. The U.S. Preventive Services Task Force (USPSTF) updated depression screening guidelines in 2016 that recommend "screening for depression in the general adult population," and "screening should be implemented with adequate systems in place to ensure accurate diagnosis, effective treatment, and appropriate follow-up" [8, 9]. In addition, the concurrence of depression with other chronic conditions and substance addiction is an understudied area where patient outcomes are known to be poor [10]. An open challenge is to design effective monitoring and treatment strategies for depression and its associated comorbid conditions.

Treatment for depression includes psychotherapy, antidepressants, or a combination of the two with supportive care. Due to potential side effects of the medications, the Food and Drug Administration (FDA) emphasizes that patients taking antidepressants should be closely monitored [3]. Finding appropriate strategies for routine monitoring is important and can be controversial [11].

Current recommendations for follow-up care of chronic depression are based almost entirely on expert opinion, which could suggest semiannual or annual monitoring intervals [12]. These recommendations do not account for significant heterogeneity in the course of depression between individuals and within individuals over time. Given that as many as 30 million Americans use antidepressants [2, 13], even minor changes in recommendations for follow-up frequency have major implications for healthcare utilization and cost.

In recent years, there has been an explosion of healthcare technology development including mobile health apps and telehealth that aim to merge big data analytics and AI to support healthcare services. Foreseeable benefits of AI-assisted decision support systems include faster, safer, cheaper, more convenient, and higher quality of care tailored to individual patients. There is strong interest from the private sector to commercialize remote monitoring and treatment platforms for chronic depression. In this chapter, we first briefly discuss the methodological challenges and relevant literature in Section 2.2, and then show highlights our recent work in developing AI-based methods for chronic depression in Section 2.3.

2.2 Methodological Challenges to Optimize Care for Chronic Depression

The ultimate goal for AI-assisted technology in the care of chronic depression is to help mental healthcare providers create patient-specific monitoring and treatment strategies that lower the risk of future recurrence of depression symptoms. This technology aims to enable healthcare systems to efficiently identify patients who would benefit from proactive management of their symptoms as well as support targeted performance metrics to evaluate the success of clinical interventions. Development of such technology requires a systems perspective and an associated computational platform, and a seamless integration with decision-analytic methods to assess their cost-effectiveness.

There are three major methodological challenges: (i) effectively analyze heterogeneous depression trajectories of a patient population and proactively probe new trajectories, (ii) adequately characterize the disease progression processes that govern these trajectories and design adaptive interventions, and (iii) design rigorous cost-effectiveness analyses to evaluate the cost and benefit of the proposed technology across subgroups of patients. To address these challenges, we conducted a literature search and identified the following research gaps.

2.2.1 Research Gaps

2.2.1.1 Gap 1: Discovering Depression Progression Patterns

Disease progression is often modeled mathematically using data that can help quantify the dynamic and temporal relationships of outcome measurements. Statistical-based learning methods have a long history. Common techniques include regression, Bayesian updating, discrete-time Markov models, hidden Markov models, semi-Markov models, hidden semi-Markov models, continuous-time Markov models, Markov random fields, neural networks, and other supervised/unsupervised machine learning approaches. Applications of these methods can be seen in modeling CD4 count decline in HIV patients [14], liver deterioration in patients on the transplant waiting list [15–17], depression progression [18, 19], and chronic obstructive pulmonary disease progression [20]. However, the majority of these studies ignore individual heterogeneity and subgroup progression patterns in the disease process and instead only consider a single stochastic process meant to reflect average, population-level outcomes.

2.2.1.2 Gap 2: Designing Adaptive Healthcare Interventions

The literature on using stochastic and dynamic models to optimize disease screening and treatment decisions over time is extensive. For example, Markov Decision Processes (MDPs), dynamic programming, and reinforcement learning have been used to decide how to optimally monitor and control disease progression [21]. Despite the successful application of these methods in a number of health applications [14–17], they are often population-based, require extensive data to estimate the transition probabilities and rewards for each possible action, and often do not incorporate real-time updating of the disease process and model parameters using all available information.

2.2.1.3 Gap 3: Linking Adaptive Technology to Cost-Effective Clinical Management

Cost-effectiveness analysis (CEA) is a crucial methodological component when designing and evaluating new technologies to enable their adoption into routine clinical practice [22, 23]. Two of the most important questions regarding depression are whether routine monitoring is justified and how to switch treatment. These questions are complicated by the heterogeneity in disease progression and treatment response within the population. With recent advancements in mobile phone apps, remote sensing, telehealth platforms, and big data, there is a considerable interest in developing commercial applications of digital therapeutics and automated remote monitoring of depression. The cost-effectiveness of this technology is uncertain and should be carefully modeled, accounting for population heterogeneity and differential treatment outcomes. A CEA of AI-assisted chronic depression management must link the data-driven design of adaptive interventions with evaluation of long-term patient health outcomes and costs in real-world implementation scenarios.

2.2.2 A New AI-Assisted Technology Framework

To remove these methodological barriers, the state-of-the-art statistical modeling, optimization, and decision-analytic modeling can help to create an AI-assisted technology framework for development and evaluation of adaptive chronic depression interventions. We proposed the following three steps to accomplish such a framework in our recent work:

Step 1: Discover patterns in chronic depression and suicide ideation trajectories using longitudinal person-level symptom severity measurements from electronic health record (EHR) data, and build models for depression progression dynamics using statistical learning methods.

Step 2: Create machine learning and optimization models to predict future risk of depression progression and treatment response. We discuss several online algorithms to conduct adaptive monitoring and treatment selection in Section 2.3.

Step 3: Evaluate the cost-effectiveness of adaptive depression interventions compared with current clinical practice and national guidelines on the population level. Outcome measures include monitoring accuracies (i.e., sensitivity and specificity of the monitoring technology), cost, life-years gained, quality-adjusted life years (QALYs) gained, and incremental cost-effectiveness ratios between strategies of interest.

Table 2.1 provides a comparison of the current depression care practice guidelines at a representative healthcare system and the proposed framework.

2.2.2.1 Guide to the Literature

For disease-trajectory modeling and depression trajectories in particular, we refer the readers to the following papers: Twisk and Hoekstra 2012 compared methods to classify developmental trajectories over time [24]; Craig and Sendi 2002 presented a tutorial on the estimation of transition matrix of a discrete-time Markov chain with healthcare examples [25]; and Musliner et al. 2015 conduced a systematic review of long-term trajectories of depressive symptoms [26]. For readers looking for technical materials on pattern recognition, classification, sequential data, neural network, and Markov models, we refer them to Bishop's textbook on pattern recognition and machine learning [27]. For readers interested in an introduction to the theory and practice in AI, we refer them to Russell and Norvig's textbook on AI [28]. For more information

Table 2.1. *Comparison of current practice and proposed framework*

	Current practice	Proposed framework
Objective	Passive information collection	Proactively prevent and treat a patient's chronic depression symptoms
Method	Routine clinic visits with fixed frequency	Enable AI-assisted interventions that are adaptive to individual disease trajectory
Capability	Assessment of depression severity and suicide risk	1) Quantify and predict individual patient's depression and suicide ideation trajectory and risk 2) Determine adaptive monitoring schedule, treatment selection, and proactively collect information
Cost-effectiveness	Not evaluated	Evaluated by decision-analytic models using simulation and scenario analyses

on how to conduct a cost-effectiveness analysis, we refer the readers to Drummond's textbook on economic evaluation in healthcare [29].

2.3 Highlights from Seven Research Studies

In this section, we present highlights from our recent work. In these studies, we are developing methods to enable the AI-assisted technology framework introduced in Section 2.2. With expanded use of EHR, many health systems can administer and store longitudinal depression measurements for a large number of patients. The majority of studies described in this section used data from the Mental Health Research Network (MHRN) – a consortium of research centers affiliated with 11 large health systems. The dataset contains depression screening and outcomes data with approximately 2 million observations from a diverse and representative sample of outpatients in 5 states (California, Colorado, Minnesota, Washington, and Idaho).

Our MHRN EHR dataset includes de-identified person-level Patient Health Questionnaire (PHQ)-9 depression measures (total scores and individual item scores) between year 2007 and 2012. PHQ-9 is a self-administered questionnaire that includes 9 multiple-choice questions with a total score ranging from 0 to 27 [30]. PHQ-9 stratifies depression into 5 severity levels including no depression (0–4), mild depression (5–9), moderate depression (10–14), moderate severe depression (15–19), and severe depression (20–27). The data set also contains relative time between measurements; type of provider (primary care, specialist, and mental health); individuals' age, sex, race/ethnicity, diagnosis, and treatment status; and the Charlson Comorbidity Index score.

The Charlson Comorbidity Index score is a summary score of medical disease burden including a total of 22 conditions (each condition is assigned a score of 1, 2, 3, or 6, depending on the associated mortality risk) that aims to predict the 1-year mortality [31]. The majority of patients are older than age 45 (age 18–29, 13%; 30–44, 27%; 45–64, 43%; 65+, 17%) and female (70%).

2.3.1 Modeling Chronic Depression Trajectories

Depression trajectories are often estimated from noisy, sparse, and irregular person-level data. Since these time series do not follow any known functional forms, several alternative methods can be used to model them: (i) **Smoothing B-spline** (Figure 2.1a) can be used to characterize nonlinear patterns. An irregular observational time interval is first transformed to the B-splines bases, then the trajectory signals are represented as linear combinations of these bases and can be computed recursively for any desired degree of the polynomial using the algorithms in Boor [32]. (ii) **Gaussian process regression** (GPR) (Figure 2.1b) is a Bayesian nonparametric method that transforms observations to a longitudinal probability distribution [33]. The rational quadratic kernel can be used,

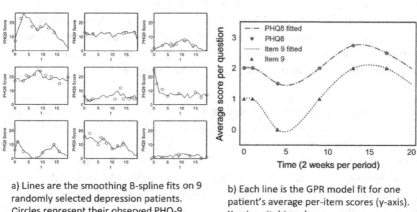

a) Lines are the smoothing B-spline fits on 9 randomly selected depression patients. Circles represent their observed PHQ-9 scores. X-axis unit: biweek.

b) Each line is the GPR model fit for one patient's average per-item scores (y-axis). X-axis unit: biweek.

c) A Markov model representation with five depression severity states.

Figure 2.1 Three alternative representations of chronic depression disease progression (panel b is from [35]).

and an optimal set of hyperparameters can be found that maximizes the marginal likelihood. (iii) **Discrete-time Markov model** is used with a state transition matrix that predicts the distribution of disease states over time (Figure 2.1c). The Expectation-Maximization (EM) algorithm can be applied to impute the missing data and obtain maximum likelihood estimators [25]. Alternatively, irregular individual observations can be first fitted with a smoothing spline and then partitioned into regular time intervals. Next, a transition matrix of movements between states is created by counting the number of transitions from each disease state to other states at each time interval [34]. The three alternative representations of the disease process may bring different advantages in the subsequent pattern discovery tasks shown in studies one, two, and four.

2.3.1.1 Pattern Discovery

We describe several studies that applied statistical learning and artificial neural networks to discover patterns in chronic depression progression. Two assumptions are made based on domain knowledge in chronic depression: (i) There are latent disease-trajectory patterns in the population (e.g., subgroups defined by stable mild, increasing severity, fluctuating severity). Patients in different subgroups may follow significantly different progression trajectories, but patients within the same subgroup may follow similar progression trajectories. (ii) Similarity information between patients can be quantified by comparing patients' demographic and clinical profiles from which features can be drawn to predict similarities in patients' future disease progressions.

Study One: Collaborative Modeling In Lin et al. 2016 [36], we analyzed patterns in the collected depression trajectories of a treatment population and compared several methods to predict individual trajectories for monitoring treatment outcomes. The data include longitudinal PHQ-9 scores over 4 years for assessing depression severity from the MHRN. We analyzed >3,000 patients with at least six PHQ-9 observations who received treatment longer than 6 months. We used smoothing splines to model individual depression trajectories. We then used K-means clustering and collaborative modeling (CM) to identify subgroup patterns. We found five broad trajectory patterns in the ongoing treatment population: stable high, stable low, fluctuating moderate, an increasing and a decreasing group (Figure 2.2a).

The CM approach assumes that the heterogeneous progression dynamics are represented by a number of canonical models in the population, where each patient's progression model is captured as variants of these canonical models [36–38]. CM considers the underlying cluster structure embedded in the

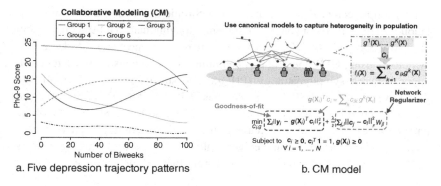

Figure 2.2 CM formulation and result [36]

population and the resemblance of the individuals to these clusters. We assign a membership vector, denoted as $c_i = [c_{i1}, \ldots, c_{iK}]^T$, to each patient i, while K is the number of canonical pattern groups. Thus, c_{ik} denotes the probability of patient i belonging to a group k. For each patient i, we assume that there are longitudinal measurements (i.e., PHQ-9 scores) at n_i time points, denoted as $y_i = [y_{i1}, \ldots, y_{in_i}]^T \in \mathbb{R}^{n_i \times 1}$, and the longitudinal measurements of the risk factors, denoted as $\mathbf{X}_i = [\mathbf{x}_{i1}, \ldots, \mathbf{x}_{in_i}]^T \in \mathbb{R}^{n_i \times p}$. CM employs a canonical model $g^k(\mathbf{X})$ for characterizing the trajectory of group k. The canonical model is flexible and can take the form of a B-spline model, a GPR, or a Markov model. Then, the progression model of patient i can be characterized by a weighted combination of the canonical models of the K latent subgroups, $f^i(\mathbf{X}) = \sum_k c_{ik} g^k(\mathbf{X})$. Furthermore, the similarity between two patients can be quantified by comparing their risk factors and past trajectory information. The similarity can be represented as a similarity matrix, $\mathbf{W}$, with each element, w_{jl}, representing the similarity between a pair of patients, j, l, and reflecting how likely the patients' progressions would be similar. To guide the learning of model parameters, we can minimize the least square loss function (Figure 2.2b) or maximize the log likelihood to measure the goodness-of-fit of the individual progression models.

Study Two: Artificial Neural Network Depression is often accompanied by thoughts of self-harm, which are a strong predictor of subsequent suicide attempt and suicide death. Few empirical data are available regarding the temporal correlation between depression symptoms and suicidal ideation. In Gong et al. 2019 [35], we investigated the traditional concern that suicidal ideation may increase during a period of depression improvement using depression trajectory data. We analyzed a chronic depression treatment population's EHR, which contained 610 patients' longitudinal PHQ-9 scores within 20 two-week periods. We discovered patterns in trajectories of depressive symptoms using GPR and artificial neural networks. We also estimated correlations between symptomatology (PHQ-8) and suicide ideation (Item 9). We found five patterns in the PHQ-8 trajectories. PHQ-8 and Item 9 scores displayed strong temporal correlations. See Figure 2.3. We also found 8% to 13% of the patients have experienced an increase in suicidal ideation during improvement of their PHQ-8. We showed some evidence that subgroups of depressive patients are at increased risk of suicide ideation during PHQ-8 improvement.

2.3.2 Designing Adaptive Interventions

2.3.2.1 Adaptive Monitoring

Study Three: Rule-Based model In Lin et al. 2018 [39], we established a rule-based method to identify a set of risk predictive patterns from person-level longitudinal depression measurements by integrating three steps: data transformation, rule discovery, and rule evaluation. We further used the identified rules to create rule-based monitoring strategies to adaptively monitor patients. To evaluate the effectiveness of rule-based monitoring, we compared several monitoring strategies by estimating the number of depressive patients (PHQ-9 $\geq$ 10) in the next 6 months that are correctly monitored (true positives). We assumed under the status quo that all patients are monitored every 6 months, which may lead to unnecessary monitoring of low-risk patients. We also considered a PHQ-9-based strategy, which monitors the patient if his/her last-period PHQ-9 score is 10 or greater. Under rule-based monitoring, we considered both using individual rules and combining all top predictive rules.

We applied the rule-based method on the EHR data of a depression treatment population containing PHQ-9 scores. Twelve risk predictive rules were identified (Table 2.2). We found the rule-based prognostic model based on the identified rules enabled more accurate prediction of disease severity than other prognostic models, including RuleFit, logistic regression, and Support Vector Machine. Two rule-based monitoring strategies outperformed the latest PHQ-9-based monitoring strategy by providing higher sensitivity and specificity. We concluded that the rule-based method can lead to a better understanding of disease dynamics and achieve more accurate prognostics of disease progressions (Figure 2.4).

Study Four: Selective Sensing In Lin et al. 2018b [38], the study's objective was to build personalized trajectory models to proactively probe new

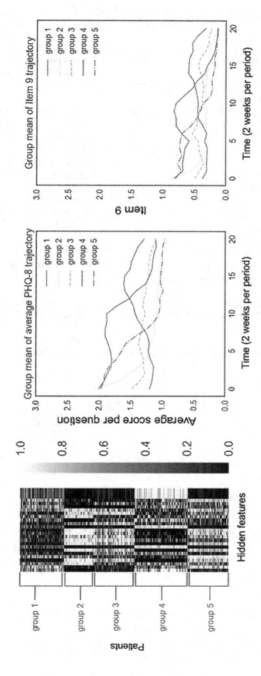

Figure 2.3 Clustering analysis for PHQ-8 (PHQ-9 total score minus the 9th question) found five subgroups in the learned features. Graphs show the mean scores of each subgroup for PHQ-8 and Item 9 (9th question on suicide ideation) scores over 20 biweeks [35].

Table 2.2. *Top rules identified by the Rulefit Model [39]*

	Decreasing risk rules		Increasing risk rules
Rule 1	Deepest increase between consecutive PHQ9 scores <7.50 & 75 percentile of PHQ9 score <14.62	Rule 7	Observing density >0.03 & Minimal PHQ9 score >8.50
Rule 2	25 percentile of PHQ9 score <6.13 & Volatility of PHQ9 score <9.64	Rule 8	Minimal PHQ9 score >9.50 & Volatility of difference between nearby PHQ9 scores <4.75
Rule 3	75 percentile of PHQ9 score <15.88 & Percentage of moderate depression <0.39	Rule 9	Latest PHQ9 score >17.50 & Volatility of PHQ9 score <7.33
Rule 4	Deepest decrease between consecutive PHQ9 scores >2.50 & 75 percentile of PHQ9 score <14.12	Rule 10	Minimal PHQ9 score >6.50 & 75 percentile of PHQ9 score > 14.88
Rule 5	Sex is male & Mean of 9th question scores <0.71 & Percentage of moderately severe <0.38	Rule 11	Age <65 & Percentage of severe depression >0.23
Rule 6	Latest PHQ9 score <8.50 & Maximal PHQ9 score <16.50	Rule 12	Deepest decrease between consecutive PHQ9 scores <13.50 & Mean of PHQ9 scores >14.73

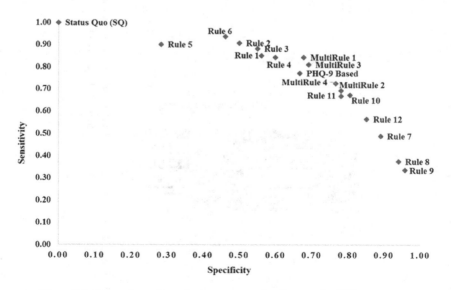

Figure 2.4 Comparison of monitoring accuracy for all strategies [39]

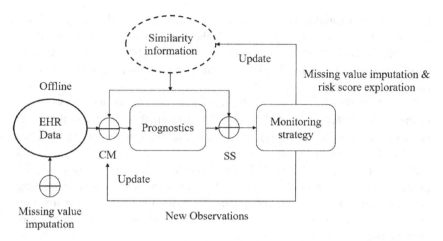

Figure 2.5 Overview: the CM-based prognosis and selective sensing for monitoring a heterogeneous patient population [38]

trajectories during online adaptive assessment and schedule the next visit under a capacity constraint. To do so, we integrated prognosis and sensing methodologies. For prognosis, a CM approach was used to predict the future progression risk of individuals. For adaptive monitoring, a selective sensing (SS) approach was developed to allocate limited sensing resources to monitor the high-risk individuals. See Figure 2.5.

We briefly describe the selective sensing method here. SS is formulated as an integer programming problem: the goal is to optimally allocate the sensing (monitoring) resources to detect a subgroup of high-risk individuals at each monitoring period. A patient's disease progression is modeled using the Markov model. Using a CM approach, we first estimated a transition matrix $\mathbf{P}_{it}$ to predict the progression risk of each individual patient i at each monitoring/sensing period t. Healthcare systems are often constrained by providers' capacity for mental health follow-up visits. For example, we learned that the demand for psychotherapy visit is much greater than supply at several health systems. We would prefer an algorithm that can optimally allocate the limited monitoring resources to detect high-risk individuals that are most likely to benefit from further interventions.

Suppose that there are N individuals and we denote the measurements of these individuals at each monitoring period as $\mathbf{x}_t = [x_{1t}, \ldots, x_{Nt}]$, where each measurement is a PHQ-9 score of the patient. We were interested in detecting the high-risk patients. Due to the limited sensing resources, we can only observe M out of N individuals at each period $(M < N)$. We introduced the binary decision variable δ_{it} for each measurement x_{it} such that $\delta_{it} = 1$ if and only if x_{it} is observed at period t. Thus, the problem is how to choose δ_{it} at each period such that the sensing constraint is satisfied and highest-risk individuals are detected. Detailed technical formulation can be found in Lin et al. 2018 [38].

New observations collected by the sensing strategy at the next period were further incorporated in the CM-based prognostic method to update the prognosis of all individuals, guiding the monitoring decision in the next period, i.e., the CM uses these observations to update the canonical models and membership vector c_i for all individual models. Adaptively monitoring the predicted high-risk individuals may lead to an increased number of missing values on predicted low-risk individuals. To guarantee an accurate estimation of the next-period major depression risk, we imputed the missing value before running risk prediction.

We applied the CM and SS methods on an EHR dataset of 610 patients that have at least 6 observations within 40 weeks under ongoing treatment [38]. We characterized patients' depression progressions using Markov models and predicted the risk to severe depression using CM. We ran the selective sensing algorithm to adaptively monitor all patients over 15 time periods (each consists of two weeks) under a sensing capability of 100 patients in each period. Prediction performance is evaluated by the correlation between predicted risks of severe depression and ground truth risks (derived from observed depression onset of the patients). Detection performance is measured by the percentage of severe patients being detected and the average true risk among detected patients. For instance, when only 10% of the patients could be monitored each time, our results showed that the selective sensing algorithm outperformed the rank and selection method.

2.3.2.2 Adaptive Treatment Selection

Adaptive treatment design aims to optimally select a series of treatments to improve the health outcomes of depression patients. Adaptive treatments are personalized based on patient characteristics, behaviors, disease history, and response to treatment [40]. Decisions on treatment may include medications, drug doses, administering schedules, behavioral interventions, or no further treatment [40]. MDPs [41], reinforcement learning [42], and multi-armed bandits [43] are among the most widely used tools. Many challenges still remain, including insufficient knowledge of personal progression dynamics and learning individual response to treatments.

Study Five: Partially Observable CM and POMDP The aforementioned studies assumed fully observable disease state and no treatment feedback. In

Gong and Liu 2019 [44], we proposed a partially observable collaborative modeling (POCM) method. Depression is modeled using a Hidden Markov Model (HMM). In an HMM, disease progression is represented using transition probabilities between true disease states, and emission probabilities are probabilities of observing some measurements of the true disease states. Similar to the CM, each patient's transition matrix and emission matrix in the HMM are assumed to be a linear combination of several canonical progression groups in the population. The weight of each patient belonging to each group is called the membership. We developed a POCM solution algorithm to estimate the parameters of the transition and emission matrices.

Next, we used a partially observable MDP (POMDP) to make a sequence of adaptive treatment decisions based on the estimated dynamics. The hidden states of the POMDP are depression severities, observations are depression assessment scores (i.e., PHQ-9), and decisions are treatment options. The objective is to optimally select between two types of treatments in each time period and maximize health outcome over time. For example, Treatment I is usual care under antidepressant medications, and Treatment II is an intensive depression management program with telephone-based treatment coordination. The objective is to maximize discounted total rewards measured using Net Monetary Benefit (defined as total health benefits × willingness-to-pay − total cost). Health benefits can be measured by quality-adjusted life years gained.

The process of creating the adaptive treatment framework includes three steps. See Figure 2.6. (i) In the **learning step**, the canonical transition and

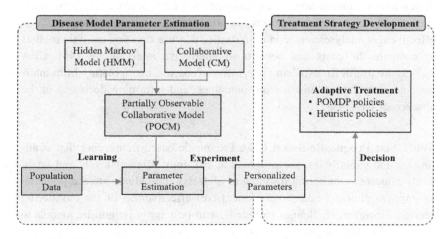

Figure 2.6 Overview of adaptive treatment design [44].

emission matrices for each progression pattern and patients' memberships are learned from an existing data set of patients under Treatment I using POCM. The population average treatment effect for Treatment II is assumed to be known from clinical trials, and such knowledge is used to estimate the canonical groups' parameters for Treatment II. (ii) In the **experiment step**, the personal dynamic for a new patient is initialized using model parameters estimated from the learning step and updated under both treatment options by running separate short trial periods; this is again accomplished by the POCM algorithm. The membership is then solved for each new patient belonging to each canonical group under either Treatment I or II. (iii) In the **decision step**, the optimal treatment strategy is obtained by solving a POMDP with the dynamic programming method (e.g., modified Monahan's algorithm [45]).

We compared the performance of the POMDP-based policies and several heuristic rule-based policies using a simulated depression treatment population. Results showed that the POCM can provide a better estimation of personal disease progression than the traditional method of solving an HMM when there are subgroup structures in the disease progression. We also demonstrated that the POCM-POMDP policies give the highest benefit for patients over the course of treatment. In addition, the POCM-based policies switch treatment less frequently than other policies. This research helps to advance the development of AI decision support tools for chronic disease care [44].

2.3.3 Cost-Effectiveness Analysis

A key missing link is how to estimate the long-term outcomes of these data-driven AI-assisted interventions in real-world clinical settings. Cost-effectiveness analyses are economic studies that use decision-analytic models to compare the costs and benefits of alternative interventions [46]. CEA models are useful for exploring alternative scenarios, extrapolating from intermediate endpoints to downstream outcomes, and informing decisions in the absence of data [47].

Study Six: Prognostic-Based CEA Prognostic-based monitoring that stratifies the individual's disease progression risk into different levels and adaptively allocates monitoring resource to high-risk individuals has the potential to improve patient health outcome and cost-effectiveness of the monitoring service. However, challenges include how to best apply prognostic models to inform the design of monitoring strategies and identify the cost-effective strategies.

In Lin et al. 2019 [48], we developed a decision support framework that integrated individual prognostics, monitoring strategy design and cost-effectiveness analysis (Figure 2.7). We applied the proposed framework to simulate the adaptive monitoring of a depression treatment population from EHR data. Several prediction algorithms with increasing complexity, including natural history matching, logistic regression, rule-based method, and Markov-based CM, were simulated to monitor the high-risk individuals for severe depression over time. We found six cost-effective monitoring strategies and demonstrated that the two routine monitoring strategies were dominated by the prognostic-based monitoring strategies (Figure 2.8). Methods from this

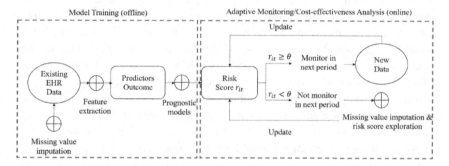

Figure 2.7 The framework of prognostic-based monitoring. Here, r_{it} denotes the risk score of individual i in tth monitoring period, and θ represents the threshold for monitoring [48].

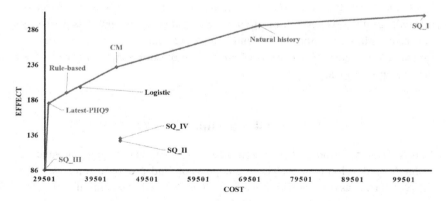

Figure 2.8 Cost-effectiveness frontier. The cost-effective strategies are represented by blue dots and the dominated strategies are denoted by red dots. SQ: status quo of routine monitoring under various frequencies [48].

research showed promise to implement prognostic-based monitoring of chronic conditions in clinical practice.

Study Seven: Cohort-Based CEA In Sun and Liu 2020 [49], we evaluated the cost-effectiveness of an adaptive remote monitoring technology for optimally switching between nine depression treatment lines. We used Markov-cohort models to simulate chronic depression patients' disease progression under monitoring and treatment over two years. Cohorts are defined by age (base case, 45 years), and sex (base case, 69% female). In addition, we considered heterogeneous disease progression patterns and clustered patients into three groups including a high-risk, a medium-risk, and a low-risk group of major depression. We considered five strategies: an adaptive technology that schedules follow-up appointment for treatment switch based on remotely monitoring patients' response to treatment with inaccuracy (i.e., imperfect sensitivity and specificity); a rule-based follow-up strategy that assigns the next follow-up time based on the patient's health state observed at the current follow-up (similar to current practice); and fixed frequency follow-up at every two-month, four-month, and six-month period. In the base case, since the monitoring accuracy and usage cost are uncertain, we simulated more than 1,000 scenarios and investigated how sensitivity, specificity, and cost of the remote monitoring technology would affect its cost-effectiveness.

Results showed for an adaptive remote monitoring technology with 0.75 sensitivity and specificity, it is cost effective with an incremental cost-effectiveness ratio ranging from \$52,600/QALYs to \$63,800/QALYs (2019 USD) gained compared to the rule-based follow-up strategy. Sensitivity analyses indicated that the imperfect technology is 63–78% cost effective depending on the risk group. In summary, a combination of methods including clustering, Markov-cohort model, and treatment simulation can be generalized to evaluate the cost-effectiveness of adaptive monitoring technology in other disease applications.

2.4 Summary

In this chapter, we presented several methodological challenges in advancing technology development for chronic depression and proposed three steps to achieve an AI-assisted technology framework. We showed highlights from seven research studies to aid in the design of adaptive monitoring and treatment strategies for chronic depression. This body of work include modeling complex disease trajectories, identifying patients at high risk of progression through predictive analytics, and recommending adaptive and cost-effective follow-up care. These methods complement and build on each other to achieve the final goal of maximizing patient health outcomes. We believe AI-assisted technology in mental health holds the promise of transforming the current reactive practice to proactive and personalized monitoring and treatment, providing value to healthcare providers, patients, and healthcare systems. Given the surge in interest in telemedicine during and post the COVID19 pandemic, and the opportunity of telemedicine to treat depression, AI-assisted technology has an increasingly important role to play in patient care.

Methods presented in this chapter are advanced and not yet implemented in clinical practice. We hope that they may serve as fundamental building blocks for future AI-assisted technology to be translated into clinical practice. Though there is growing interest from academia, large healthcare systems, and private entrepreneurs to develop applications in remote monitoring and digital thera-peutics, and some efforts have shown early success [50], the effectiveness and cost-effectiveness of these novel technologies still need to be proven and evaluated in long-term observational studies and comparative effectiveness trials. Ultimately, implementation success will depend on user acceptance, ease of use, system maintenance, and integration with EHR and the workflow of routine mental health services.

References

1. Centers for Disease Control and Prevention: Depression. www.cdc.gov/nchs/fas tats/depression.htm.
2. Centers for Disease Control and Prevention: Depression morbidity. www.cdc.gov/nchs/data/nhis/earlyrelease/EarlyRelease202009-508.pdf.
3. National Institute of Mental Health: Depression. www.nimh.nih.gov/health/topics/depression/index.shtml. 2018
4. Centers for Disease Control and Prevention: Facts about suicide. www.cdc.gov/suicide/facts/index.html.
5. Insel, T.: Thomas Insel: toward a new understanding of mental illness. TED Talk. www.youtube.com/watch?v=PeZ-U0pj9LI. 2013
6. National Institute of Mental Health: Suicide. www.nimh.nih.gov/health/statistics/suicide.
7. Klein M. Bloomberg visual data: how Americans die. www.bloomberg.com/data view/2014-04-17/how-americans-die.html. 2014.
8. Ribeiro J, Franklin J, Fox KR, et al. Self-injurious thoughts and behaviors as risk factors for future suicide ideation, attempts, and death: a meta-analysis of longitu-dinal studies. *Psychological Medicine*. 2016; **46**(2):225–236.
9. USPSTF. Screening for depression in adults: U.S. preventive services task force recommendation statement. *Annals of Internal Medicine*. 2009; **151** (11):784–792.

10. Parekh AK, Barton MB. The challenge of multiple comorbidity for the US health care system. *JAMA*. 2010; **303**(13):1303–1304.

11. Simon GE, VonKorff M, Rutter C, Wagner E. Randomised trial of monitoring, feedback, and management of care by telephone to improve treatment of depression in primary care. *BMJ*. 2000; **320**(7234):550–554.

12. Reynolds CFR, Frank E. US Preventive Services Task Force Recommendation Statement on Screening for Depression in Adults: not good enough. *JAMA Psychiatry*. 2016; **73**(3):189–190.

13. Pratt L, Brody D, Gu Q. *Antidepressant Use in Persons Aged 12 and Over: United States, 2005–2008*. NCHS Data Brief, No. 76. Hyattsville, MD: National Center for Health Statistics. 2011.

14. Shechter SM, Bailey MD, Schaefer AJ, Roberts MS. The optimal time to initiate HIV therapy under ordered health states. *Operations Research*. 2008; **56**(1):20–33.

15. Alagoz O, Maillart LM, Schaefer AJ, Roberts MS. The optimal timing of living-donor liver transplantation. *Management Science*. 2004; **50**(10):1420–1430.

16. Alagoz O, Maillart LM, Schaefer AJ, Roberts MS. Determining the acceptance of cadaveric livers using an implicit model of the waiting list. *Operations Research*. 2007; **55**(1):24–36.

17. Burhaneddin S, Maillart, LM, Shaefer, AJ, Alagoz O. Estimating the patient's price of privacy in liver transplantation. *Operations Research*. 2008; **56**(6):1393–1410.

18. Sutin AR, Terracciano A, Milaneschi Y, et al. The trajectory of depressive symptoms across the adult life span. *JAMA Psychiatry*. 2013; **70**(8):803–811.

19. Gunn J, Elliott P, Densley K, et al. A trajectory-based approach to understand the factors associated with persistent depressive symptoms in primary care. *Journal of Affective Disorders*. 2013; **148**(2-3):338–346.

20. Wang X, Sontag D, Wang F. Unsupervised learning of disease progression models. *Proceedings of the 20th ACM SIGKDD International Conference on Knowledge Discovery and Data Mining*. 2014:85–94.

21. Brandeau ML, Sainfort F, Pierskalla WP. *Operations Research and Health Care: A Handbook of Methods and Applications*. Boston: Kluwer Academic 2004.

22. Weinstein MC, Siegel JE, Gold MR, Kamlet MS, Russell LB. Recommendations of the Panel on Cost-effectiveness in Health and Medicine. *JAMA*. 1996; **276** (15):1253–1258.

23. Weinstein MC, O'Brien B, Hornberger J, et al. Principles of good practice for decision analytic modeling in health-care evaluation: report of the ISPOR Task Force on Good Research Practices – modeling studies. *Value in Health*. 2003; **6** (1):9–17.

24. Twisk J, Hoekstra T. Classifying developmental trajectories over time should be done with great caution: a comparison between methods. *Journal of Clinical Epidemiology,* 2012; **65**(10):1078–1087.

25. Craig BA, Sendi PP. Estimation of the transition matrix of a discrete-time Markov chain. *Health Economics*, 2002; 11(1):33–42.

26. Musliner KL, Munk-Olsen T, Eaton WW, Zandi PP. Heterogeneity in long-term trajectories of depressive symptoms: patterns, predictors and outcomes. *Journal of Affective Disorders*, 2016; **192**:199–211.

27. Bishop CM. *Pattern Recognition and Machine Learning*. New York: Springer 2006.

28. Russell SJ, Norvig P, Davis E. *Artificial Intelligence: A Modern Approach.* 3rd ed. Upper Saddle River, NJ: Prentice Hall 2010.

29. Drummond M. *Methods for the Economic Evaluation of Health Care Programmes.* 4th ed. Oxford: Oxford University Press 2015.

30. Kroenke K, Spitzer RL, Williams JB. The PHQ-9: validity of a brief depression severity measure. *Journal of General Internal Medicine.* 2001; **16**(9):606-613.

31. Charlson ME, Pompei P, Ales KL, MacKenzie CR. A new method of classifying prognostic comorbidity in longitudinal studies: development and validation. *Journal of Chronic Diseases.* 1987; **40**(5):373–383.

32. Boor CD. *A Practical Guide to Splines*: New York: Springer 1978.

33. Lasko TA, Denny JC, Levy MA. Computational phenotype discovery using unsupervised feature learning over noisy, sparse, and irregular clinical data. *PloS One.* 2013; **8**(6):e66341.

34. Shechter S. When to initiate, when to switch, and how to sequence HIV therapies: a Markov decision process approach. Doctoral thesis, University of Pittsburgh, Pittsburgh, PA; 2006.

35. Gong J, Simon GE, Liu S. Machine learning discovery of longitudinal patterns of depression and suicidal ideation. *PloS One.* 2019; **14**(9):e0222665.

36. Lin Y, Huang S, Simon GE, Liu S. Analysis of depression trajectory patterns using collaborative learning. *Mathematical Biosciences.* 2016; **282**:191–203.

37. Lin Y, Liu K, Byon E, et al. A collaborative learning framework for estimating many individualized regression models in a heterogeneous population. *IEEE Transactions on Reliability.* 2018; **67**(1):328–341.

38. Lin Y, Liu S, Huang S. Selective sensing of a heterogeneous population of units with dynamic health conditions. *IISE Transactions.* 2018; **50**(12):1076–1088.

39. Lin Y, Huang S, Simon GE, Liu S. Data-based decision rules to personalize depression follow-up. *Scientific Reports.* 2018; **8**(1):5064.

40. Kosorok MR, Moodie EE. *Adaptive Treatment Strategies in Practice: Planning Trials and Analyzing Data for Personalized Medicine.* ASA-SIAM Series on Statistics and Applied Mathematics. Philadelphia: Society for Industrial and Applied Mathematics 2016.

41. Schaefer AJ, Bailey MD, Shechter SM, Roberts MS. Modeling medical treatment using Markov decision processes. In: Brandeau ML, Sainfort F, Pierskalla WP, eds. *Operations Research and Health Care: A Handbook of Methods and Applications.* Boston: Springer 2004:593–612.

42. Vincent RD, Pineau J, Ybarra N, Naqa IE. Chapter 16: Practical reinforcement learning in dynamic treatment regimes. In: *Adaptive Treatment Strategies in Practice* 2016:263–296.

43. Negoescu D, Bimpikis K, Brandeau M, Iancu DA. Dynamic learning of patient response types: an application to treating chronic diseases. *Management Science.* 2017; **64**(8):3469–3970.

44. Gong J, Liu S. Partially observable collaborative model for optimizing personalized treatment selection. Paper presented at the 40th SMDM Annual Meeting; 2018; Montreal, Quebec, Canada.

45. Monahan GE. A survey of partially observable Markov decision processes: theory, models, and algorithms. *Management Science.* 1982; **28**(1):1–16.

46. Gold M. Panel on cost-effectiveness in health and medicine. *Medical Care.* 1996; **34**(12 Suppl):DS197–DS199.
47. Buxton MJ, Drummond MF, et al. Modelling in economic evaluation: an unavoidable fact of life. *Health Economics.* 1997; **6**(3):217–227.
48. Lin Y, Huang S, Simon GE, Liu S. Cost-effectiveness analysis of prognostic-based depression monitoring. *IIE Transactions on Healthcare Systems Engineering.* 2019; **9**(1):41–54.
49. Sun X, Liu S. A decision-analytic framework to evaluate the cost-effectiveness of adaptive monitoring technology: the case of chronic depression. Paper presented at the 42nd Annual SMDM Annual Meeting; 2020; virtual.
50. Wu S, Vidyanti I, Liu P, et al. Patient-centered technological assessment and monitoring of depression for low-income patients. *Journal of Ambulatory Care Management.* 2014; **37**(2):138–147.

3

Personalizing Medicine

Estimating Heterogeneous Treatment Effects

Tony Duan and Sanjay Basu

Summary of the Problem

Personalized medicine requires patient-specific estimates of the risks and benefits of treatment based on the patient's preferences, characteristics, and medical history. Estimating the risks and benefits of a given therapy for a given patient requires estimation of "heterogeneous treatment effects" – or the different ways that the same treatment might impact different people.

Summary of the Solution

We describe fundamental challenges to estimating heterogeneous treatment effects in the context of the statistical causal inference literature, proposed algorithms for addressing those challenges, and methods to evaluate how well heterogeneous treatment effects have been estimated. We illustrate the proposed algorithms using data from two large randomized trials of blood pressure treatments. We describe directions for future research in medical statistics and machine learning in this domain.

Summary of Relevance in a Post-COVID World

The United States saw significant disparities in the rates of COVID-19 mortality and morbidity associated with race, ethnicity, and socioeconomic status. This has brought more attention to an old problem; gaps in access to and quality of US healthcare for under-served populations. Many of the clinical trials underlying evidence-based treatments failed to include representatively diverse patient populations. Estimating heterogeneous treatment effects from previous studies may allow for the evaluation of therapies for populations insufficiently represented in the original works.

3.1 Introduction

In this chapter we discuss applications of artificial intelligence to estimating heterogeneous treatment effects (HTEs) in medicine. More generally, this problem is known as *causal inference*, especially in econometrics and computer science. We observe a patient with a set of covariates, and we can choose from a set of possible treatments. In order to make the best decision, we need to predict the personalized effect that each treatment option would have on some outcome of interest (such as mortality, or cardiovascular event).

Causal inference is a difficult problem. Broadly speaking, there are two relevant settings when we are interested in personalizing medicine: estimating causal effects from *randomized controlled trials (RCTs)* and estimating causal effects from *observational data*. Both settings have seen recent advances in methodology with the advent of larger data sets and machine learning methods, though in this chapter we will primarily analyze the randomized controlled trial setting.

At a high level, what we will see is that machine learning can be used as a black-box method that helps make better predictions, which can then be plugged into existing causal inference methods. As data sets are made increasingly available, better predictions will improve the accuracy of causal estimators. The field is quickly evolving, and remains a very active area of research.

In this chapter we will assume basic familiarity with statistics and machine learning methods (such as logistic regression and random forests). The focus will be on how flexible machine learning methods can improve causal estimators, especially in the RCT setting. For readers unfamiliar with statistical learning methods, we refer to Hastie et al. (2009) for an accessible introduction.

3.1.1 Motivating Example: SPRINT versus ACCORD

As a motivating example, we will focus on the question of how to prescribe blood-pressure-lowering medications to prevent atherosclerotic cardiovascular disease (CVD; manifest as heart attacks and strokes). Two strategies have been debated: intensive (target systolic blood pressure [SBP] < 120 mmHg) versus standard (target SBP $<$ 140 mmHg) blood pressure therapy. We want to keep blood pressure low by prescribing medications to help reduce the risk of heart attacks and strokes, but at the same time we don't want to over-prescribe due to the adverse side effects that may be associated with excessive blood pressure treatment, such as kidney failure.

The issue of whether to treat an intensive target has been extensively debated due to conflicting data from large, randomized trials (Figure 3.1). In 2010, the ACCORD study group reported the results of a large, well-designed RCT of 4733 participants that did not find a statistically significant benefit in intensive blood pressure therapy (hazard ratio [HR] of a CVD event such as heart attack or stroke = 0.88, 95% CI: 0.73 − 1.06) and even suggested a potentially higher mortality rate among those experiencing intensive treatment (The ACCORD Study Group, 2010). In 2015, however, the SPRINT study group reported the results of a large, well-designed RCT of 9361 participants that found a statistically significant benefit in intensive blood pressure therapy (HR of a CVD event = 0.75, 95% CI: 0.64 − 0.89), and was actually stopped early because it was considered unethical to continue treating subjects in the control arm with only standard therapy (The SPRINT Research Group, 2015). See Table 3.1 for summary statistics on the populations of these two trials.

These discordant results added uncertainty in the debate over how to prescribe treatments in the clinic. While there were a few differences between the study populations (for example, all ACCORD participants had diabetes whereas SPRINT participants did not), both had large populations with results that should generalize (and blood pressure medicines are thought to work equivalently in people with and without diabetes).

One approach to this problem is to say: perhaps intensive blood pressure therapy is not universally helpful or harmful to all patients, but rather some patients will benefit and others will experience more harm than benefit, depending on their unique characteristics. In the rest of this chapter we test the hypothesis that there may be HTEs that could be identified using data from these two blood pressure treatment RCTs, and determine whether machine learning could better identify who benefits and who does not, compared to conventional statistical regression methods.

3.2 A Primer on Causal Inference Methods

In this section we formalize the problem of causal inference with regard to HTE identification for blood pressure therapy. First, we need to define relevant variables for each patient. Each observes a binary *treatment* variable W, where

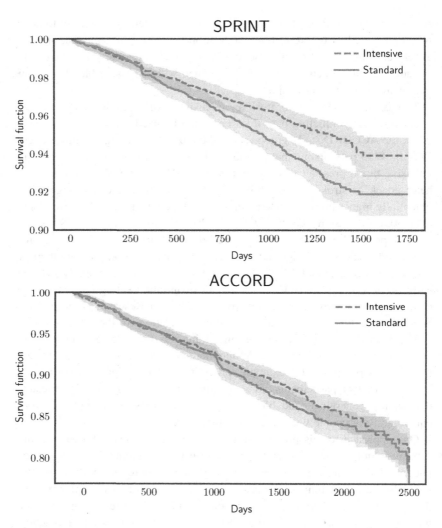

Figure 3.1 Kaplan-Meier plots of the SPRINT and ACCORD randomized controlled trials for intensive blood pressure therapy. ACCORD (right) did not show a statistically significant benefit for intensive therapy whereas SPRINT (right) did.

$W = 0$ denotes standard blood pressure therapy and $W = 1$ denotes intensive blood pressure therapy. We similarly define a binary *outcome* variable Y, where $Y = 1$ denotes that a CVD event occurred within a fixed window (for example, 3 years) of follow-up and $Y = 0$ denotes it did not. Finally, we regress using a set of d numerical and categorical covariates X which may

Table 3.1. *Summary statistics of mean (standard deviation) of covariates from the SPRINT and ACCORD trials*

Covariate	SPRINT ($N = 9{,}361$)	ACCORD-BP ($N = 4{,}733$)
Age (years)	67.84 (9.40)	63.19 (6.68)
Female (%)	35 (48)	49 (50)
Black (%)	32 (46)	24 (42)
Hispanic (%)	11 (0.31)	7 (26)
Systolic blood pressure (mm Hg)	139.65 (15.59)	139.62 (15.75)
Diastolic blood pressure (mm Hg)	78.16 (11.92)	75.94 (10.34)
Number of blood pressure treatment classes	1.84 (1.04)	1.70 (1.08)
Current Smoker (%)	13 (34)	1 (10)
Former Smoker (%)	43 (49)	48 (50)
Aspirin use (%)	51 (50)	52 (50)
Statin use (%)	44 (50)	65 (48)
Serum creatinine (mg/dL)	1.07 (0.34)	0.91 (0.25)
Total cholesterol (mg/dL)	190.10 (41.22)	192.88 (43.77)
High-density lipoprotein cholesterol (mg/dL)	52.82 (14.45)	46.74 (13.50)
Triglycerides (mg/dL)	126.13 (90.29)	186.86 (164.58)
Body mass index (kg/m^2)	29.87 (5.76)	32.23 (5.46)

include baseline blood pressure; and demographics and health features that may relate to the effectiveness of blood pressure therapy or risk of CVD, such as tobacco smoking. Mathematically, we summarize with:

$$X \in \mathbb{R}^d \text{ a set of covariates}$$

$$Y \in \{0, 1\} \text{ binary outcome}$$

$$W \in \{0, 1\} \text{ binary treatment}$$

We assume the *potential outcomes framework* (Imbens and Rubin, 2015). Let $Y(0)$ denote the outcome when $W = 0$ and $Y(1)$ denote the outcome when $W = 1$. For each participant, we only observe one of these two potential outcomes, depending on the value of W. We observe a data set of n participants which consists of realizations

$$\left\{ X^{(i)}, Y^{(i)}, W^{(i)} \right\}_{i=1}^{n},$$

and for each participant i we have $Y^{(i)} = Y^{(i)}\left(W^{(i)}\right)$.

Traditionally an RCT is used to estimate and make recommendations based on the *average treatment effect (ATE)*,

$$\tau = \mathbb{E}[Y(1) - Y(0)].$$

The interpretation of τ is: on average (over the population), what is the difference in outcomes within the pre-specified window of follow-up due to the treatment arm versus the control arm? A positive value indicates higher likelihood of CVD event due to intensive blood pressure therapy, whereas a negative value indicates a lower likelihood of CVD event due to intensive blood pressure therapy. Note that τ here is a single scalar only, and estimating it will not allow us to make different recommendations depending on covariates x.

This motivates the setting we'll be focusing on, in which we actually want to estimate the *conditional average treatment effect (CATE)*,

$$\tau(x) = \mathbb{E}[Y(1) - Y(0) \mid X = x].$$

Estimating the CATE allows us to make *personalized* treatment decisions that account for heterogeneity, instead of recommending the same treatment to every participant. Returning to our example of blood-pressure therapy, $-\tau(x)$ denotes the absolute risk reduction (ARR) for a CVD event associated with intensive treatment for a patient with covariates x, within the pre-specified window of follow-up.

The *fundamental problem of causal inference* is that for each participant i, we only ever observe $Y^{(i)}(0)$ or $Y^{(i)}(1)$, but never both. That is, we only ever know the potential outcome for a participant that matches the treatment they were prescribed. In a sense, this is a missing data problem: we are missing the complete data set and need to use causal methods to adjust for this missingness.

The main issue that arises in causal inference is *confounding*. We may have some variables Z that affect both the treatment assignment W and the outcome Y, which would bias our attempts to estimate the causal effect of W. For example, suppose we want to estimate the effect of intensive blood pressure therapy on reducing CVD event risk (the risk of heart attack or stroke). However, in the intensive arm we enroll only participants over the age of 80, while in the standard arm we enroll only participants under the age of 80. Since older adults tend to have significantly higher CVD risk, a naive examination of the absolute risks in each arm would show a significant risk increase associated with intensive treatment, even if there is actually a slight reduction in risk associated with intensive treatment.

In an observational data set, to proceed we first need to assume *unconfoundedness* (also known as ignorability). Loosely speaking, this assumes that the treatment assignment mechanism can be determined from observed covariates and there is no additional unobserved confounding:

$$\{Y(0), Y(1)\} \perp W \mid X.$$

That is, the potential outcomes are conditionally independent of the treatment, given covariates. In this setting we let $e(x) = \mathbb{E}[W|X = x]$ denote the *propensity score*, i.e. the likelihood of being assigned to a particular treatment arm conditioned on covariates. We will see that estimating the propensity score is often critical. Another quantity that we will later employ is the marginal outcome probability, $m(x) = \mathbb{E}[Y|X = x]$. This is simply the expected outcome given observed covariates, irrespective of treatment.

The second assumption we need is *overlap*; that is, there is some non-zero probability that each patient can be assigned to either of the treatment arms. If all patients were deterministically assigned to their respective arms, there would be no observable information about the missing potential outcomes from the data. Formally, the overlap assumption can be written as

$$0 < e(x) < 1, \text{for all } x.$$

The RCT setting simplifies the assumptions significantly, since we have a completely random treatment assignment mechanism. Not only can we assume unconfoundedness, we can make the even stronger assumption that potential outcomes are independent of the treatment (unconditional of X), i.e.

$$\{Y(0), Y(1)\} \perp W.$$

Moreover, all propensity scores are $e(x) = \Pr[W = 0] = \Pr[W = 1] = \frac{1}{2}$. Recalling that our motivating example is to use data from the SPRINT and ACCORD trials, we will focus on the RCT setting. We leave references in the Guide to the Literature at the end of this chapter for readers interested in the observational setting.

3.2.1 Conventional Approaches

The traditional method for assessing heterogeneity in RCTs is via *subgroup analyses*, which analyze subsets of the RCT participants that belong to each particular subgroup (for example, by race, or gender). Unfortunately, by subdividing the trial participants into subgroups, the statistical power to detect benefit for each subgroup is significantly reduced (Hayward et al., 2006). Moreover, subgroup analyses need to be corrected for multiple hypothesis testing and have generally been criticized due to the risk of false positives (Wallach et al., 2017).

What has instead been recommended is a multivariate regression approach to identifying HTEs (Kent et al., 2010, 2016). This approach predicts HTEs by regressing the treatment term and interaction between treatment and covariates against the outcome. For a logistic regression approach, the model would look like

$$Y \sim X_1 + \ldots + X_d + W + X_1 W + \ldots + X_d W.$$

Such a model can then be used with future patients to predict heterogeneous treatment effects, by estimating

$$\hat{\tau}(x) = \hat{p}(Y|X, W = 1) - \hat{p}(Y|X, W = 0).$$

Note that the notation $\hat{\tau}$ denotes an *estimator* of the true CATE, which is instead denoted as τ. Likewise, $\hat{p}$ denotes an estimator of the probability of outcome under the logistic regression model given covariates and treatment. We do not have any guarantees in general that the estimated quantities correspond to the true quantities of interest, especially when the model is mis-specified.

Two studies that applied logistic regression to the SPRINT and ACCORD data found that there was indeed heterogeneity in the populations (Patel et al., 2017; Basu et al., 2017). In Figure 3.2, for example, we exhibit the heterogeneity in distributions of predicted ARR from a simple logistic regression approach on the SPRINT and ACCORD data sets. As one might expect, we find that there is greater predicted ARR (i.e. benefit from treatment) for the SPRINT population than for the ACCORD population.

However, logistic regression is relatively naive in that it is unable to account for nonlinear relationships between covariates and the outcome. Instead, more powerful machine learning models (such as random forests and neural networks) can be combined with individual participant data to potentially make better predictions.

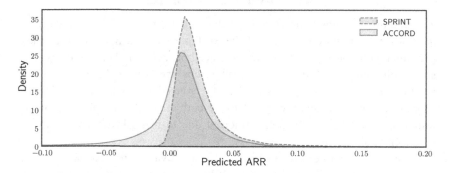

Figure 3.2 Heterogeneity in the predicted treatment benefit from a simple logistic model approach, adapted from Basu et al. (2017).

3.2.2 Machine Learning Approaches

We describe four machine learning (ML) approaches for causal inference in this section. There exist more causal inference methods beyond this list, but our intention is to highlight several of the recent proposals that leverage machine learning to perform causal inference.

The first three of these approaches are *meta-learning* methods (Künzel et al., 2019). This term meta-learning refers to the fact that they rely on an underlying choice of supervised learning model as a "base learner", but are agnostic to the particular choice of base learner and can therefore treat it as a black box. The practitioner can choose the supervised learning method that best suits the size and modality of their data set.

3.2.2.1 S-Learner

We build a *single* machine learning model to predict $p(Y|X,W)$, then estimate

$$\hat{\tau}(x) = \hat{p}(Y|X, W = 1) - \hat{p}(Y|X, W = 0).$$

This is perhaps the most intuitive method to predict treatment effects with generic machine learning: by simply including the treatment as an additional covariate. It is equivalent to the conventional approach described in the previous section, with a logistic regression model as the choice of base learner.

3.2.2.2 T-Learner

We build *two* machine learning models; one to predict $p(Y|X, W = 1)$ and one to predict $p(Y|X, W = 0)$. Then we estimate

$$\hat{\tau}(x) = \hat{p}(Y|X, W = 1) - \hat{p}(Y|X, W = 0)$$

The difference between the S-learner and T-learner methods is that the relationship between Y and W no longer needs to follow a rigid model specification. With a logistic regression base learner, for example, the outcome logit no longer needs to depend linearly on W. Another valuable example to consider when a random forest is chosen as a base learner. In the T-learner, the model effectively *forces* each decision tree to split on W as the first partition. On the other hand, in the S-learner W is simply treated like any other covariate, and each tree may or may not choose to use it as the first split.

3.2.2.3 X-Learner

The X-learner is a three-step process which attempts to control for potential confounding (Künzel et al., 2019).

1. Estimate marginal outcomes conditional on treatment using any machine learning base learner. The quantities of interest are:

$$\mu_0(x) = \mathbb{E}[Y(0)|X, W = 0] \qquad \mu_1(x) = \mathbb{E}[Y(1)|X, W = 1]$$

We estimate by learning separately on control and treatment groups. Results in the learned functions $\hat{\mu}_0(x)$ and $\hat{\mu}_1(x)$.

2. Impute treatment effects for each participant, using the model corresponding to the un-observed outcome for each participant. Specifically, the i-th participant is imputed with either:

$$\tau_1^{(i)} = Y^{(i)} - \hat{\mu}_0\left(X^{(i)}\right) \text{ if } W^{(i)} = 1$$

$$\tau_0^{(i)} = \hat{\mu}_1\left(X^{(i)}\right) - Y^{(i)} \text{ if } W^{(i)} = 0$$

Then we fit models using imputed treatment effects and any machine learning base learner. Results in the learned functions $\hat{\tau}_0(x)$ and $\hat{\tau}_1(x)$.

3. Finally we estimate the CATE with

$$\hat{\tau}(x) = \hat{e}(x)\hat{\tau}_0(x) + (1 - \hat{e}(x))\hat{\tau}_1(x)$$

Recall that $\hat{e}(x)$ estimates the propensity scores $p(W|X = x)$. In the case of an RCT we know that $e(x) = \frac{1}{2}$. But in the case of an observational data set these propensity scores must be estimated via a learning method as well. For the interested reader we have published an implementation of the X-learner with random forest base learners in R (Duan et al., 2019).

A crucial step in the X-learner method is cross-fitting (Chernozhukov et al., 2018). In step 2 we're imputing treatment effects for each participant, and then fitting models to them in step 3. For participant i, it is important that the prediction $\hat{\mu}_0\left(X^{(i)}\right)$ or $\hat{\mu}_1\left(X^{(i)}\right)$ must *not* have included i in its training set. We can view this as leaving i in the held-out set when making predictions for the marginal outcomes, thus limiting the degree of overfitting. This can be implemented by implementing a k-fold cross-validation, making predictions for each fold as a held-out set while training on remaining folds. When using random forests as base learners, we can make predictions for each participant i using only trees for which i is out-of-bag (i.e. not in the training set) (Breiman, 2001).

3.2.2.4 Causal Forests

The causal forest builds on random forests for inference of causal effects (Wager and Athey, 2018). The idea is to build on standard regression trees by estimating the causal effect as the difference in observed outcomes in a leaf L corresponding to data point x,

$$\hat{\tau}(x) = \frac{\sum_{i:i\in L,\, W^{(i)}=1} Y^{(i)}}{|i \in L : W^{(i)} = 1|} - \frac{\sum_{i:i\in L,\, W^{(i)}=0} Y^{(i)}}{|i \in L : W^{(i)} = 0|}$$

Similar to how standard regression trees make splits on variables that maximize the variance of predicted values, the causal trees make splits to maximize variance of predicted causal effects.

One important aspect of causal forests is *honesty*, which arises from using separate data partitions (for example, a 50/50 split of the training data); one devoted to splitting each tree and one devoted to estimating causal effects. This ensures that no data point is used in *both* splitting the tree and estimating causal effects in a leaf – a necessary criterion for ensuring consistency of inference.

3.2.3 Evaluation Methods

How do we determine the accuracy of our CATE estimates? Importantly, we'll follow standard machine learning practice and evaluate on a held-out test set of participants. However, due to the fundamental problem of causal inference, we do not actually observe the ground truth CATE for participants – so evaluation is more challenging than in a traditional prediction task.

3.2.3.1 Evaluation for Traditional Classifiers

To motivate the metrics we'll use, we first consider how to evaluate traditional predictive models built for risk stratification over a binary outcome (for example, consider a model that predicts 10-year probability of CVD events). The most useful model is one that achieves high discrmimination while remaining well-calibrated (Alba et al., 2017). Discrimination is a measure of the predictive performance of a classifier, in terms of how well high risk individuals are separated from low risk individuals. Calibration is a measure of how well the predicted classifier probabilities match long-term frequencies of events.

Discrimination: C-Statistic. The C-Statistic is defined based on pairs with discordant outcomes. The C-statistic is the proportion of pairs in which the $Y = 1$ event was assigned a higher probability by the model than the $Y = 0$ event. In other words, the C-Statistic can be interpreted as: "if we have two

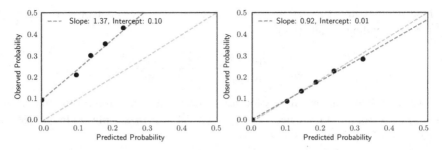

Figure 3.3 Examples of a poorly calibrated model (left) and a well-calibrated model (right) for 10-year CVD risk prediction. We group data points into quantiles of predicted risk and compare against the observed outcome rate in each quantile.

people with different outcomes, what is the model's probability of correctly choosing the one that is higher risk for the outcome of interest?" Higher C-Statistics are better; and the best possible model achieves a C-Statistic of 1. C-Statistic turns out to be equivalent to the area under the receiver operating characteristic curve (AUROC or ROC), which is a traditional metric for diagnostic models determined by plotting the range of model sensitivity against its specificity (Davis and Goadrich, 2006).

Calibration: Calibration Curve. A model is well-calibrated if predicted probability of events matches the observed probability of events. For example, out of all patients for which a model predicts an outcome probability of 20%, approximately 20% of those patients should actually observe the event. The traditional calibration curve and associated Hosmer-Lemeshow statistic (Harrell, 2001) can be constructed by partitioning patients into quantiles of predicted probability, and calculating the observed event rate in each quantile. Plotting the predicted against the observed event rates should ideally yield a curve that lies along the diagonal; the line of best fit should have slope 1 and intercept 0 (Figure 3.3). The calibration curve's slope essentially says "given two people, does my model not just predict which one is higher risk (as with a C-Statistic), but actually correctly predict the numerical probability of each of them getting the outcome?"

3.2.3.2 Evaluation for the HTE setting

Now let's consider the causal inference setting. Unlike simply determining the risk of an outcome (CVD events), for HTE analysis, we wish to determine the risk of an outcome being increased or decreased by the treatment of

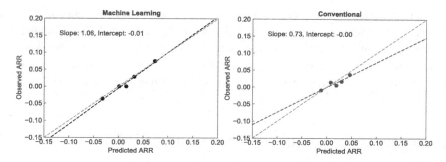

Figure 3.4 Calibration-for-benefit curves from our machine learning versus conventional HTE comparison.

intensive blood pressure treatment. Here we will constrain ourselves; the evaluation methods that we describe below are designed for the RCT setting and not for the observational data setting. We note that evaluation in the observational setting is challenging and remains an open area of research (Gottesman et al., 2019).

Discrimination: C-Statistic for Benefit. C-Statistic for benefit is calculated as the proportion of all matched pairs with unequal observed benefit, in which the patient pair receiving greater treatment benefit was predicted to do so (van Klaveren et al., 2018). To calculate we must match pairs of patients together such that each pair of patients has one with $W = 1$ and one with $W = 0$, and the two have identical predicted CATE. The C-Statistic for benefit thus represents the probability that two randomly chosen matched patient pairs with unequal observed benefit, the pair with greater observed benefit also has a higher predicted benefit.

Calibration: Calibration for Benefit Curve Here, we construct the analogue of calibration using CATE estimates. We partition individuals into quantiles of predicted CATE, and compare the empirical average treatment effect in each quantile against the predicted average treatment effect. The empirical average treatment effect can simply be calculated by taking the difference in event rates across each arm of the trial. Again, ideally the curve should lie along the diagonal with a slope of 1 and an intercept of 0 (Figure 3.4).

3.2.4 Time to Event Considerations

So far we have assumed that we have access to data sets with binarized outcomes for which we can apply causal inference methods. However, one practical consideration is that in many RCT data sets (and observational data sets) in healthcare, events are often right-censored. In an RCT, for example, participants may be lost to follow-up and so instead of knowing exactly when an event occurred, we only know that the event did not occur up to a certain time. This setting is known as a *time to event* (or survival) data set, of the form

$$\left\{ X^{(i)}, T^{(i)}, E^{(i)}, W^{(i)} \right\}_{i=1}^{n}.$$

This corresponds to the following random variables.

$$X \in \mathbb{R}^d \text{ covariates}$$

$$T \in \mathbb{R}_+ \text{ time to event or censorship}$$

$$E \in \{0, 1\} \text{ censorship indicator}$$

$$W \in \{0, 1\} \text{ treatment}$$

For example, in the SPRINT RCT we are interested in whether a CVD event occurred within 3 years of the baseline measurement. But we only know definitely whether this is the case for 67.3% of patients. The remaining participants were censored prior to the 3 year mark, so we don't know whether or not they truly observed a CVD event within 3 years of the baseline measurement. It isn't obvious how to adapt these remaining patients into the causal framework previously described, which assumes binary outcomes $Y^{(i)}$.

Generally, suppose we are interested in binary outcomes by a time of interest ψ. There are four cases that need to be accounted for when using a time to event data set:

1. The participant observed the event after the time of interest. Then we know for sure that $Y^{(i)} = 0$.
2. The participant was censored after the time of interest. Then we know for sure that $Y^{(i)} = 0$.
3. The participant observed the event before the time of interest. Then we know for sure that $Y^{(i)} = 1$.
4. The participant was censored before the time of interest.

In this setting, cases 1–3 have well-defined outcomes by the time of interest, but case 4 does not. How do we proceed?

One approach is inverse propensity of censorship weighting (IPCW) (Vock et al., 2016). We'll only use data points from cases 1–3, but re-weight them appropriately to adjust for the fact that we're not including data points in case 4. The intuition is that if participant i has a 1/3 chance to be censored after $T^{(i)}$, we'll want to weight them by 3 to account for the fact that there were 2

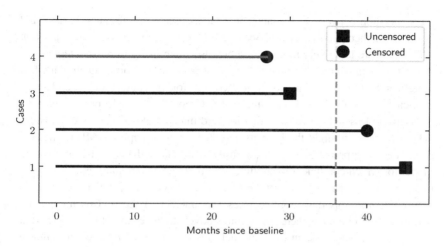

Figure 3.5 Time-to-event data needs to be adjusted for censorship. If a participant in the trial is censored prior to the followup time of interest (for example 3 years), then their data cannot be included as necessarily reflecting either a positive or negative outcome.

"copies" of i that were censored before $T(i)$, plus i itself. Mathematically, the weights are:

$$\omega(i) = \frac{1\{T^{(i)} \geq \psi\}}{\hat{p}\left(\text{cens after } \psi \mid X^{(i)}\right)} + \frac{1\{T^{(i)} < \psi, C^{(i)} = 0\}}{\hat{p}\left(\text{cens after } T^{(i)} \mid X^{(i)}\right)}.$$

The relevant probabilities of the time-to-censorship in the denominators can be estimated using Cox regression (Harrell, 2001) (Figure 3.5).

Last, we need to account for censoring not only when training causal estimators, but also when evaluating causal estimators. C-statistic for benefit can be weighted by the IPCW weights for each pair. The calibration curve for CATE can still be constructed by partitioning participants into quantiles of predicted CATE, but to calculate observed CATE, Kaplan-Meier estimates should be used to calculate the observed event rates in each arm of the trial.

3.3 Clinical Implications for Blood Pressure Treatment

There are three major clinical implications of this work on HTEs. First, the process of estimating HTEs is imperfect but can be evaluated as standard clinical risk scores are evaluated (through discrimination and calibration metrics). Hence, personalized treatment recommendations based on HTE/CATE estimates should be viewed similarly to how risk scores are viewed – as helpful but imperfect tools to facilitate a conversation between physicians and patients regarding the inherent risks and benefits of a therapeutic decision. Second, HTE estimation helps us recognize that ATE effect are less likely to be biased but also more likely to be an average that doesn't account well for personalized characteristics and important treatment effect modifiers that a physician needs to account for in clinical practice. Hence, explicit HTE analyses and reporting in RCT reports may help practically even if it appears less scientifically straightforward than simple ATE reporting. Third, HTE estimates highlight the benefits and challenges of applying ML to medical data. The ML approaches may be less easily interpretable than a logistic regression model for which coefficient magnitudes and directions help interpret the model's treatment of a given variable; yet the ML approaches can be far more accurate by accounting for important nonlinearities and interaction terms. Communicating ML models to clinicians therefore requires novel strategies to help visualize what the model is doing, to gain trust and help incorporate such models into clinical practice. We demonstrate some of these strategies in the following section.

3.3.1 Results: SPRINT versus ACCORD

Here, we present the results of our analysis of HTEs for intensive versus standard blood pressure therapy, using the SPRINT and ACCORD data sets. After experimenting with alternative machine learning methods, we found that the X-learner with random forests performed best. Confidence intervals were constructed via bootstrap re-sampling of the data set with optimism correction (Harrell, 2001).

The machine learning methods achieve statistically significantly better C-Statistic for Benefit compared to conventional logistic regression (Table 3.2). Moreover, the predicted ARRs tend to be better calibrated, with predicted event probabilities matching up better to observed event probabilities. Machine learning revealed a greater range of heterogeneity as well, i.e. a wider range of predicted ARR (Figure 3.6).

Table 3.2 *Summary statistics comparing a machine learning approach to a conventional approach to HTE analysis to identify benefits of intensive blood pressure therapy, using data from the SPRINT and ACCORD trials*

	Machine learning	Conventional
Discrimination		
C-for-benefit	0.60 (0.58 to 0.63)	0.51 (0.49 to 0.53)
Calibration		
Slope (ideally 1)	1.06 (0.74 to 1.32)	0.73 (0.30 to 1.14)
Intercept (ideally 0)	0.00 (-0.01 to 0.00)	0.00 (-0.01 to 0.01)

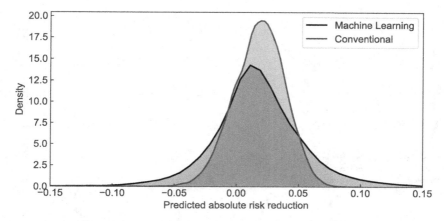

Figure 3.6 Distributions of predicted 3-year absolute risk reduction using machine learning (X-learner) and conventional (logistic regression) approaches, using data from the SPRINT and ACCORD trials. The machine learning approach resulted in a wider range of predicted risk reduction, exposing more potential heterogeneity in treatment effect while remaining well-calibrated.

3.3.2 Interpretation of ML Methods

A major challenge in applying machine learning to healthcare is that machine learning methods more complex than simple linear models are extremely difficult to interpret. Nonlinear relationships and complex interactions that are present in random forests and neural networks can be difficult to reason about. This has been, understandably, commonly cited as a reason for hesitation when looking to deploy artificial intelligence methods in healthcare. There has been considerable recent research activity in the area of interpretability to bring machine learning models closer to production (Murdoch et al., 2019). Here we will highlight two traditional methods of model interpretation that we applied to our work estimating HTEs for blood pressure therapy.

Partial Dependence Plots (Friedman, 2001) For each covariate, we can examine the effect of changes in that covariate on the predicted outcome, averaged over the entire held-out test set where other covariates are held fixed. This gives us a picture of the *average* dependence of the CATE predictions on each covariate. For example, we find in our setting that the predicted ARR due to intensive blood pressure therapy tends to increase with age among our participants (Figure 3.7).

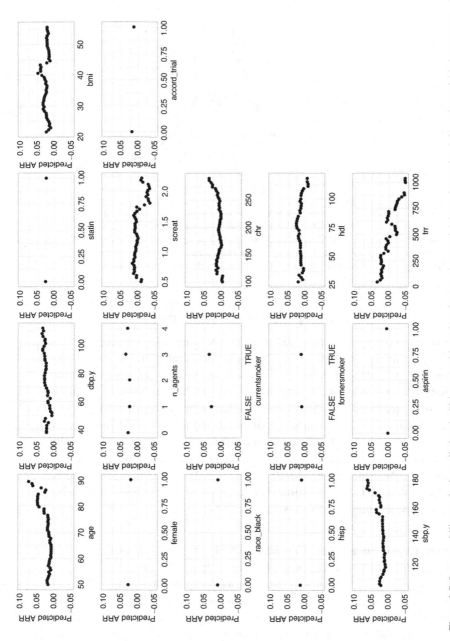

Figure 3.7 Interpretability methods applied to the X-learner with random forests, via a partial dependence plot (left) and a variable importance plot (right).

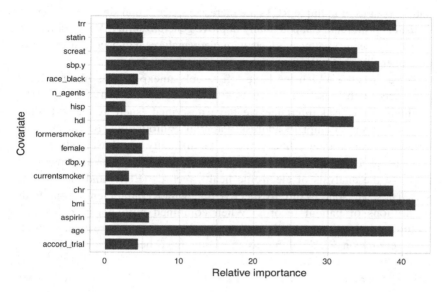

Figure 3.7 (*cont.*)

Variable Importance Plots (Breiman, 2001) When using random forest base learners, we can estimate the relative importance of each variable. This is done by examining how much out-of-bag error increases when each covariate is randomly permuted among out-of-bag participants instead of being held intact. For example, we find in our setting that the most important variables are: age, body mass index, total cholesterol, and number of blood pressure treatment classes (Figure 3.7).

3.3.3 Challenges Moving Forward

There remain many open questions that continue to drive research in the causal inference field forward. First, further studies are necessary to confirm the generalization of potential HTEs revealed through our machine learning analyses. Increased flexibility of machine learning models carry with them an increased risk of overfitting due to spurious correlations. While our work has been validated in part through our evaluations, further validation is necessary in external cohorts (i.e. ones not used in the derivation process). A prospective RCT would be particularly valuable.

Second, we have limited ourselves to a setting with a direct comparison between treatment options. However, meta-analyses that leverage individual patient data from multiple RCTs are increasingly common since they improve statistical power and can potentially improve generalizability. Valid estimation of heterogeneous treatment effects with meta-analyses will need to account for heterogeneity across RCT sites.

Third, an area which we have left largely unexplored is observational data sets with observed or potentially unobserved confounding. The methods for causal inference we have described (such as the X-learner and R-learner) attempt to address potential confounding, but there is no consensus yet on their efficacy due to the difficulty of robust evaluation in this setting. Developing methodology for observational data sets may help improve the analysis of electronic health records (EHR) and claims data sets. These are sources of retrospective data which contain tens or hundreds of millions of patient records. When combined with machine learning methods, they can potentially reveal more heterogeneous treatment effects than relying on RCTs alone, as the latter have been criticized for non-diverse patient selection.

Fourth, we have restricted ourselves to the setting in which we want to make a decision for a single treatment. In reality however, clinical practice involves a series of medical decision-making steps, in which each decision affects the future outcome. For example, in sepsis treatment a series of decisions must continually be made to maintain patient stability (Komorowski et al., 2018). Causal inference is especially challenging in this setting because any one of the decisions in the trajectory could have caused the adverse outcome, and it is difficult to pin down which ultimately caused it. The computer science literature on reinforcement learning studies multiple timestep decision making and has recently seen much activity in applications to healthcare.

3.4 Conclusion

So how can artificial intelligence help personalize medicine?

First, we can apply machine learning to help contextualize the average treatment effect from a randomized trial in the context of more personalized HTE-based personalized treatment effects. This will help facilitate shared decision-making between physicians and patients who wish to identify an individual's risks and benefits for a therapeutic decision.

Second, machine learning methods can help us identify why a particular treatment may be more or less beneficial in complex ways. There are physiological reasons to believe, for example, that the benefits or risks of a drug therapy will not just depend on a person's weight or age or sex, but complex combinations of – for example – their weight, kidney function, liver function, and prior medical history. Machine learning methods can account for such complexities with potentially much greater accuracy than traditional statistical regression-based risk scores.

Third, at a conceptual level, machine learning methods can help us transition from a clinical focus on the risk of an outcome to a more appropriate focus on the risk reduction or risk increase afforded by an intervention. It is one thing to say that a person has a high risk for a heart attack because of their blood pressure or cholesterol level; it is a much more useful thing to say that a particular intervention will lower that risk or increase that risk. Machine learning methods to assess HTE help us to better understand the effects of our decisions, not just the effects of exposures or demographics, allowing us to move towards a better understanding of how we can improve medical decision-making for personalized medical therapy.

Further Reading

For a clinical perspective, we refer the reader to the following review papers: Kent et al. (2020) provides guidelines for analyzing and reporting HTE in the medical literature, Davidoff (2017) provides guidance for how to interpret the results of HTE analyses, and Dahabreh et al. (2017) compares typical approaches for HTE analysis. For a causal inference perspective, the following textbooks and papers are more technical: Imbens and Rubin (2015) provides a theoretical causal inference framework, Coppock et al. (2018) explores the limitations to HTE analysis generalizability in the social science literature, and Athey and Imbens (2016) provide details on a generalized random forest approach for HTE analysis using machine learning.

References

Alba, Ana Carolina, Agoritsas, Thomas, Walsh, Michael, Hanna, Steven, Iorio, Alfonso, Devereaux, P. J., McGinn, Thomas, and Guyatt, Gordon. 2017. Discrimination and calibration of clinical prediction models: Users' guides to the medical literature. *JAMA*, **318**(14), 1377–1384.

Athey, Susan, and Imbens, Guido. 2016. Recursive partitioning for heterogeneous causal effects. *Proceedings of the National Academy of Sciences*, **113**(27), 7353–7360.

Basu, Sanjay, Sussman, Jeremy B., Rigdon, Joseph, Steimle, Lauren, Denton, Brian T., and Hayward, Rodney A. 2017. Benefit and harm of intensive blood pressure treatment: Derivation and validation of risk models using data from the SPRINT and ACCORD trials. *PLOs Medicine*, **14**(10), e1002410.

Breiman, Leo. 2001. Random forests. *Machine Learning*, **45**(1), 5–32.

Chernozhukov, Victor, Chetverikov, Denis, Demirer, Mert, Duflo, Esther, Hansen, Christian, Newey, Whitney, and Robins, James. 2018. Double/debiased machine learning for treatment and structural parameters. *The Econometrics Journal*, **21**(1), C1–C68.

Coppock, Alexander, Leeper, Thomas J., and Mullinix, Kevin J. 2018. Generalizability of heterogeneous treatment effect estimates across samples. *Proceedings of the National Academy of Sciences*, **115**(49), 12441–12446.

Dahabreh, Issa J., Trikalinos, Thomas A., Kent, David M., and Schmid, Christopher H. 2017. Heterogeneity of treatment effects. Pages 227–272 of: *Methods in Comparative Effectiveness Research*, edited by Constantine Gatsonis and Sally C. Morton. New York: Chapman and Hall/CRC.

Davidoff, Frank. 2017. Can knowledge about heterogeneity in treatment effects help us choose wisely? *Annals of Internal Medicine*, **166**(2), 141–142.

Davis, Jesse, and Goadrich, Mark. 2006. The relationship between precision-recall and ROC curves. Pages 233–240 of: *Proceedings of the 23rd International Conference on Machine Learning*. ICML '06, Pittsburgh, Pennsylvania, USA. New York: ACM.

Duan, Tony, Pranav, Rajpurkar, Dillon, Laird, Ng, Andrew Y., and Sanjay, Basu. 2019. Clinical value of predicting individual treatment effects for intensive blood pressure therapy. *Circulation: Cardiovascular Quality and Outcomes*, **12**(3), e005010.

Friedman, Jerome H. 2001. Greedy function approximation: A gradient boosting machine. *The Annals of Statistics*, **29**(5), 1189–1232.

Gottesman, Omer, Johansson, Fredrik, Komorowski, Matthieu, Faisal, Aldo, Sontag, David, Doshi-Velez, Finale, and Celi, Leo Anthony. 2019. Guidelines for reinforcement learning in healthcare. *Nature Medicine*, **25**(1), 16–18.

Harrell, Frank. 2001. *Regression Modeling Strategies: With Applications to Linear Models, Logistic Regression, and Survival Analysis*. Springer Series in Statistics. New York: Springer-Verlag.

Hastie, Trevor, Tibshirani, Robert, and Friedman, Jerome. 2009. *The Elements of Statistical Learning: Data Mining, Inference, and Prediction*, 2nd ed. Springer Series in Statistics. New York: Springer-Verlag.

Hayward, Rodney A., Kent, David M., Vijan, Sandeep, and Hofer, Timothy P. 2006. Multivariable risk prediction can greatly enhance the statistical power of clinical trial subgroup analysis. *BMC Medical Research Methodology*, **6**(1), 18.

Imbens, Guido W., and Rubin, Donald B. 2015. *Causal Inference for Statistics, Social, and Biomedical Sciences: An Introduction*. New York: Cambridge University Press.

Kent, David M., Rothwell, Peter M., Ioannidis, John P. A., Altman, Doug G., and Hayward, Rodney A. 2010. Assessing and reporting heterogeneity in treatment effects in clinical trials: A proposal. *Trials*, **11**(August), 85.

Kent, David M., Nelson, Jason, Dahabreh, Issa J., Rothwell, Peter M., Altman, Douglas G., and Hayward, Rodney A. 2016. Risk and treatment effect heterogeneity: Re-analysis of individual participant data from 32 large clinical trials. *International Journal of Epidemiology*, **45**(6), 2075–2088.

Kent, David M., Paulus, Jessica K., van Klaveren, David, D'Agostino, Ralph, Goodman, Steve, Hayward, Rodney, Ioannidis, John P. A., Patrick-Lake, Bray,

Morton, Sally, Pencina, Michael, Raman, Gowri, Ross, Joseph S., Selker, Harry
P., Varadhan, Ravi, Vickers, Andrew, Wong, John B., and Steyerberg, Ewout W.
2020. The Predictive Approaches to Treatment effect Heterogeneity (PATH)
statement. *Annals of Internal Medicine*, **172**(1), 35–45.

Komorowski, Matthieu, Celi, Leo A., Badawi, Omar, Gordon, Anthony C., and Faisal,
A. Aldo. 2018. The Artificial Intelligence Clinician learns optimal treatment
strategies for sepsis in intensive care. *Nature Medicine*, **24**(11), 1716–1720.

Künzel, Sören R., Sekhon, Jasjeet S., Bickel, Peter J., and Yu, Bin. 2019. Metalearners
for estimating heterogeneous treatment effects using machine learning.
Proceedings of the National Academy of Sciences, **116**(10), 4156–4165.

Murdoch, W. James, Singh, Chandan, Kumbier, Karl, Abbasi-Asl, Reza, and Yu, Bin.
2019. Definitions, methods, and applications in interpretable machine learning.
Proceedings of the National Academy of Sciences, **116**(44), 22071–22080.

Patel, Krishna K., Arnold, Suzanne V., Chan, Paul S., Tang, Yuanyuan, Pokharel,
Yashashwi, Jones, Philip G., and Spertus, John A. 2017. Personalizing the intensity of blood pressure control: Modeling the heterogeneity of risks and benefits
from SPRINT (Systolic Blood Pressure Intervention Trial). *Circulation:
Cardiovascular Quality and Outcomes*, **10**(4), e003624.

The ACCORD Study Group. 2010. Effects of intensive blood-pressure control in type
2 diabetes mellitus. *New England Journal of Medicine*, **362**(17), 1575–1585.

The SPRINT Research Group. 2015. A randomized trial of intensive versus standard
blood-pressure control. *New England Journal of Medicine*, **373**(22), 2103–2116.

van Klaveren, David, Steyerberg, Ewout W., Serruys, Patrick W., and Kent, David M.
2018. The proposed 'concordance-statistic for benefit' provided a useful metric
when modeling heterogeneous treatment effects. *Journal of Clinical
Epidemiology*, **94**(February), 59–68.

Vock, David M., Wolfson, Julian, Bandyopadhyay, Sunayan, Adomavicius,
Gediminas, Johnson, Paul E., Vazquez-Benitez, Gabriela, and O'Connor, Patrick
J. 2016. Adapting machine learning techniques to censored time-to-event health
record data: A general-purpose approach using inverse probability of censoring
weighting. *Journal of Biomedical Informatics*, **61**(June), 119–131.

Wager, Stefan, and Athey, Susan. 2018. Estimation and inference of heterogeneous
treatment effects using random forests. *Journal of the American Statistical
Association*, **113**(523), 1228–1242.

Wallach, Joshua D., Sullivan, Patrick G., Trepanowski, John F., Sainani, Kristin L.,
Steyerberg, Ewout W., and Ioannidis, John P. A. 2017. Evaluation of evidence of
statistical support and corroboration of subgroup claims in randomized clinical
trials. *JAMA Internal Medicine*, **177**(4), 554–560.

4

Proceed with Care

Integrating Predictive Analytics with Patient Decision Making

Hamsa Bastani and Pengyi Shi

Summary of the Problem

While state-of-the-art machine learning models have demonstrated impressive results in many domains, these models are limited by the quality of their training data. This poses a significant challenge in healthcare, since electronic medical record data suffers from a number of causal issues and biases, thereby calling into question the reliability of resulting predictive models. Furthermore, even when a reliable machine learning model is available, it is unclear how its predictions can be leveraged in complicated decision problems embedded in dynamic, uncertain environments. Specifically, hospital decision makers must additionally account for the dynamics in patient disease progression and take a system-level operational perspective.

Summary of the Solution

To address the first challenge, we advocate for *human-in-the-loop* machine learning, which involves domain experts in an interactive process of developing predictive models. Interpretability offers a promising way to facilitate this interaction. We describe an approach that offers a simple decision tree interpretation for any complex blackbox machine learning model. In a case study with physicians, we find that they were able to use the interpretation to discover an unexpected causal issue in a personalized patient risk score trained on electronic medical record data.

To address the second challenge, we advocate for building decision models that integrate predictions of the disease progression at the individual patient level with system models capturing the dynamic operational environments. We describe a case study on hospital inpatient management, showing how to build a Markov decision framework that leverages predictive analytics on patient readmission risk and prescribes the optimal set of patients to be discharged each day.

Summary of Relevance in a Post-COVID World

The COVID-19 pandemic highlighted the need to allocate limited hospital resources to patients with the highest risk (and potential benefit). This involves both accurately identifying heterogeneous treatment effects through predictive analytics and making operational decisions accordingly to maximize patient welfare subject to capacity constraints. This chapter describes how to use predictive and prescriptive analytics to facilitate hospitals' management of limited resources.

4.1 Introduction

Predictive analytics holds great promise for data-driven decision making in healthcare operations. However, it is important to carefully account for biases in observational patient data and operational structure to ensure successful implementation of predictive analytics. This chapter describes two case studies that integrate predictive analytics with patient decision making in hospitals: one targets personalized interventions to patients, and the other seeks to improve patient flow in complex inpatient ward settings.

In the personalized intervention setting, we consider a machine learning model that uses electronic medical record data to predict which patients are at risk for diabetes. While state-of-the-art machine learning models achieve strong predictive performance, they are known to suffer from causal issues or biases. To address this concern, physicians were presented with a human-understandable explanation of the predictive model. Interestingly, physicians were successfully able to leverage the explanation to discover an unexpected but important causal issue in the data. Thus, caution must be exercised when deploying predictive models to aid decision making on actual patients; explainable artificial intelligence (AI) presents an attractive bridge for integrating domain expertise with high-performing machine learning models.

In the patient flow setting, we consider a discharge decision-making problem to balance the trade-off between patient readmission risk and inpatient ward congestion. Even with a predictive tool that is calibrated from observational data and addresses the possible biases, it is still non-trivial to translate the prediction into day-to-day operational decisions, particularly when the environment is dynamic and uncertain. We describe in this case study how to build a system model for the patient flow and how to integrate a personalized readmission prediction tool to dynamically prescribe both how many and which patients to discharge on each day.

Through these two case studies, we illustrate that predictive analytics alone may not lead to better decisions. It must be implemented in tandem with careful consideration of domain expertise and operational structure.

4.2 Personalized Interventions

Predictive analytics holds great promise for improving medical decision making. However, a key challenge is that predictive models are highly specialized to perform well on the data on which they are trained. Yet, for a number of reasons, the training data may not be representative of the data observed by the deployed model. One common reason is that the patient mix may differ significantly across domains. For instance, patients that visit the intensive care unit (ICU) tend to be far sicker than the general population, so a model that is trained to achieve good performance on ICU patients may perform poorly on general patients. Similarly, different hospitals often have systematic differences in how they code diagnoses for patients; these differences can cause a predictive model that is trained to perform well for patients at one hospital to perform very poorly at a different hospital (see, e.g., Bastani 2020 [1]). Temporal shifts introduce additional challenges. For instance, Nestor et al. 2019 [2] find that system-wide record-keeping changes in ICU data can render machine learning models with time-agnostic features useless; in these cases, one must be careful to discard old unrepresentative data or explicitly model the change in dynamics.

A more subtle challenge is that predictive models are often trained on *observational data* – i.e., data that are obtained from monitoring existing patients rather than by running a randomized clinical trial. However, these patients are already subject to medical care, which systematically biases the observed data. To illustrate, in one case study, Caruna et al. 2015 [3] built a machine learning model predicting mortality for pneumonia patients. Oddly, the model predicted that patients with a history of asthma have lower mortality risk than the general population; this is unexpected since asthmatics generally have higher asthmatic risk (if untreated). Yet, the model was not wrong – this pattern was reflected in the observational data due to systematic differences in treatment decisions. In particular, pneumonia patients with a history of asthma were usually admitted directly to the ICU, where they received aggressive care that was so effective that it lowered their mortality risk relative to even the general population. Unfortunately, as a consequence machine learning models trained on the data incorrectly learn that asthma lowers mortality risk. In other words, even though the model performs well on predicting patient outcomes in the observational data, it is not useful for decision making since it does not correctly distinguish which patients are in need of treatment.

These challenges are particularly problematic for *blackbox models*, which are models such as deep neural networks (DNNs) and random forests that are difficult or impossible for humans to understand due to their complex, opaque structure together with their use of a large number of explanatory variables. Simple models such as decision trees are much easier to understand, yet they are often outperformed by blackbox models. That is, there has traditionally been a tension between predictive performance (maximized by using blackbox models) and human understandability to diagnose potential issues or biases in the data (achieved by using interpretable models).

4.2.1 Explaining Blackbox Models

A promising middle ground is to train a blackbox model, but then leverage techniques to interpret the prediction made by the blackbox model in a human-understandable way. Broadly speaking, there are two kinds of techniques for interpreting blackbox models. The first kind produce *local explanations*, which describe how the model made a prediction for a single input. For instance, suppose we train a random forest model that predicts whether a patient has diabetes based on their demographics, vitals, past diagnoses, and current lab results. For a given patient – say, Bob – a local explanation may be that the blackbox model predicts that Bob has diabetes due to his high glucose level. For a different patient – say, Alice – a local explanation may be that the blackbox model predicts that Alice has diabetes since she is currently taking insulin. In other words, local explanations can help physicians understand the reasoning behind a single prediction made by the blackbox model.

In contrast, *global explanations* attempt to explain the high-level reasoning performed by the blackbox model across all patients in a given population. For instance, given the machine learning model trained to predict diabetes together with a data set of patients, such a technique might approximate the blackbox model using a simpler, interpretable model (e.g., a decision tree). Since the simpler model approximates the blackbox model, we expect that major issues with the blackbox model will also be reflected in the simple model. Thus, a human decision maker can use the global explanation to detect issues in the blackbox model *before* it is deployed to be used in a real-world setting.

To this end, Bastani et al. 2017 [4] propose the Decision Tree Extraction (DTExtract) algorithm, which approximates an arbitrary blackbox model with a simple, accurate decision tree. It uses a greedy strategy similar to CART [5], where it grows the decision tree iteratively from the root down. At each step, it chooses the most promising branch to add to the tree using a metric called the Gini coefficient, which captures the "diversity" of the data in terms of its labels, preferring branches that reduce diversity. A common challenge in constructing accurate decision trees is that they easily overfit the training data. To overcome this difficulty, the DTExtract algorithm leverages the ability to generate arbitrarily large amounts of training data, by sampling new inputs and labeling them using the blackbox model. In such problems, random sampling of the training data can be extremely inefficient. Instead, one can use *active learning* to generate inputs that flow down a given path in the decision tree. Thus, DTExtract uses active learning to efficiently sample new data points, labels them using the blackbox model, and uses the resulting augmented training data set to construct an interpretable decision tree.

4.2.2 Case Study

The remainder of this section is based on a case study from Bastani et al. 2017, 2018 [4, 6], which demonstrates how global explanations can be used to diagnose issues in blackbox models. In this setting, the authors sought to build a machine learning model predicting diabetes risk for patients. Diabetes is a leading cause of cardiovascular disease, limb amputation, and other health problems; by preemptively predicting which patients are likely to be diagnosed with diabetes, physicians can propose health interventions such as exercise and improved diet to reduce patient risk. Indeed, clinical trials have demonstrated the effectiveness of preventive interventions in reducing risk for diabetes.

The blackbox model was trained using de-identified electronic medical record data from multiple providers. Each patient was associated with several hundred features extracted from their electronic medical records from previous visits to the healthcare provider in the past three years. These features spanned demographics, ICD-9 diagnosis codes, prescription medications, and lab test results. The binary outcome variable was whether the patient received a type II diabetes diagnosis in their most recent visit to the healthcare provider. This data set was preprocessed by domain experts to ensure that only information prior to the diabetes diagnosis was available to the predictive model.

The authors first considered data from just the largest provider, which included 578 unique patients. Following standard practice, 70 percent of the data was used as a training set, while 30 percent was used as a test set. Multiple machine learning models were tested, and the random forest model was found to be the best in terms of predictive performance. However, as noted earlier, electronic medical record data constitutes observational data which may suffer from various biases; thus, a high-performing predictive model may form incorrect conclusions. Thus, the authors applied the aforementioned DTExtract algorithm, which constructs a decision tree that *approximates* the random forest. The resulting global explanation of the random forest model is shown in Figure 4.1.

This global explanation was then shown to physicians to see if it was reasonable. They derived a number of insights based on this explanation, some of which suggested possible issues in the underlying random forest.

4.2.2.1 Bias in Diagnosis for Sicker Patients

Most notably, the model appears to reason about prior diagnoses that are unrelated to diabetes. In particular, consider the subtree of Figure 4.1 rooted at the node labeled "Dermatophytosis of nail." This subtree applies to the subpopulation of patients who are over 50 years of age, have high cholesterol, and furthermore have not had a preoperative medical exam. According to the explanation, these factors are all indicators for higher diabetes risk.

However, for this subpopulation, the decision tree predicts that patients with medical diagnoses such as dermatophytosis of nail, abdominal pain, and red blood cells in urine are *less* likely to have diabetes. In other words, it says that patients who already have other medical conditions have lower diabetes risk. Physicians found this effect to be counterintuitive, since dermatophytosis of nail has no known negative relation to diabetes; if anything, patients with this condition should be *more* likely to have diabetes.

Upon further reflection, the physicians suggested a possible explanation: it might be the case that patients who have these other health conditions are more likely to have visited the physician recently. Thus, they are likely to have received preventive measures to reduce their risk of diabetes. In contrast, patients without prior health conditions may not have visited the physician, and therefore may not have been recommended to undertake preventive measures. An alternative explanation could be that patient records selected for training the blackbox model were systematically riskier, inducing a similar unwarranted bias in predictions. Statistical checks on the original random forest model suggested that it also suffers from the same biases.

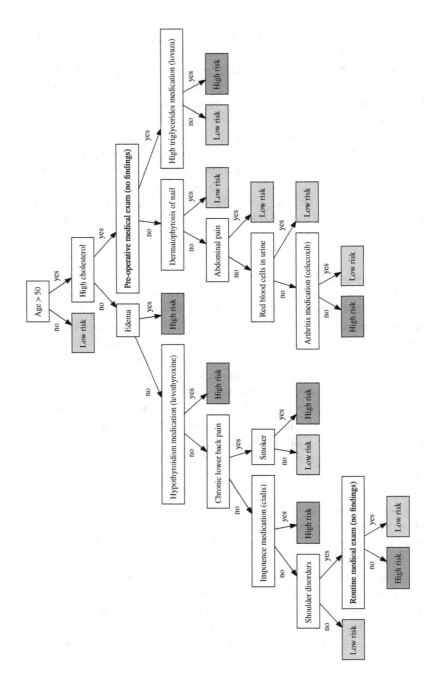

Figure 4.1 Global explanation for the blackbox random forest trained to predict diabetes for patients in the largest provider [6].

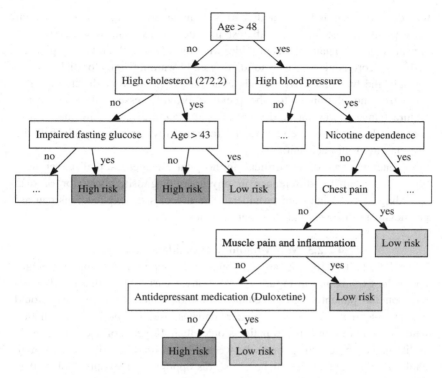

Figure 4.2 Global explanation for the blackbox random forest trained to predict diabetes for patients in the second-largest provider [6].

As described above, using this random forest to make decisions could lead physicians to underestimate the diabetes risk of patients in this subpopulation, and fail to recommend preventive measures to high-risk patients. The global explanation enabled physicians to diagnose an important issue with using the random forest. Once discovered, such issues can be addressed using standard techniques (e.g., adding the number of recent visits as a control variable).

4.2.2.2 Comparison to Different Provider

The authors then repeated the same process on data from the second-largest provider, which included 402 unique patients. They trained a new random forest model and used DTExtract to explain it; the resulting decision tree is shown in Figure 4.2.

This explanation was also shown to physicians, and they were asked to interpret how it differed from the explanation trained on data from the first provider. A key observation they had is that, unlike the previous explanation, this decision tree includes a diagnosis "Impaired fasting glucose," which corresponds to the standard lab test intended to evaluate diabetes risk. It appears that physicians at this provider were more active about having patients undergo rigorous glucose tests to identify early warning signs for diabetes. As a result, the two predictive models treated this feature very differently. The predictive model trained for the previous provider essentially ignored the feature (since it was rarely diagnosed, and therefore rarely informative); in contrast, the predictive model trained for this provider significantly benefits from taking it into account.

In general, it can be very difficult for hospital management to discover these types of systematic differences in physician diagnosing behavior or data recording across healthcare providers. The use of such explanations can aid physicians to discover and shed light on these biases.

4.2.2.3 Non-Monotone Dependence on Age

Bastani et al. 2018 [6] note an additional observation made by the physicians about the explanation in Figure 4.2. The physicians noticed that the dependence on the patient's age is actually non-monotone. Normally, one would expect older patients to have higher diabetes risk. Indeed, the explanation tends to assign higher risk to patients older than 48 years of age. However, it additionally singles out patients between 43 and 48 years of age with high cholesterol as having high diabetes risk (as opposed to all patients older than 43 years of age with high cholesterol). The physicians hypothesized the following explanation for this effect: high cholesterol is more common in older patients, but for younger patients, it is particularly abnormal and therefore suggests a greater risk for diabetes. In this manner, explanations can yield novel data-driven insights that can be tested in the future to further improve patient targeting or care management.

4.3 Patient Flow Management

The previous case study illustrates the importance of leveraging domain knowledge to correct possible biases in building predictive models from observational data. Yet, even with a properly calibrated predictive tool, it could still be challenging for hospital managers to directly use prediction in solving complicated decision problems, particularly in a dynamic, uncertain environment. Properly accounting for the dynamics in individual patient disease progression and, more importantly, the system-level operational perspective is critical when integrating predictive tools in decision making. In the second case study, we describe an illustrative example integrating predictive and prescriptive analytics to provide a powerful yet easy-to-implement decision support tool in solving a critical issue faced by many hospitals around the world: inpatient discharge management.

4.3.1 Background

A hospitalist makes many decisions that influence the cost of an inpatient stay ... but probably none has more impact than "Should this patient go home today or tomorrow?"
–Cover story for *American College of Physicians (ACP) Hospitalist,*
October 2014 [7].

Inpatient discharge decision plays an important role in patient outcomes, hospital financial performance, and patient flow management, impacting all care providers from small community hospitals to major teaching hospitals. This cover story further highlights the key trade-off in making discharge decisions: "Under the Affordable Care Act, it is still in hospitals' financial interest to discharge patients as soon as possible, but also to facilitate post-discharge care and prevent 30-day readmissions. Rather than just lowering LOS (length-of-stay), hospitals now aim to optimize it at the intersection of quality and cost" [7].

In other words, the key trade-off in making discharge decisions lies at the intersection of quality of care and cost. To alleviate inpatient ward overcrowding, hospitals may discharge patients early; this practice shifts the burden to the early discharged patients, who may experience increased risk of readmission, mortality, and other adverse outcomes. On the other hand, when occupancy levels are low, hospitals may keep patients longer, which can have a positive impact on patient outcomes. How to balance this trade-off in a dynamic, uncertain environment has broad implications for patient flow, inpatient unit congestion, quality of care, and post-discharge risk.

Currently, most hospitals engage in adaptive discharge practices in a reactive and ad hoc manner. For example, as illustrated by Adepoju et al. 2019 [8], when a hospital becomes overcrowded, a communication is sent to all physicians asking them to discharge as many patients as possible to free up beds. This unstructured approach may end up discharging too many or too few patients, or discharging a suboptimal set of patients. Adepoju et al. [8] note that the individual physicians lacking a system perspective could be one reason why they react to occupancy crises poorly. There is a growing need for analytically guided tools to help hospital managers balance the delicate trade-off between individual patient outcomes and the system-level ward crowding [9].

4.3.2 Case Study

The remainder of this section is based on a case study from Shi et al. 2020 [10], which develops a decision support tool in discharge management to improve hospital patient flow and reduce readmissions. Along with a data analytics company, the authors have done a pilot implementation of this decision tool at a local community hospital in the state of Indiana.

The first component that the community hospital asked for is a predictive tool of patient readmission risk evolution as a function of her length of stay (LOS) in the hospital. A substantial amount of effort was expended to develop this predictive tool. Similar to the first case study, Shi et al. 2020 [10] also faced challenges from building the predictive tool based on observational data. Specifically, most existing readmission prediction tools treat LOS as an exogenous variable. Directly applying these tools by varying LOS suffers from endogeneity (sicker patients tend to stay longer and have a higher readmission risk), which leads to the incorrect conclusion that extending length of stay for an individual patient results in higher readmission risk. In addition, when applying the classical Cox proportional hazard model to predict readmission timing, there were additional challenges including the excess zero count issue (i.e., most patients are *not* readmitted [11]) and patient heterogeneity in the readmission timing. Shi et al. 2020 [10] integrated several statistical methods and proposed one prediction model that works reasonably well. Specifically, to overcome the three major barriers – (i) excess zero count, (ii) patient heterogeneity, and (iii) endogeneity – the authors leveraged a two-stage framework. The framework predicted the readmission probability in the first stage and the timing of readmission in the second stage, eliminating the bias caused by the large proportion of non-readmissions and addressing (i). In the second stage, a mixture component was added to the Cox model to capture patient heterogeneity in readmission timing, addressing (ii). On top of this two-stage framework, an Instrumental Variable approach was used as a preprocessing stage to eliminate endogeneity, addressing (iii). Figure 4.3 gives an example of the output from their prediction tool. Each curve is the readmission risk "trajectory" of a patient produced from the predictive tool, showing how the readmission probability would change with each additional day that the patient spends in the hospital.

4.3.2.1 Nuances with Using the Predictive Tool in Discharge Decisions

After this predictive tool was developed, hospital management still faced complex decisions on how to turn the prediction into decision making, in particular, how to use this predictive tool in the day-to-day dynamic

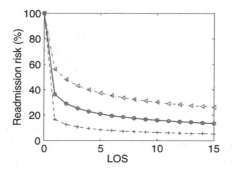

Figure 4.3 Predicted readmission risk trajectory against length of stay (LOS) from [10]. The plot shows the 90-day cumulative probability as a function of LOS for three random patients selected from the testing data.

environment to decide on how many patients and whom to discharge on a given day. Discharge decisions must not only account for the risk of each patient, but also for each patient's risk evolution over future days in conjunction with current and future occupancy levels. The inpatient arrival day-of-week phenomenon further complicates discharge decisions. To explain, consider the following simple illustrative example: Patient A has a relatively high risk currently, but this risk is unlikely to improve significantly by keeping the patient longer. Then the best decision readmissions may be to discharge patient A now. The reverse may be true for a patient with lower discharge risk that may improve significantly by staying one day longer. This contradicts the common industry notion that a simple risk threshold is sufficient (i.e., discharge all patients when their risk drops below a certain level). In addition, the decisions are modulated by considering current and future occupancy levels rather than risk alone. These complexities necessitate a forward-looking, dynamic approach that cannot be easily intuited.

4.3.2.2 Accounting for Operational Aspects
As discussed, the discharge decisions need to account not only for the medical aspect (patient's risk evolution) but also for the system's operational aspects (occupancy levels and future arrivals). One needs to build a system model to capture the patient flow dynamics, which then provides the basis for making dynamic discharge decisions.

Figure 4.4 illustrates a schematic representation for the system model built in Shi et al. 2020 [10]. Consider a hospital ward that has a fixed number of beds (denote this number of beds as N, e.g., $N = 50$ beds for a 50-bed inpatient unit). The first box presents the inpatient ward, where the upper arrow coming

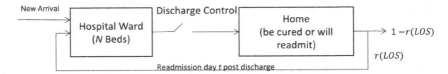

Figure 4.4 Patient flow model of the hospital ward.

to the box represents new patient arrivals to this ward – often referred to as a service station in the literature. The patient's hospital length-of-stay corresponds to the time of the patient receiving "service" in this station. The arrow coming from this first box corresponds to the main decision we are considering here: whether to discharge a certain patient that is currently in the box to home. If the patient is discharged, she enters the recovery process represented by the second box in Figure 4.4. After this recovery process, the patient could be either discharged and not come back to the system, with probability $1 - r(LOS)$, or be re-hospitalized with probability $r(LOS)$. This readmission probability $r(LOS)$ is from the predictive model and depends on the individual patient characteristics and how long the patient spent in the previous hospital stay (LOS). The readmitted patients come back to the first box, forming a second stream of input to the hospital station in addition to the new patient arrivals.

Two key features need to be accounted for when making dynamic decisions based on this system model: (i) each patient may have her own readmission risk trajectory (patient heterogeneity): it is important and increasingly common to have personalized risk predictions; (ii) the resource – inpatient beds – is limited, which means the decisions to discharge each patient currently "in service" are not independent but connected through the resource constraint. This also corresponds to interplay between the individual patient perspective and the system perspective presented in the discharge problem. To capture these two features and reflect the key trade-off, one needs to set up an appropriate dynamic decision framework – the output from which is the optimized recommendation on "which and how many" patients will be discharged. A powerful and commonly used tool for such dynamic decision is the Markov Decision Process (MDP) framework.

The first step to set up an MDP framework is to specify the "state variable" – the information that hospital managers would take into account when making the discharge decision, for example, how many patients are currently in the system, how long each of these patients have already spent in the system, and their current predicted readmission risk and future risk trajectory. The next step is to specify the "action" to be taken and the "cost" associated with the action.

Action corresponds to the discharge decision – how many patients and whom to discharge each day in this setting. The cost associated with an action is to capture the key trade-off in a decision problem. Given that the trade-off we consider in this case study is the inpatient congestion versus patient readmission risk, two cost terms are incorporated: the first is a *congestion cost* that depends on the number of patients exceeding the bed capacity N, i.e., the overage cost that reflects capacity shortage and ward congestion; the second is a *readmission cost* that captures the predicted readmission penalty if we discharge a patient on a certain day. Discharging patients early reduces the congestion cost but increases the readmission cost; discharging fewer patients increases the congestion cost but reduces the readmission cost. This tension is exactly why one needs to find an *optimal* decision each day. The values of these two competing costs would be dependent on management goals and how much emphasis (weight) is placed on one or the other. One could conduct empirical or behavior study to infer these cost parameters from data such as those from Thompson et al. 2009 [12]; alternatively, Shi et al. 2020 [10] developed a trade-off curve to show the performance under different combinations of the cost parameters. This trade-off curve allows managers to see what levels of readmission risk they could achieve at a given hospital congestion level so that they could choose the desired operating regime.

In a typical MDP framework, the decision maker is often assumed to aim at minimizing the average cost over a certain period (e.g., a week or a month), not just the current day. For example, hospital managers may want to proactively discharge patients in anticipation of a large volume of arrivals showing up the next day. Myopic decisions that only focus on what happened today are often suboptimal. To account for future periods, one needs to describe how the state would transition after an action is taken today. In the discharge setting, the transition dynamic is in fact simple: those who are not discharged today will stay in the hospital tomorrow, with their LOS being updated by one day (readmission risk is updated accordingly); new patients arriving today will occupy a bed or wait for a bed depending on the capacity and current occupancy level. Mathematically, let

$$X_k = (X_k^0, X_k^1, \ldots, X_k^J)$$

denote the system state at day k, where $X_k^j = (X_k^{1,j}, X_k^{2,j}, \ldots, X_k^{M,J})$ and $X_k^{m,j}$ denotes the number of type m patients who have spent j days in the system, $m = 1, \ldots, M, j = 0, \ldots, J$. The decision variables $\{D_k^{m,j}\}$ represent the numbers of patients, for each type m and each past length-of-stay j days, that should be discharged on day k. Let $A_k^{m,0}$ denote the number of type m new arrivals on day k, and $A_k^{\prime m,0}$ denote the number of readmissions belonging to type m. For each m, the state evolution follows:

$$X_{k+1}^{m,0} = A_k^{m,0} + A_k^{\prime m,0}; \qquad (4.1)$$

$$X_{k+1}^{m,j} = X_k^{m,j-1} - D_k^{m,j-1}, \quad j = 1, \ldots, J. \qquad (4.2)$$

Equation (4.1) captures the total arrivals to the hospital ward on day k. Equation (4.2) says that patients who have stayed $j - 1$ days in k become patients who have stayed j days in $k + 1$, except for those who are discharged, $D_k^{m,j-1}$. Readers are referred to Shi et al. 2020 [10] for more details of the transition probabilities and MDP specification.

4.3.2.3 Whom and How Many to Discharge

Once the MDP framework is formulated, solving the MDP is often non-trivial with standard methods such as value or policy iteration. A main reason is that there are often millions of states or actions to consider for a realistic size problem. To overcome this well-known curse-of-dimensionality, one often needs to identify structural properties in the optimal policy and leverage approximation methods.

For the discharge problem, an interesting finding from Shi et al. 2020 [10] is that there is a priority ranking in terms of the readiness to discharge. That is, the optimal policy will discharge all patients of a higher readiness before discharging any patients of a lower readiness. The ranking of the readiness depends on *marginal* change in the readmission risk between today and a future day, not the absolute value of the readmission risk. At a high level, when deciding between two patients on whom to discharge, since the congestion cost each causes is the same (as each occupies one bed), it is preferable to discharge the patient with a smaller marginal change in the readmission risk between today and tomorrow. This priority ranking also answers the "whom to discharge" question.

Regarding the "how many to discharge" question, the intuition is to discharge more patients when the occupancy is high and fewer when low. However, computing the optimal number is much more complicated. Shi et al. 2020 [10] leveraged an approximation for the cost-to-go for all future periods based on the exact solution of the main problem for a quadratic cost structure. The closed-form solution from this quadratic-cost problem preserves the aforementioned structural properties on the priority ranking and leads to a univariate optimization. The univariate optimization not only is computationally efficient for implementation, but also allows one to incorporate full patient heterogeneity into decision making and is robust enough to adapt to a complex hospital environment such as time-varying arrivals on different days of a week.

4.3.2.4 Tool Implementation and Results

To demonstrate the value of such an analytically guided tool, Shi et al. 2020 [10] developed a counterfactual study using a trace-based simulation to compare how the hospital would have performed using their discharge tool versus what the hospital actually did in the historical data. They showed that the dynamic policy produced from their MDP framework could significantly reduce readmission risk for medium- and high-risk groups (from 32% to 28%) when extending the LOS slightly (from 3.33 to 3.55 days). The dynamic policy was also able to correctly recommend intervention (i.e., extending LOS) on over 50% of the patients that were readmitted in the data set.

Further, using an extensive simulation analysis, they showed that the dynamic policy produced from the MDP framework always dominated a *static policy* that also used the predictive information. The improvement gained by the dynamic policy is particularly significant for smaller hospitals and patients with shorter average LOS. This finding again shows that, even with a predictive tool, it is nontrivial to use the tool properly, particularly in a dynamic, changing environment that has many uncertainties. A sophisticated dynamic decision support tool is often necessary.

Conversely, the MDP framework, though sophisticated, was designed for easy integration with hospital IT system and EHR. Together with their partner hospital and a data analytics company, Shi et al. 2020 [10] tested and implemented a cloud-based tool to provide discharge decision support. Figure 4.5 shows a screen shot of the tool, which has recently been integrated into the hospital's IT infrastructure and provider workflow. The tool displays (a) patients currently in the hospital unit (represented by each block), ranked with different color codes in terms of their discharge readiness (the priority ranking mentioned above); (b) discharge risk curve for future possible LOS of each patient (with past LOS and generally recommended LOS).

4.4 Conclusion

Through the two case studies, we illustrate that caution must be exercised when integrating predictive analytics with patient decision making. In the first case study, we demonstrate the importance of model interpretability and domain knowledge in building predictive tools from observational data. Tools from interpretable machine learning are critical to ensure that we do not entrust faulty or biased predictive models with patient decision making. In the second case study, we further show that it is nontrivial to apply a readily developed predictive tool in complex decision making.

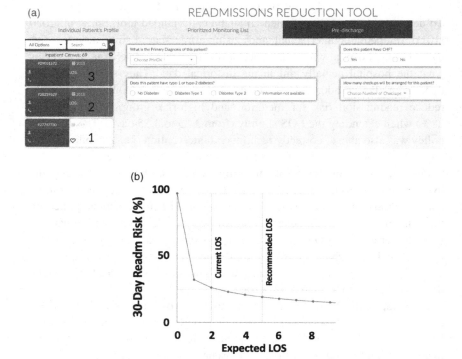

Figure 4.5 Screenshot of the discharge decision support web portal implemented in the partner hospital of [10].

The prediction–decision framework in the second case study has the potential to overcome many common challenges faced more broadly in risk prediction in healthcare and other fields. Combining both of these approaches paves a new road for personalized dynamic decision problems, which are becoming increasingly necessary in healthcare and other services industries. Potential applications include chronic disease management, adverse event prediction for hospital inpatients due to conditions such as deep vein thrombosis screening and sepsis, and proactive interventions for adverse events in the elderly population.

Further Reading

Many have studied directly building interpretable predictive models via rule lists [13] or decision trees [14, 15]. Yet, blackbox predictive models often continue to outperform interpretable models on a range of predictive tasks. Consequently, a literature has emerged interpreting blackbox model predictions. While the first case study discussed DTExtract for approximating a blackbox model, other methods seek to better understand different aspects of the model. For example, LIME learns an interpretable model locally around a given prediction [16], allowing one to reason about a particular patient's prediction; saliency maps perform a similar role for deep neural networks [17]. SHAP assigns each feature an importance value for a particular prediction [18]. However, recent literature warns that the resulting interpretations may be misleading since they identify correlations rather than causal effects [19]. Alternatively, if one is concerned about data corruption or outliers, Wei Koh and Liang 2017 [20] use influence functions to identify (potentially problematic) training points that are most responsible for a given prediction.

Discharge management to improve patient flow has received much attention in the operations management literature. Berk and Moinzadeh's 1998 paper [21] is one of the earliest to study the trade-off between discharge risk and inpatient occupancy. The authors focus on steady-state performance analysis under two fixed policies (with and without early discharge). Chan et al. 2012 [22] consider the scenario of a new patient's arrival to a full ICU and doctors must decide which patient to discharge to free a bed. Ouyang et al. 2019 [23] consider the joint decision of ICU admission and discharge, where the decision maker determines whether to admit an arriving patient to the ICU or to the general ward and also whom to discharge early if a patient needs to be admitted to a full ICU. Bavafa et al. 2019 [24] study the joint problem of coordinating elective case-mix and discharge policies. The authors find that coordination has benefits over a siloed approach when costs of either the operating room and/or inpatient beds are sufficiently high.

For tackling high-dimensional MDP problems with large state or action size, Approximate Dynamic Programming (ADP) is a powerful technique; see Bertsekas 2012 [25] and Powell 2011 [26] for details and the references there. The approximation used in Shi et al. 2020 [10] is connected to the broad literature of value function approximation, i.e., approximating the value function by a linear combination of basis functions. Commonly used methods for value function approximations include the temporal-difference learning method [27], Q-learning [28], and the linear programming approach [29, 30]. Policy-gradient-based methods [31, 32] help address issues with large action space.

References

[1] Hamsa Bastani. Predicting with proxies: transfer learning in high dimension. *Management Science*, **67**(5), 2020.

[2] Bret Nestor, Matthew McDermott, Willie Boag, et al. Feature robustness in non-stationary health records: caveats to deployable model performance in common clinical machine learning tasks. *arXiv preprint arXiv:1908.00690*, 2019.

[3] Rich Caruana, Yin Lou, Johannes Gehrke, et al. Intelligible models for healthcare: predicting pneumonia risk and hospital 30-day readmission. *Proceedings of the 21th ACM SIGKDD International Conference on Knowledge Discovery and Data Mining*, 1721–1730. 2015.

[4] Osbert Bastani, Carolyn Kim, and Hamsa Bastani. Interpreting blackbox models via model extraction. *arXiv preprint arXiv:1705.08504*, 2017.

[5] Leo Breiman, Jerome Friedman, Charles J Stone, and Richard A Olshen. *Classification and Regression Trees*. CRC Press, 1984.

[6] Hamsa Bastani, Osbert Bastani, and Carolyn Kim. Interpreting predictive models for human-in-the-loop analytics. *arXiv preprint arXiv:1705.08504*, 1–45, 2018. https://hamsabastani.github.io/interp.pdf.

[7] Janet Colwell. Length of stay: timing it right. Strategies for achieving efficient, high-quality care. *ACP Hospitalist*, 2014. www.acphospitalist.org/archives/2014/10/los.htm.

[8] Temidayo Adepoju, Anita Tucker, Helen Jin, and Chris Manasseh. The impact of two managerial responses on hospital occupancy crises. *SSRN Electronic Journal*, 2019.

[9] David Frenz. Not too long, not too short, just right. *Today's Hospitalist*, 2014. www.todayshospitalist.com/not-too-long-not-too-short-just-right/.

[10] Pengyi Shi, Jonathan Helm, Jivan Deglise-Hawkinson, and Julian Pan. Timing it right: balancing inpatient congestion versus readmission risk at discharge. *Operations Research*, 2020. Forthcoming.

[11] Indranil Bardhan, Jeong-ha Oh, Zhiqiang Zheng, and Kirk Kirksey. Predictive analytics for readmission of patients with congestive heart failure. *Information Systems Research*, **26**(1):19–39, 2014.

[12] Steven Thompson, Manuel Nunez, Robert Garfinkel, and Matthew D Dean. Or practice – efficient short-term allocation and reallocation of patients to floors of a hospital during demand surges. *Operations Research*, **57**(2):261–273, 2009.

[13] Hongyu Yang, Cynthia Rudin, and Margo Seltzer. Scalable Bayesian rule lists. *Proceedings of the 34th International Conference on Machine Learning*, **70**:3921–3930, 2017.

[14] Jerome H Friedman. Greedy function approximation: a gradient boosting machine. *Annals of Statistics*, **29**(5):1189–1232, 2001.

[15] Dimitris Bertsimas and Jack Dunn. Optimal classification trees. *Machine Learning*, **106**(7):1039–1082, 2017.

[16] Marco Tulio Ribeiro, Sameer Singh, and Carlos Guestrin. Why should I trust you? Explaining the predictions of any classifier. *Proceedings of the 22nd ACM SIGKDD International Conference on Knowledge Discovery and Data Mining*, 1135–1144. 2016.

[17] Karen Simonyan, Andrea Vedaldi, and Andrew Zisserman. Deep inside convolutional networks: visualising image classification models and saliency maps. *arXiv preprint arXiv:1312.6034*, 2013.

[18] Scott M Lundberg and Su-In Lee. A unified approach to interpreting model predictions. In *Advances in Neural Information Processing Systems*, 4765–4774, 2017.

[19] Himabindu Lakkaraju and Osbert Bastani. "How do I fool you?": manipulating user trust via misleading black box explanations. *AIES*, 2020.

[20] Pang Wei Koh and Percy Liang. Understanding black-box predictions via influence functions. In *Proceedings of the 34th International Conference on Machine Learning*. Volume 70, 1885–1894. JMLR. org, 2017.

[21] Emre Berk and Kamran Moinzadeh. The impact of discharge decisions on health care quality. *Management Science*, **44**(3):400–415, 1998.

[22] Carri W Chan, Vivek F Farias, Nicholas Bambos, and Gabriel Escobar. Optimizing intensive care unit discharge decisions with patient readmissions. *Operations Research*, **60**(6):1323–1341, 2012.

[23] Huiyin Ouyang, Nilay Tanik Argon, and Serhan Ziya. Allocation of intensive care unit beds in periods of high demand. *Operations Research*, 2019. Forthcoming.

[24] Hessam Bavafa, Lerzan Ormeci, Sergei Savin, and Vanitha Virudachalam. Surgical case-mix and discharge decisions: does within-hospital coordination matter? Working Paper, 1–40, 2019.

[25] Dimitri P. Bertsekas. *Dynamic Programming and Optimal Control: Approximate Dynamic Programming*. Volume II. Belmont, MA: Athena Scientific, 2012.

[26] Warren B. Powell. *Approximate Dynamic Programming: Solving the Curses of Dimensionality*. Wiley Series in Probability and Statistics. Hoboken, NJ: Wiley-Interscience, 2011.

[27] Richard S. Sutton. Learning to predict by the methods of temporal differences. *Machine Learning*, 3(1):9–44, 1988.

[28] Christopher J.C.H. Watkins and Peter Dayan. *Technical note: Q-learning*. *Machine Learning*, 8(3):279–292, 1992.

[29] D. P. de Farias and B. Van Roy. The linear programming approach to approximate dynamic programming. *Operations Research*, 51(6):850–865, 2003.

[30] Daniel Adelman and Adam J. Mersereau. Relaxations of weakly coupled stochastic dynamic programs. *Operations Research*, 56(3):712–727, 2008.

[31] John Schulman, Sergey Levine, Pieter Abbeel, Michael Jordan, and Philipp Moritz. Trust region policy optimization. In *International Conference on Machine Learning*, 1889–1897, 2015.

[32] John Schulman, Filip Wolski, Prafulla Dhariwal, Alec Radford, and Oleg Klimov. Proximal policy optimization algorithms. *arXiv preprint arXiv:1707.06347*, 2017.

PART II

Optimizing Healthcare Systems

5

Using Algorithmic Solutions to Address Gatekeeper Training Issues for Suicide Prevention on College Campuses

Anthony Fulginiti, Aida Rahmattalabi, Jarrod Call,
Phebe Vayanos, and Eric Rice

Summary of the Problem

Suicide is a major concern in college populations. Utilization of mental health services during a crisis can reduce suicide risk, but most students who experience suicidal thoughts and behaviors do not seek treatment. Gatekeeper training (GT), which involves teaching people to recognize and support someone in crisis, is a popular approach to promote service utilization. However, the impact of training can be limited by critical gatekeeper, population, and institutional issues that are often not accounted for in practice.

Summary of the Solution

The goal of GT is to select people for training in an effort to achieve good coverage of the student population (i.e., high proportion of students are connected to someone who has received training). GT in college settings usually involves a combination of voluntary drop-in GT sessions for the affiliated community (i.e., passive recruitment) and targeted enlistment of Resident Assistants for GT (i.e., active recruitment). In practice, these "baseline" strategies crudely approximate random and degree centrality processes whereby people are selected for training, respectively; a degree centrality approach is the most common way to select peer change agents in the context of network interventions. We propose modeling the student social network as a graph and then present deterministic and robust algorithmic optimization solutions that can address key gatekeeper, population, and institutional issues while achieving more desirable coverage than baseline strategies.

Summary of Relevance in a Post-COVID World

COVID-19 precipitated significant changes in the higher learning environment. Many students are facing unprecedented life adversity that can increase suicide risk. At the same time, students' social interaction in the college environment has been fundamentally altered – a serious concern given that social connectedness can protect against suicide. Students are learning remotely rather than living on campus, and even those on campus are changing the way they interact with fellow students. Moreover, legitimate worries exist about the long-term impact of COVID-19 on the higher learning environment, including persistent changes in how students learn (e.g., online) and interact with one another (e.g., on-campus housing). These changes may further undermine traditional gatekeeper recruitment that relies heavily on resident advisors in dormitory settings. Therefore, the ability to recruit well-connected students from social networks that transcend place-based boundaries will only increase in importance in the future. This chapter presents network-based methods to identify those best positioned to benefit an organization with gatekeeper training.

Chapter Outline

In this chapter, we (1) detail the problem scope and gatekeeper training as a solution to it, (2) delineate key issues that can impact GT as well as the consequences of ignoring them, (3) explore the value of social network information for GT recruitment, (4) explain the mathematical model of GT and an algorithmic solution approach that can account for gatekeeper, population, and institutional issues, and (5) describe experimental results that compare a novel algorithmic solution for GT recruitment with recruitment approaches that approximate common GT practice.

5.1 Prevalence of Suicidal Thoughts and Behavior

Suicide is the second-leading cause of death among college students (Centers for Disease Control and Prevention [CDC], 2019; Turner, Leno, & Keller, 2013). More than 1,000 college students die by suicide on an annual basis in the United States (National Mental Health Association & the Jed Foundation, 2002). Prevalence rates and trends with respect to suicidal thoughts and behaviors (STB) among college students have led to growing concerns in higher education. Lifetime STB prevalence estimates among college students range from 22% to 33% for suicidal ideation, 6% to 18% for suicide plans, and 2% to 8% for suicide attempts (Becker, Holdaway, & Luebbe, 2018; Drum et al., 2009; Mortier, Auerbach et al., 2018; Mortier, Cuijpers et al., 2018). Additionally, a recent meta-analysis found that within the past 12 months, 10.6% of college students had seriously considered suicide, 3% had made a plan, and 1.2% had attempted suicide (Mortier, Cuijpers et al., 2018). STB rates and related risk factors, such as mental health diagnoses, have also increased over time (e.g., Oswalt et al., 2018). Lifetime rates of suicidal ideation and suicide attempt have increased from 25% to 36% and 8% to 11% over the past decade, respectively (Center for Collegiate Mental Health, 2009, 2019).

5.2 Prevalence of Help-Seeking Behaviors

Seeking professional care during a mental health crisis can help to reduce suicide risk. Yet, most college students who experience STB do not seek treatment or utilize mental health services (Downs & Eisenberg, 2012; Drum et al., 2009). Roughly 20% to 35% of college students experiencing STB have sought professional help (Bruffaerts et al., 2019; Han et al., 2016). Of college students who die by suicide, only 10% to 20% of them have received services at their college-based counseling center (Kisch, Leino, & Silverman 2005). Making matters worse, individuals experiencing suicidal ideation are actually *less* likely to seek help than their non-suicidal counterparts (Deane, Wilson, & Ciarrochi, 2001; Rudd, Joiner, & Rajab, 1995). When students in suicidal crises do seek help, nonprofessional sources of support (e.g., friends, family) are often viewed as a more attractive option than professional care (Arria et al., 2011). Therefore, informal supports play a pivotal role in getting students into professional care. Indeed, approximately two-thirds of students in treatment report that encouragement from others influenced their decision to seek professional help (Downs & Eisenberg, 2012).

5.3 Gatekeeper Training: Rationale, Goals, & Implementation

Gatekeeper training (GT) is a widely used suicide prevention strategy in university settings (Wolitzky-Taylor et al., 2020). Since the establishment of the Garrett Lee Smith Memorial Youth Suicide Prevention Program, more than

144 grants have been awarded to universities (Walrath et al., 2015) and more than 96% of them have implemented gatekeeper training (Robinson-Link et al., 2019). The rationale for GT is to train informal support persons to facilitate professional help-seeking and mental health service utilization among students who typically avoid it (Goldsmith et al., 2002). These *gatekeepers* are "individuals in a community who have face-to-face contact with large numbers of community members as part of their usual routine" (U.S. Department of Health and Human [HHS] Services Office of the Surgeon General and National Action Alliance for Suicide Prevention, 2012). Training involves teaching this subset of the population skills to *recognize* and *refer* people in suicidal crises to professional mental health services (Coleman et al., 2019; Isaac et al., 2009). Specifically, GT focuses on changing gatekeepers' knowledge and attitudes/beliefs about suicide as well as their self-efficacy to intervene with at-risk persons as mechanisms to increase intervention behavior (i.e., approach and linkage activity; Burnette, Ramchand, & Ayer, 2015). See Figure 5.1 for an illustration of how GT is purported to affect suicide outcomes; GT promotes professional help-seeking (Figure 5.1a), which can interrupt the progression of crises to suicide (Figure 5.1b). Even though

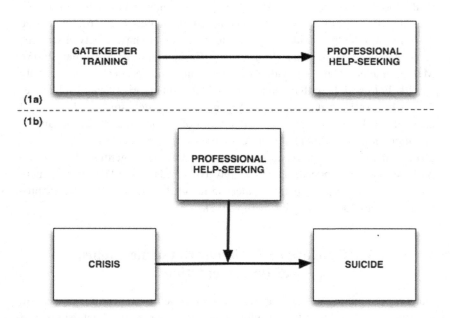

Figure 5.1 Gatekeeper training in the prevention of suicide.

multiple endpoints are not depicted for the sake of clarity, the interruption of this process can lead to the abatement of or recovery from crises.

A broad variety of GT programs have been designed for or implemented on college campuses throughout the United States. According to the Suicide Prevention Research Center, programs intended for use with university audiences include Campus Connect, Connect Suicide Prevention/Intervention Training, Kognito, Sources of Strength, and the Student Support Network. Many other GT programs, especially Question Persuade Refer (QPR), have also been used on college campuses (Litteken & Sale, 2018; Reetz, Barr, & Krylowicz, 2014; Wolitzky-Taylor et al., 2020). These programs generally use a combination of didactic education to improve knowledge about suicide warning signs and risk factors as well as behavioral modeling and rehearsal to improve one's preparedness, efficacy, and ability to effectively engage and link someone in crisis to mental health services (Coleman et al., 2019). Yet, individual programs can differ in content, delivery method (face-to-face vs. online), duration (hours-to-days), setting, training group size, cost, and target audience (e.g., Robinson-Link et al., 2019).

An important point of consideration involves *how* gatekeeper training is implemented on college campuses; this is critical given that implementation decisions can influence the effectiveness of GT programs (Mo, Ko, & Xin, 2018). Many colleges disseminate information about drop-in GT sessions on campus that affiliated students, staff, and faculty can attend at no cost (i.e., passive recruitment); this passive recruitment strategy crudely approximates a *random approach* – random in the sense of an apparent lack of predictability with respect to who attends training – wherein individuals are randomly selected for training. However, active recruitment for GT is typically focused on enlisting a strategically identified subgroup of people who are required to attend training based on their position in the social structure of campus life. Resident Assistants (RAs) constitute a group of student leaders who have been a popular target for gatekeeper training (Tompkins & Witt, 2009; Wolitzky-Taylor et al., 2020).

Colleges and universities in the United States employ roughly 60,000 RAs each year (U.S. Census Bureau, 2010). As a group, they are tasked with a multitude of responsibilities geared toward facilitating student development (e.g., personal, social, academic, and professional; Paladino et al., 2005); building a sense of community; and cultivating a safe environment (McCarthy, 2019). These responsibilities have increased as the RA role has expanded beyond a disciplinary function to a helper function; RAs now serve as front-line paraprofessionals in residence halls who triage a diverse range of student issues and help to resolve them (McLaughlin, 2018). Given that colleges institutionalize routine contact between RAs and students – positioning RAs to be central in the social fabric of student residential life – this active recruitment strategy crudely approximates a *degree centrality approach* wherein people with high numbers of connections are selected for training.[1]

5.4 Gatekeeper Training: Issues to Address for Program Improvement

In general, gatekeeper training has resulted in favorable outcomes in college settings; a recent meta-analysis found that GT had a large effect on gatekeepers' knowledge about suicide and self-efficacy to address suicidality as well as a moderate effect on suicide prevention skills (Wolitzky-Taylor et al., 2020).[2] The growing implementation of GT (Tompkins & Witt, 2009; Walrath et al., 2015) holds the potential to appreciably reduce the burden of suicide-related morbidity and mortality on college campuses. Yet, consistent with the notion that individual (e.g., sex/gender; occupation/education; mental health) and social-contextual factors (e.g., organizational support) can affect GT effectiveness (e.g., Burnette et al., 2015; Midorikawa et al., 2020), the impact of GT may be limited because college campuses have not (1) accounted for certain *gatekeeper, population, and institutional* issues or (2) leveraged *social network information* to guide active GT recruitment. Of note, the following is a targeted discussion of select issues and not an exhaustive review of all issues that contribute to the success of GT.

5.4.1 Gatekeeper Issues

To date, the principal attribute guiding active recruitment on college campuses has been Resident Assistant Status. The basic logic of RA recruitment is sound: many students in on-campus housing are assigned to an RA, so RA training means that much of the student body is connected to someone who has

---

[1] A true degree centrality approach involves collecting social network information to identify people who are most central in a network. Instead, RAs are often selected based on their *assumed* centrality. A major advantage of the true degree centrality approach is that gatekeeper recruitment is based on empirical information about social ties (i.e., a nomination process is used to identify recruits who have the most social ties), whereas a major advantage of the assumed centrality approach is that gatekeeper recruitment is based on social roles (which requires fewer resources and simplifies recruitment).

[2] For a broader perspective, see systematic reviews about GT training that have not focused on college settings (Isaac et al., 2009; Mo, Ko, & Xin, 2018; Yonemoto et al., 2019).

completed GT. Having RAs as the focal group for GT also allows for efficient recruitment and regulatory oversight. However, the effectiveness of a gatekeeper is largely a function of their *social influence*[3] – characterized by being *highly connected* and/or a subject matter *expert who others seek out for advice or support* (Boster et al., 2011) – and *ability to satisfactorily perform gatekeeping behaviors*. As discussed below, we believe that RAs are mistakenly assumed to possess these attributes; the critique of these assumptions parallels work that emphasizes the potential advantages of identifying "natural gatekeepers" (Robinson-Link et al., 2019).[4]

Whether students seek advice and support from RAs when struggling with a mental health issue is complicated because RAs possess some attributes that potentially encourage and others that discourage help-seeking behavior. On the one hand, RAs are *peers* with whom students are expected to have *routine contact* – two attributes that might make them more attractive as sources of help for personal mental health and suicide-related issues (Fulginiti, Pahwa et al., 2016; Michelmore & Hindley, 2012). On the other hand, RAs are *in authority positions* (Everett & Loftus, 2011), which can make it difficult for them to build trust with students; it is not uncommon for students to be wary of and hold negative or ambivalent attitudes toward RAs (Porter & Newman, 2016). This is highly problematic because young people will usually only open up about personal and emotional issues in the context of established, familiar, and trusting relationships (Rickwood et al., 2005). Indeed, research finds that individuals overwhelmingly choose to disclose their suicidal ideation to friends (Becker & Drum, 2015; Pisani et al., 2012) as well as other close and socially supportive people (Fulginiti, Pahwa et al., 2016). Moreover, the reality is that RAs may have *infrequent contact* with residents (Reingle et al., 2010), which can undermine relationship building. Making matters worse, RAs must regularly enforce breaches of residence hall policy (Twale & Burrell, 1994), which often involve student behaviors that also constitute risk factors for suicide (e.g., substance use and antisocial activities). In the wake of enforcement-related conflict, a subgroup of particularly vulnerable students may be even more reluctant to reach out to RAs for help.

[3] An extensive body of work focuses on influential social actors – people who are variously referred to as peer leaders, opinion leaders, peer change agents, community leaders, influencers, and other terms (e.g., Borgatti, 2006; Ford-Paz et al., 2015) – but identifying them can be a complicated endeavor.
[4] The term "natural gatekeepers" refers to people who are more likely to engage in gatekeeper behaviors *before* training (i.e., pre-intervention characteristics can affect gatekeeper outcomes). This is supported by work showing that positive GT effects are more often observed among people engaging in gatekeeping behavior at baseline (e.g., Robinson-Link et al., 2019; Wyman et al., 2008).

Whether RAs are well positioned to reach a large segment of the student population is also questionable. First, RAs are not assigned to all settings where students reside (e.g., particularly off-campus housing) and, consequently, many students are not connected to an RA who has received training. This observation raises concern given that graduate students and students living in off-campus settings are more likely to experience certain suicidogenic factors (e.g., substance use; Benz et al., 2017; Evans et al., 2018). Second, the positions of people in a network depend on the criteria used to define the boundaries of and social ties within it; networks are often defined based on interaction (e.g., interpersonal contact), role-relations (e.g., friendship), affective qualities (e.g., closeness), and social support exchange (Marin & Hampton, 2007). There is no denying that RAs occupy reasonable network positions when *interaction* constitutes evidence of a social tie. However, RA positions in the network will change if we define the network based on friendship – a more ideal relational context for promoting mental health and suicide-related communication. As a result, many students do not find themselves connected to a *trusted* source of help who has received training. See Figure 5.2 for a visual depiction of how the RA position (black) in relation to students (gray = connected to RA; white = not connected to RA) can change when the network is defined based on interaction (left) versus friendship (right). In the interaction network, we see a well-positioned RA whose training would mean that 100% of students are connected to someone who received GT (i.e., complete network protection/coverage). In the friendship network, we see a poorly positioned RA whose training would mean that only 40% of students are connected to someone who received GT (i.e., incomplete network protection/coverage).

Whether RAs can be expected to attend GT and satisfactorily perform gatekeeper functions following training is another debatable contention. A university can certainly mandate GT as a condition of enrollment or employment. However, the RA position has become more stressful and

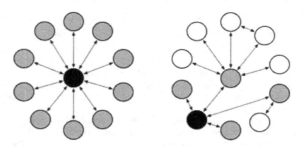

Figure 5.2 Impact of RA position on coverage as a function of network type.

demanding over time (McLaughlin, 2018) – an issue that could cause a pendulum shift away from mandated GT as questions emerge about treating RAs as front-line paraprofessionals. Of course, nonattendance is a major threat when training is voluntary, particularly when a subgroup of people is *actively recruited* for GT based on their *collective* position in relation to students. For example, if an RA does not attend training, then none of the students in their residence hall wing or floor may be connected to a gatekeeper. Moreover, the magnitude of nonattendance in a voluntary GT context could be sizable. Cross and colleagues (2010) found that only 33.8% of invitees who were actively recruited accepted the training invitation. Inadequate gatekeeper performance produces the same consequences as nonattendance (i.e., subgroups of students are not connected to a *capable* gatekeeper), but it is an undoubtedly more widespread and insidious issue. Individuals who attend training and/or score above an assessment threshold are essentially treated as equals in their performance readiness. An attendance-based criteria is troubling given that attendance does not necessarily translate to effective gatekeeper performance; for instance, one study found that 54% of attendees showed adequate skills following training (Cross et al., 2010). And the truth is that assessment thresholds are imperfect for predicting adequate performance and performance varies among qualified gatekeepers. See Figure 5.3 for an illustration that shows the impact of variation in attendance and performance. In the network

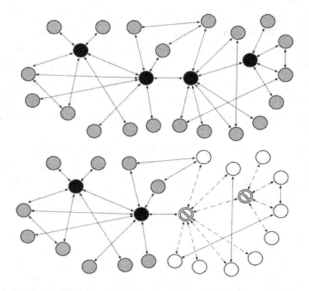

Figure 5.3 Impact of RA nonattendance/inadequate performance on coverage.

on the top, we see complete network coverage when all four recruited gate-keepers are trained *and* effectively perform gatekeeping activities. In the network on the bottom, we see incomplete network coverage when two recruited gatekeepers are either not trained *or* ineffective in their performance.

Gatekeeper Issues: What Do I Need To Know?

Active recruitment for gatekeeper training frequently targets RAs. Yet, we cannot assume that RAs are influential social actors in student networks. It is also unwise to assume that people who are actively recruited for training will invariably attend it and adequately perform gatekeeper behaviors following it. The consequence of not accounting for these assumptions is that many students are not connected to a capable gatekeeper who holds the social cache to facilitate mental health service utilization. We need recruitment tools that can help us to better select influential social actors for training and account for uncertainty in attendance/performance.

5.4.2 Population Issues

To date, gatekeeper training on college campuses has been implemented in a way that could be regarded as information-naïve – no information about suicide risk or professional help-seeking behavior in the student population is accounted for in the implementation approach.[5] The ostensible goal of this naïve approach is to connect every student with a single trained RA. There are at least two major factors that lend merit to a naïve approach: (1) suicide risk immunity is impossible and (2) suicide risk prediction is extraordinarily diffi-cult (Franklin et al., 2017). However, it is a relatively crude approach that fails to capitalize on extant knowledge and forecasting progress in the field of suicide prevention.

With respect to (1), although no student is ever at zero risk, we know that students differ in suicide risk vulnerability based on certain attributes; for example, prior suicidal crises, particularly a suicide attempt, are robust predict-ors of future suicide (Van Orden et al., 2010), but belonging to a marginalized

---

[5] First- and second-year students (i.e., students most likely to be housed with RAs) are often viewed as particularly vulnerable, so some might argue that targeting RAs for GT is accounting for at least a modicum of risk information in the population. However, to our knowledge, this rationale is not explicitly outlined anywhere and thus cannot be assumed.

racial/ethnic or sexual minority group (Goodwill & Zhou, 2020), depression, hopelessness, stressful life experiences, sleep problems, disconnection from others, and perceived burdensomeness (Li, Dorstyn, & Jarmon, 2020), as well as a history of nonsuicidal self-injury, bipolar disorder, and substance use, all elevate suicide risk among college students (Paul et al., 2015). Moreover, we know that disparities exist in mental health service utilization based on certain attributes; for example, students of color are less likely to seek out professional care than white students (Busby et al., 2021; Lipson et al., 2018). With respect to (2), technological solutions, like machine learning, are being increasingly leveraged to improve suicide risk prediction (Burke, Ammerman, & Jacobucci, 2019; Walsh, Ribeiro, & Franklin, 2017). Mortier and colleagues (2017) developed a risk screening algorithm to examine persistence of STB in college.

Therefore, a reasonable argument can be made for targeted GT, which calls for active recruitment that integrates information about risk and help-seeking variation in a population (e.g., Fulginiti, Rice et al., 2016). Using a data-informed approach, we can work to align gatekeeper distribution with patterns of risk and help-seeking behavior as well as prioritize connections and/or build in redundancies between gatekeepers and students based on differential student vulnerability. Notably, issues of fairness need to be considered in the implementation of GT to ensure that students from marginalized groups (e.g., people of color, LGBTQ, undocumented status) are given the same opportunity to benefit from GT as other students.

Population Issues: What Do I Need To Know?

Gatekeeper training in college settings has adopted an information-naïve approach wherein data about student vulnerability is not used to inform active recruitment approaches. We need recruitment tools that can help us to select people for training to achieve customizable coverage goals based on student attributes that impact suicide vulnerability (e.g., differential coverage for students at higher or lower risk; equitable coverage for students from marginalized groups).

5.4.3 Institutional Issues

To date, the impact of institutional factors on the feasibility, effectiveness, and sustainability of GT on college campuses has been conspicuously under-studied (Burnette et al., 2015). However, institutions clearly make a difference in the success of any programming. Burnette and colleagues (2015) pointed to the importance of support from one's organization, supervisor, and coworkers in contributing to effective gatekeeping behavior. Positive associations have been observed between organizational and supervisor support and use of gatekeeper intervention skills (Moore et al., 2011). Alternatively, one's competing occupational demands can impede gatekeeping behavior (Moore et al., 2011). Although universities that decide to implement GT are thoughtful about the provision of support for gatekeepers, the reality is that gatekeeping responsibilities are unevenly distributed across social groups. Specifically, universities have increasingly relied on RAs to be peer helpers and gatekeepers, which can exact a heavy toll on RAs and the student community. For instance, managing the full-time demands of a student *and* front-line paraprofessional (e.g., helping peers who engage in self-destructive behaviors) can lead to burnout and secondary trauma (McCarthy, 2020; McLaughlin, 2018). The excessive burdens of the RA role can also compromise the performance of gatekeeping behavior (Moore et al., 2011). Hence, RAs and the student community may benefit from active strategies that do not confine recruitment to a small subgroup of already overburdened students.

The procurement and allocation of financial resources are especially critical for universities to adopt, administer, and sustain effective GT. However, large disparities exist between universities as they relate to resources that can be leveraged for gatekeeper training. For some universities, the use of institutional resources to fund GT in perpetuity is a nonissue. However, most universities operate under financial constraints, particularly given the precariousness of the higher education landscape (e.g., Dennis, 2017). Thankfully, there are more opportunities now than ever before for suicide prevention funding that can be applied toward GT in college settings. For example, the Garrett Lee Smith Campus Suicide Prevention Grant is funded by the Substance Abuse and Mental Health Services Administration (SAMHSA) to support suicide prevention work in campus communities. Moreover, many gatekeeper training programs are reasonably priced for use (see www.sprc.org). Yet, many universities do not have the requisite institutional support, such as grants management personnel or behavioral health specialists, to oversee grant awards and GT programming processes (e.g., planning/delivery; Taub et al., 2013). Additionally, the sustainability of an effective GT program is a long-term challenge regardless of whether a university obtains funding to launch it (e.g., Shtivelband, Aloise-Young, & Chen, 2015). After all, universities not only need to train gatekeepers but may need to *re-train* them (i.e., booster sessions) to prevent declines in gatekeeper knowledge, self-efficacy, and skills over time (Robinson-Link et al., 2019; Tompkins & Witt, 2009; Zinzow et al., 2020). Tools that can aid planning and decision making about GT implementation may help to offset such challenges. For example, decision makers can benefit from information about anticipated student coverage conditional on expenditure (e.g., If I have a budget of x, what proportion of the population can I expect to be connected to someone who has received GT?) or vice versa (e.g., If I want x proportion of the population connected to someone who has received GT, what budget will I need?). These kinds of tools can support the efficient and fiscally responsible allocation of resources, but no known tools are currently available for implementation efforts.

Institutional Issues: What Do I Need To Know?

Institutional support AND demands can influence gatekeeper training effectiveness. Overreliance on RAs as gatekeepers in college settings may limit the impact of gatekeeper training. We need to expand the pool of candidates for active recruitment beyond a small subgroup of already overburdened students. Moreover, resource distribution is fundamental to adopting, implementing, and sustaining gatekeeper training. We need tools that help us to plan and make decisions about gatekeeper training delivery based on trade-offs between coverage and resources.

5.4.4 Relevance of Social Network Information for Gatekeeper Recruitment

To date, universities have not employed a social network approach – a process that involves collecting information from individuals about themselves (i.e., nodes) and their social ties (i.e., edges) – to guide active GT recruitment.[6] From our perspective, this is a missed opportunity, given the substantial value of using social network information in the context of intervention programming (Valente, 2010, 2012, 2017).

Therefore, in contrast to RA recruitment, we recommend collecting relational data from students to build a sociocentric friendship network (i.e., the web of direct and indirect friendship ties among university students) and then using a novel algorithmic approach to select a subset of influential social actors (i.e., student peers) for GT that will provide efficient coverage of the student population; coverage refers to the proportion of the student population

---

[6] Informed by network theory, a couple of studies in high school settings have used a staff nomination approach to identify peer leaders (i.e., degree centrality; Wyman et al., 2010) and a sociocentric approach to identify peers (i.e., closeness centrality; Pickering et al., 2018).

connected to someone who has received GT, which is important given that students with direct ties to trained peer leaders have greater exposure to the intervention (Pickering et al., 2018). The network-informed approach to gatekeeper training that we recommend was informed by several critical points drawn from network intervention scholarship.

First, network interventions that involve the recruitment of influential social actors, especially peers, are common and generally effective at promoting behavior change (Valente, 2012). Second, there are distinct advantages to explicitly modeling sociocentric or whole social networks – networks constructed based on information gathered from an *entire set of actors* in a population about their social ties to other people in that population – to identify influential social actors (e.g., higher data validity/reliability; mapping entire community; Schneider, Zhou, & Laumann, 2015; Valente & Pumpuang, 2007). Pickering and colleagues (2018) illustrate the utility of modeling networks for GT. Third, the effectiveness of network interventions that recruit influential social actors may depend on their attributes and *how* those actors are identified or selected (e.g., Schneider et al., 2015). Relatedly, pilot work suggests that algorithm-driven recruitment approaches for identifying influential social actors may outperform traditional recruitment methods (i.e., selecting people with the greatest number of social ties, i.e., highest degree centrality) when addressing certain public health issues (e.g., HIV; Rice et al., 2018).

Social Networks & GT: What Do I Need To Know?

Social network information can be used to identify influential social actors for active GT recruitment; this selection of gatekeepers may be critical to the effectiveness of GT. Yet, college settings have not explicitly modeled student social networks to help guide the recruitment of gatekeepers. We propose modeling sociocentric student friendship networks because communication about mental health and suicide is more likely to occur among friends and then designing algorithms to guide active recruitment efforts.

5.5 Gatekeeper Training: Algorithmic Approaches

In this section, we explain the mathematical model of gatekeeper training and the solution approach. We primarily focus on the deterministic case in which we assume that there is no uncertainty in individuals' availability or performance. We note that uncertainty makes the problem significantly more difficult, and we refer the reader to a paper in which we extensively investigate a model that accounts for uncertainty.

5.5.1 Mathematical Model (Deterministic)

We model the social network as a directed graph $G = (\mathcal{N}, \mathcal{E})$, in which $\mathcal{N}$ is the set of nodes (individuals) and $\mathcal{E}$ is the set of edges (social ties). An edge from node n to node v exists if n reports v as a friend. Therefore, an edge from n to v indicates that n can "protect" or "cover" v.

We use $\delta(n) := \{v \in \mathcal{N} : (v, n) \in \mathcal{E}\}$ to denote the set of neighbors (friends) of n in G (i.e., the set of nodes that can cover node n). Each node $n \in \mathcal{N}$ is characterized by a set of "protected" attributes (e.g., race/ethnicity, gender), for which fair treatment is important. Based on these node characteristics, we partition $n \in \mathcal{N}$ into C disjoint groups $\mathcal{N}_c, c \in C := \{1, \ldots, C\}$, such that $\cup_{c \in C} \mathcal{N}_c = \mathcal{N}$.

We consider the problem of selecting a set of I {nodes} from $\mathcal{N}$ to act as gatekeepers for their neighbors. We encode the choice of gatekeepers using a binary vector x of dimension N whose nth element is one iff (i.e., "if and only if") the nth node is chosen. We require $x \in \mathcal{X} := \{x \in \{0,1\}^N : e^\top x \leq I\}$, where e is a vector of all ones of appropriate dimension.

A node n is counted as "covered" if at least one of its neighbors has attended the GT. We let $y_n(x)$ denote if n is covered for the gatekeeper choice x. In other words,

$$y_n(x) := \mathbb{I}\left(\sum_{v \in \delta(n)} x_v \geq 1 \right),$$

in which $\mathbb{I}(.)$ is the indicator function that is equal to 1 iff its argument is true. Finally, the total coverage is the sum of the $y_n(x)$ over the entire set of individuals, i.e., we measure the coverage as $\sum_{n \in \mathcal{N}} y_n(x)$.

5.5.2 Optimization Model (Deterministic)

We aim to solve the following optimization problem:

$$\max_{x \in \mathcal{X}, y \in \{0,1\}^N} \sum_{n \in \mathcal{N}} y_n : y_n \geq \sum_{v \in \delta(n)} x_v.$$

In the above formulation, y is a binary vector of dimension N, where y_n indicates whether node n is covered. Each constraint $y_n \geq \sum_{v \in \delta(n)} x_v$ indicates that an individual is covered only if one of their neighboring friends has attended the training.

The goal is to choose x such the total coverage is maximized. This problem does not take the individual's characteristics into account. Thus, it is possible that the outcome coverage is not evenly distributed among different subpopulations. We now introduce another variant of this problem in which we incorporate fairness constraints to ensure every group receives a minimum level of coverage given by W:

$$\max_{x \in \mathcal{X}, y \in \{0, 1\}^N} \sum_{n \in \mathcal{N}} y_n$$

$$\text{s.t. } y_n \geq \sum_{v \in \delta(n)} x_v$$

$$\sum_{n \in \mathcal{N}_c} y_n \geq |\mathcal{N}_c| \, W, \, \forall c \in \mathcal{C}$$

We want to emphasize that our model allows different choices of W for different groups. For example, a practitioner may desire a higher level of coverage for groups who are at higher risk for suicide (e.g., people with a history of suicidal ideation/attempt). In the present work, we do not explore such aspects of the problem; thus, we consider the same level of coverage for every group.

5.5.3 Mathematical Model (Robust)

The previous model assumes that all individuals who are actively recruited for training will attend training and adequately perform gatekeeping functions post training. Yet, in practice, we cannot guarantee attendance or adequate performance. We can hedge against this type of uncertainty by explicitly incorporating it into the model. The uncertainty, however, adds another layer of complication both in the modeling and solution approach.

From the modeling side, there are two approaches to model the uncertainty: in a Stochastic Model, we assume that we have distributional information about the uncertain parameters (availability or performance). In this case, typically, we are interested in finding a solution that maximizes the coverage in expectation. In a Robust Model, distributional information is no longer required, and we model uncertainty as a set (i.e., set of possible/likely scenarios). The optimization is then performed against the worse-case realization of the uncertain parameter in the set. Thus, we make decisions that are guaranteed to perform well even in the worst-case scenarios. In the context of gatekeeper training, we have fairly limited data to help inform the probabilities that any individual will attend training and perform well. In addition, robustness is desirable. This motivates the robust model for the uncertainty. In particular, we assume that out of the invited individuals, at most, a certain percentage of them will not attend training or perform well. We use α to denote this "failure rate." We note that α can be easily tuned using historical data, which renders our model very data efficient.

From the optimization perspective, uncertainty often makes the problem more challenging to solve because one needs to reason about *all* possible scenarios, of which there are typically many. We have also investigated the gatekeeper training model under uncertainty and developed a robust optimization model with a tractable solution scheme. We have shown that our model can cater for group fairness constraints similar to those in the deterministic model. In tests of our model on several real social networks, we have demonstrated competitive coverage relative to state-of-the-art methods and significant improvement in group fairness. Notably, we do not detail the model and algorithmic solution here due to space considerations but interested readers can find that information in other works (Rahmattalabi, Vayanos, Fulginiti, et al., 2019; Rahmattalabi, Vayanos, Fulginiti, & Tambe, 2019). However, we do present empirical results in the next section to show the importance of modeling the uncertainty and to demonstrate the effectiveness of our approach.

5.6 Gatekeeper Training: Algorithmic Results

We now present results from a series of experiments in which we compare our selection approach against two baseline selection strategies that are motivated by current practices: (1) Random, which selects individuals at random; (2) Degree-Centrality (DC), which selects individuals with the most social connections; (3) Our Approach, which selects the gatekeepers based on the optimal solution to the optimization model we introduced. It leverages the entire social network in order to choose the best gatekeepers. To reiterate, the Random approach serves to approximate drop-in GT sessions during which anyone can be trained, and the DC approach serves to approximate targeted GT where RAs are trained. All of the following experiments are conducted using real-world social network data collected as part of a study described elsewhere (Fulginiti, Rice, et al., 2016). The network includes 165 individuals who provided information about themselves (e.g., race/ethnicity and suicidal ideation) and their social ties. Of note, we collected similar network data at the University of Denver but did not use them in the following experiments because they lack specific population information that is necessary to illustrate certain benefits of our algorithmic approach (e.g., limited racial/ethnic diversity). The results section is organized to illustrate that our algorithmic approach can account for different gatekeeper, population, and institutional issues delineated earlier.

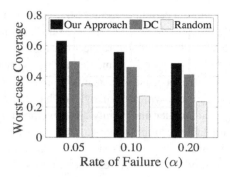

Figure 5.4 Worst-case coverage with respect to α. We compare the worst-case coverage, the coverage in the worst-case failure of α fraction of gatekeepers, against DC and random baselines.

5.6.1 Gatekeeper Issues

With respect to gatekeeper issues, we conducted a set of experiments focused on prospective gatekeepers' training attendance and performance. We compared our approach with baseline algorithms in terms of the worst-case coverage under different failure rate conditions; we set the budget (number of gatekeepers to train) to 20% of the network size and varied the failure rate (α) from 5% to 20%. The results are included in Figure 5.4.

Figure 5.4 demonstrates how worst-case coverage changes across different rates of failure. We observed a decrease in worst-case coverage as the failure rate increased; this emphasizes the importance of uncertainty modeling and the potential loss of coverage when we do not model it. Further, we found that our approach consistently and significantly outperformed the baseline algorithms across all failure rates.

5.6.2 Population Issues

With respect to population issues, we conducted a set of experiments focused on the race/ethnicity and suicide risk of the population. We compared our approach with baseline algorithms in terms of consistency of coverage across different racial/ethnic and risk groups (i.e., similarity in the proportion of people who are covered across groups); we set the number of gatekeepers to be 20% of the network size and $\alpha = 0.0$ (i.e., no uncertainty).

Turning first to the race/ethnicity of the population, Figure 5.5 compares the coverage breakdown for the different algorithms across five groups (i.e., White, Black/African American, Hispanics, Mixed, and Other); for each algorithm, the bars correspond to different racial/ethnic groups. Unlike the DC and

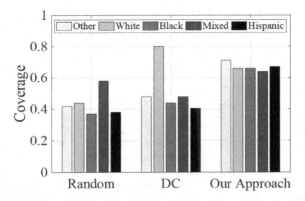

Figure 5.5 Coverage breakdown across five different racial groups. We compare the coverage against DC and random baselines.

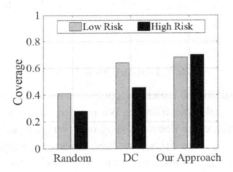

Figure 5.6 Coverage breakdown across groups with and without suicide ideation. We compare the coverage against DC and random baselines.

Random algorithms, we found that our approach significantly improved the coverage of groups in a fair manner.

Turning next to the suicide risk of the population, Figure 5.6 compares the coverage breakdown for the different algorithms across two groups (i.e., higher risk = people with a history of suicidal ideation; lower risk = people without a history of suicidal ideation); for each algorithm, the bars correspond to different risk groups (i.e., black = higher risk; gray = lower risk). As compared to DC and Random algorithms, we found that our approach led to better coverage of higher *and* lower risk groups while achieving equitable coverage across groups. Notably, the baseline algorithms resulted in poor coverage of the higher risk group, and a type of inequitable coverage that bodes poorly for suicide prevention – the higher risk group was *less* likely to be connected to a

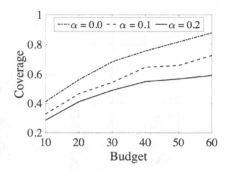

Figure 5.7 Coverage with respect to training budget which is the number of individuals to train as gatekeepers. We compare the coverage for different failure rates.

gatekeeper than the lower risk group. Pickering and colleagues (2018) high-lighted the concern that certain at-risk groups may have lower exposure to GT intervention.

5.6.3 Institutional Issues

With respect to institutional issues, we conducted a set of experiments focused on budgeting for gatekeeper training. We used our approach to estimate the budget needed to achieve a desirable level of coverage under different failure rate conditions (α). Figure 5.7 shows how coverage changes as the budget increases from 10 to 60 under different failure rate conditions. Thus, our approach can be used as a tool to help decision makers when faced with a common cost-coverage trade-off – training more people may lead to greater intervention exposure (Pickering et al., 2018) and/or coverage in a population but also incurs greater cost. For example, a decision maker with a budget of 10 can expect to cover roughly 40% of the population whereas a decision maker with a budget of 50 can expect to cover approximately 80% of the population (in the zero failure rate condition). Notably, a decision maker can start with a coverage goal and use the chart to determine the anticipated budget to achieve that goal.

5.7 Practical Challenges and Limitations of Our Algorithm

Although our algorithm holds promise for improving gatekeeper program-ming, several practical challenges for deploying it warrant consideration.

First, valid and complete social network information remains difficult to collect; algorithm-driven recruitment can be undermined when there is a mismatch between the social network used for planning and the true network (e.g., different social structures). Second, social networks can be dynamic so the time between network data collection and use of the algorithm for recruitment needs to be relatively brief; the ability to expedite this process will benefit from advances on multiple fronts, such as streamlined network data collection as well as an end-user interface for gatekeeper program coordinators. Relatedly, dynamic networks call for periodic assessments of network coverage and periodic (algorithm-driven) recruitment to account for network coverage changes; periodic assessments and recruitment can be demanding. Last, social isolates remain uncovered when using our algorithm for gatekeeper recruitment; this underscores the need for comprehensive suicide prevention programming in colleges, including efforts to promote social connectedness.

5.8 Prospective Applications of Our Algorithm in Different Contexts

There are a multitude of potential applications for our algorithm beyond gatekeeper recruitment on college campuses. With respect to suicide prevention, gatekeeper programming is widely used in high schools and gaining more traction in other settings (e.g., workplaces, correctional facilities); our algorithm can be a useful tool for recruitment in any of these settings. Additionally, our algorithm may be useful in guiding recruitment for network interventions that address other public health behaviors (e.g., substance use; sexually transmitted infections); this can include any intervention that involves teaching a subgroup of people skills to facilitate professional help-seeking behavior for a given problem in an at-risk population. Our algorithm can also be applied in non-health contexts. For instance, the algorithm can be utilized to effectively plan an emergency landslide response; a subgroup of people in a community can be recruited and trained to notify select others as part of a collective landslide response so that all community members are warned of an impending disaster.

5.9 Conclusions

Gatekeeper training is a widely implemented suicide prevention approach in college settings. However, the feasibility, effectiveness, and sustainability of

GT may be affected by gatekeeper, population, and institutional issues that are often unaddressed in practice. Moreover, the impact of GT has been limited by the underutilization of student social network information to guide active GT recruitment. We have critically analyzed these outstanding issues, delineated algorithmic approaches to address them, and provided preliminary results to demonstrate their value. We showed that our algorithm leads to better overall population coverage as well as more equitable coverage across different sub-populations than alternative approaches that approximate common GT and broader peer leader recruitment practices. We also showed that our approach can effectively aid decision makers when planning GT implementation.

Further Reading

For additional perspective on the major issues covered in this chapter, we refer the interested reader to the following papers: Mortier, Cuijpers et al. (2018) provides a robust review focused on suicidal ideation and behaviors among college students. Bruffaerts et al. (2019) offers a similarly strong review of treatment utilization among college students who report mental health and suicide-specific experiences. Wolitzky-Taylor et al. (2020) systematically details the evidence regarding the effectiveness of gatekeeper training on college campuses. Valente (2010) is an excellent text for an accessible intro-duction to social networks, particularly how social network information can be leveraged for intervention programming. Rahmattalabi, Vayanos, Fulginiti, and Rice (2019) discuss the technical development and performance of our algorithmic approach for recruiting gatekeepers.

References

Arria, A. M., Winick, E. R., Garnier-Dykstra, L. M., et al. (2011). Help seeking and mental health service utilization among college students with a history of suicide ideation. *Psychiatric Services*, **62**(12), 1510–1513. https://doi.org/10.1176/appi.ps .005562010

Becker, M. A. S., & Drum, D. J. (2015). The influence of suicide prevention gatekeeper training on resident assistants' mental health. *Journal of Student Affairs Research and Practice*, **52**(1), 76–88. https://doi.org/10.1080/19496591.2015.996055

Becker, S. P., Holdaway, A. S., & Luebbe, A. M. (2018). Suicidal behaviors in college students: frequency, sex differences, and mental health correlates including slug-gish cognitive tempo. *Journal of Adolescent Health*, **63**(2), 181–188.

Benz, M. B., DiBello, A. M., Balestrieri, S. G., et al. (2017). Off-campus residence as a risk factor for heavy drinking among college students. *Substance Use & Misuse*, *52*(9), 1236–1241. https://doi.org/10.1080/10826084.2017.1298620

Borgatti, S. P. (2006). Identifying sets of key players in a social network. *Computational & Mathematical Organization Theory*, *12*(1), 21–34. https://doi .org/10.1007/s10588-006-7084-x

Boster, F. J., Kotowski, M. R., Andrews, K. R., & Serota, K. (2011). Identifying influence: development and validation of the Connectivity, Persuasiveness, and Maven scales. *Journal of Communication*, *61*(1), 178–196. https://doi.org/10 .1111/j.1460-2466.2010.01531.x

Bruffaerts, R., Mortier, P., Auerbach, R. P., et al. (2019). Lifetime and 12-month treatment for mental disorders and suicidal thoughts and behaviors among first year college students. *International Journal of Methods in Psychiatric Research*, *28*(2), e1764. https://doi.org/10.1002/mpr.1764

Burke, T. A., Ammerman, B. A., & Jacobucci, R. (2019). The use of machine learning in the study of suicidal and non-suicidal self-injurious thoughts and behaviors: a systematic review. *Journal of Affective Disorders*, *245*, 869–884. https://doi.org/ 10.1016/j.jad.2018.11.073

Burnette, C., Ramchand, R., & Ayer, L. (2015). Gatekeeper training for suicide prevention. *Rand Health Quarterly*, *5*(1). Retrieved from www.ncbi.nlm.nih.gov/ pmc/articles/PMC5158249/

Busby, D. R., Zheng, K., Eisenberg, D., et al. (2021). Black college students at elevated risk for suicide: barriers to mental health service utilization. *Journal of American College Health*, *69*(3), 308–314. https://doi.org/10.1080/07448481.2019.1674316

Center for Collegiate Mental Health. (2009). *2009 Annual Report*. https://ccmh.psu .edu/assets/docs/2009_CCMH_Report-zwcspm.pdf

Center for Collegiate Mental Health. (2019). *2019 Annual Report*. https://ccmh.psu .edu/assets/docs/2019-CCMH-Annual-Report_3.17.20.pdf

Centers for Disease Control and Prevention (CDC). (2019, September 11). *Preventing suicide |violence prevention|injury center|CDC*. www.cdc.gov/violencepreven tion/suicide/fastfact.html

Coleman, D., Black, N., Ng, J., & Blumenthal, E. (2019). Kognito's avatar-based suicide prevention training for college students: results of a randomized controlled trial and a naturalistic evaluation. *Suicide and Life-Threatening Behavior*, *49*(2). https://doi.org/10.1111/sltb.12550

Cross, W., Matthieu, M. M., Lezine, D., & Knox, K. L. (2010). Does a brief suicide prevention gatekeeper training program enhance observed skills? *Crisis*, *31*(3), 149–159. https://doi.org/10.1027/0227-5910/a000014

Deane, F. P., Wilson, C. J., & Ciarrochi, J. (2001). Suicidal ideation and help-negation: not just hopelessness or prior help. *Journal of Clinical Psychology*, *57*(7), 901–914.

Dennis, M. J. (2017). Bumpy road ahead for U.S. higher education. *Enrollment Management Report*, *21*(9), 1–3. https://doi.org/10.1002/emt.30362

Downs, M. F., & Eisenberg, D. E. (2012). Help seeking and treatment use among suicidal college students. *Journal of American College Health*, *60*(2), 104–114. https://doi.org/10.1080/07448481.2011.619611

Drum, D. J., Brownson, C., Burton Denmark, A., & Smith, S. E. (2009). New data on the nature of suicidal crises in college students: shifting the paradigm. *Professional Psychology: Research and Practice*, **40**(3), 213–222. https://doi.org/10.1037/a0014465

Evans, T. M., Bira, L., Gastelum, J. B., Weiss, L. T., & Vanderford, N. L. (2018). Evidence for a mental health crisis in graduate education. *Nature Biotechnology*, **36**(3), 282–284. https://doi.org/10.1038/nbt.4089

Everett, D. D., & Loftus, Z. V. (2011). Resident assistants as rule enforcers versus friends: an exploratory study of role conflict. *Journal of College and University Student Housing*, **37**(2), 72–89.

Ford-Paz, R. E., Kuebbeler, A., Contreras, R., Garduño, M., & Sánchez, B. (2015). Training community opinion leaders to raise awareness and promote early intervention for depressed Latino adolescents. *Progress in Community Health Partnerships: Research, Education, and Action*, **9**(2), 191–201. https://doi.org/10.1353/cpr.2015.0039

Franklin, J., Ribeiro, J., Fox, K., et al. (2017). Risk factors for suicidal thoughts and behaviors: a meta-analysis of 50 years of research. *Psychological Bulletin*, **143**(2), 187–232. https://doi.org/10.1037/bul0000084

Fulginiti, A., Pahwa, R., Frey, L. M., Rice, E., & Brekke, J. S. (2016). What factors influence the decision to share suicidal thoughts? a multilevel social network analysis of disclosure among individuals with serious mental illness. *Suicide and Life-Threatening Behavior*, **46**(4), 398–412. https://doi.org/10.1111/sltb.12224

Fulginiti, A., Rice, E., Hsu, H.-T., Rhoades, H., & Winetrobe, H. (2016). Risky integration. *Crisis*, **37**(3), 184–193. https://doi.org/10.1027/0227-5910/a000374

Goldsmith, S. K., Pellmar, T. C., Kleinman, A. M., & Bunney, W. E. (Series Eds.). (2002). *Reducing Suicide: A National Imperative*. Washington, DC: National Academies Press.

Goodwill, J. R., & Zhou, S. (2020). Association between perceived public stigma and suicidal behaviors among college students of color in the U.S. *Journal of Affective Disorders*, **262**, 1–7. https://doi.org/10.1016/j.jad.2019.10.019

Han, B., Compton, W. M., Eisenberg, D., et al. (2016). Prevalence and mental health treatment of suicidal ideation and behavior among college students aged 18–25 years and their non-college-attending peers in the United States. *Journal of Clinical Psychiatry*, **77**(6), 815–824. https://doi.org/10.4088/JCP.15m09929

Isaac, M., Elias, B., Katz, L. Y., et al. (2009). Gatekeeper training as a preventative intervention for suicide: a systematic review. *The Canadian Journal of Psychiatry*, **54**(4), 260–268. https://doi.org/10.1177/070674370905400407

Kisch, J., Leino, E. V., & Silverman, M. M. (2005). Aspects of suicidal behavior, depression, and treatment in college students: results from the Spring 2000 National College Health Assessment Survey. *Suicide and Life-Threatening Behavior*, **35**(1), 3–13.

Li, W., Dorstyn, D. S., & Jarmon, E. (2020). Identifying suicide risk among college students: a systematic review. *Death Studies*, **44**(7), 450–458. https://doi.org/10.1080/07481187.2019.1578305

Lipson, S. K., Kern, A., Eisenberg, D., & Breland-Noble, A. M. (2018). Mental health disparities among college students of color. *Journal of Adolescent Health*, **63**(3), 348–356. https://doi.org/10.1016/j.jadohealth.2018.04.014

Litteken, C., & Sale, E. (2018). Long-term effectiveness of the Question, Persuade, Refer (QPR) Suicide Prevention Gatekeeper Training Program: lessons from Missouri. *Community Mental Health Journal*, **54**(3), 282–292. https://doi.org/10.1007/s10597-017-0158-z

Marin, A., & Hampton, K. N. (2007). Simplifying the personal network name generator: alternatives to traditional multiple and single name generators. *Field Methods*, **19**(2), 163–193. https://doi.org/10.1177/1525822X06298588

McCarthy, K. (2020). Resident assistant secondary trauma and burnout associated with student nonsuicidal self-injury. *Journal of American College Health*, **68**(7), 673–677. https://doi.org/10.1080/07448481.2019.1590374

McLaughlin, W. G. (2018). Overloaded and overlooked: improving resident advisors' self-care. *Journal of American College Health*, **66**(8), 831–833. https://doi.org/10.1080/07448481.2018.1440573

Michelmore, L., & Hindley, P. (2012). Help-seeking for suicidal thoughts and self-harm in young people: a systematic review. *Suicide and Life-Threatening Behavior*, **42**(5), 507–524. https://doi.org/10.1111/j.1943-278X.2012.00108.x

Midorikawa, H., Tachikawa, H., Nemoto, K., et al. (2020). Mental health of gatekeepers may influence their own attitudes toward suicide: a questionnaire survey from a suicide-prevention gatekeeper training program. *Asian Journal of Psychiatry*, **47**, 101842. https://doi.org/10.1016/j.ajp.2019.101842

Mo, P. K. H., Ko, T. T., & Xin, M. Q. (2018). School-based gatekeeper training programmes in enhancing gatekeepers' cognitions and behaviours for adolescent suicide prevention: a systematic review. *Child and Adolescent Psychiatry and Mental Health*, **12**(1), 29. https://doi.org/10.1186/s13034-018-0233-4

Moore, J. T., Cigularov, K. P., Chen, P. Y., Martinez, J. M., & Hindman, J. (2011). The effects of situational obstacles and social support on suicide-prevention gatekeeper behaviors. *Crisis*, **32**(5), 264–271. https://doi.org/10.1027/0227-5910/a000090

Mortier, P., Auerbach, R. P., Alonso, J., et al. (2018). Suicidal thoughts and behaviors among college students and same-aged peers: results from the World Health Organization World Mental Health Surveys. *Social Psychiatry and Psychiatric Epidemiology*, **53**(3), 279–288.

Mortier, P., Cuijpers, P., Kiekens, G., et al. (2018). The prevalence of suicidal thoughts and behaviours among college students: a meta-analysis. *Psychological Medicine*, **48**(4), 554–565.

Paladino, D. A., Murray, T., Newgent, R. A., & Goiin, L. A. (2005). Resident assistant burnout: factors impacting depersonalization, emotional exhaustion, and personal accomplishment. *Journal of College and University Student Housing*, **33**, 18–27.

Paul, E., Tsypes, A., Eidlitz, L., Ernhout, C., & Whitlock, J. (2015). Frequency and functions of non-suicidal self-injury: associations with suicidal thoughts and behaviors. *Psychiatry Research*, **225**(3), 276–282. https://doi.org/10.1016/j.psychres.2014.12.026

Pickering, T. A., Wyman, P. A., Schmeelk-Cone, K., et al. (2018). Diffusion of a peer-led suicide preventive intervention through school-based student peer and adult networks. *Frontiers in Psychiatry*, **9**. https://doi.org/10.3389/fpsyt.2018.00598

Pisani, A. R., Schmeelk-Cone, K., Gunzler, D., et al. (2012). Associations between suicidal high school students' help-seeking and their attitudes and perceptions of social environment. *Journal of Youth and Adolescence*, **41**(10), 1312–1324. https://doi.org/10.1007/s10964-012-9766-7

Porter, S. C., & Newman, L. (2016). A brief measure of attitudes toward resident advisors. *College Student Journal*, **50**(1), 107–111.

Rahmattalabi, A., Vayanos, P., Fulginiti, A., Rice, E., et al (2019). Exploring algorithmic fairness in robust graph covering problems. In H. Wallach, H. Larochelle, A. Beygelzimer, F. Alché-Buc, E. Fox, & R. Garnett (Eds.), *Advances in Neural Information Processing Systems 32*, 15750–15761. http://papers.nips.cc/paper/ 9707-exploring-algorithmic-fairness-in-robust-graph-covering-problems.pdf.

Rahmattalabi, A., Vayanos, P., Fulginiti, A., & Tambe, M. (2019). Robust peer-monitoring on graphs with an application to suicide prevention in social networks. *Proceedings of the 18th International Conference on Autonomous Agents and MultiAgent Systems*, 2168–2170. http://dl.acm.org/citation.cfm?id=3306127.3332046

Reetz, D. R., Barr, V., & Krylowicz, B. (2014). *The Association of University and College Counseling Center Directors Annual Survey*. www.aucccd.org/assets/ documents/2014%20aucccd%20monograph%20-%20public%20pdf.pdf

Reingle, J., Thombs, D., Osborn, C., Saffian, S., & Oltersdorf, D. (2010). Mental health and substance use: a qualitative study of resident assistants' attitudes and referral practices. *Journal of Student Affairs Research and Practice*, **47**(3), 325–342. https://doi.org/10.2202/1949-6605.6016

Rice, E., Yoshioka-Maxwell, A., Petering, R., et al. (2018). Piloting the use of artificial intelligence to enhance HIV prevention interventions for youth experiencing homelessness. *Journal of the Society for Social Work and Research*, **9**(4), 551–573. https://doi.org/10.1086/701439

Rickwood, D., Deane, F. P., Wilson, C. J., & Ciarrochi, J. (2005). Young people's help-seeking for mental health problems. *Australian E-Journal for the Advancement of Mental Health*, **4**(3), 218–251. https://doi.org/10.5172/jamh.4.3.218

Robinson-Link, N., Hoover, S., Bernstein, L., et al. (2019). Is gatekeeper training enough for suicide prevention? *School Mental Health* **12**(2): 239–249. https://doi .org/10.1007/s12310-019-09345-x

Rudd, M. D., Joiner, T. E., & Rajab, M. H. (1995). Help negation after acute suicidal crisis. *Journal of Consulting and Clinical Psychology*, **63**(3), 499–503.

Schneider, J. A., Zhou, A. N., & Laumann, E. O. (2015). A new HIV prevention network approach: sociometric peer change agent selection. *Social Science & Medicine*, **125**, 192–202. https://doi.org/10.1016/j.socscimed.2013.12.034

Shtivelband, A., Aloise-Young, P. A., & Chen, P. Y. (2015). Sustaining the effects of gatekeeper suicide prevention training. *Crisis*, **36**(2), 102–109. https://doi.org/10 .1027/0227-5910/a000304

Taub, D. J., Servaty-Seib, H. L., Miles, N., et al. (2013). The impact of gatekeeper training for suicide prevention on university resident assistants. *Journal of College Counseling*, **16**(1), 64–78. https://doi.org/10.1002/j.2161-1882.2013.00027.x

Tompkins, T. L., & Witt, J. (2009). The short-term effectiveness of a suicide prevention gatekeeper training program in a college setting with residence life advisers. *The Journal of Primary Prevention*, **30**(2), 131–149. https://doi.org/10.1007/s10935-009-0171-2

Turner, J. C., Leno, E. V., & Keller, A. (2013). Causes of mortality among American college students: a pilot study. *Journal of College Student Psychotherapy*, **27**(1), 31–42.

Twale, D. J., & Burrell, L. F. (1994). Resident assistants on Black and White campuses assess resident student problems. *Journal of College Student Development*, **35**(1), 29–34.

U.S. Census Bureau. (2010). Group quarters population in college/ university housing. 2010 Census Congressional District Summary File (113th Congress). http://factfinder2.census.gov.

U.S. Department of Health and Human Services (HHS) Office of the Surgeon General and National Action Alliance for Suicide Prevention. (2012, September). *2012 National Strategy for Suicide Prevention: Goals and Objectives for Action*. Washington, DC: HHS. www.ncbi.nlm.nih.gov/books/NBK109917/

Valente, T. W. (2010). *Social Networks and Health: Models, Methods, and Applications*. Oxford University Press.

Valente, T. W. (2012). Network interventions. *Science*, **337**(6090), 49–53. https://doi.org/10.1126/science.1217330

Valente, T. W. (2017). Putting the network in network interventions. *Proceedings of the National Academy of Sciences of the United States of America*, **114**(36), 9500–9501. https://doi.org/10.1073/pnas.1712473114

Valente, T. W., & Pumpuang, P. (2007). Identifying opinion leaders to promote behavior change. *Health Education & Behavior*, **34**(6), 881–896. https://doi.org/10.1177/1090198106297855

Van Orden, K. A., Witte, T. K., Cukrowicz, K. C., et al. (2010). The interpersonal theory of suicide. *Psychological Review*, **117**(2), 575–600. https://doi.org/10.1037/a0018697

Walrath, C., Garraza, L. G., Reid, H., Goldston, D. B., & McKeon, R. (2015). Impact of the Garrett Lee Smith Youth Suicide Prevention Program on suicide mortality. *American Journal of Public Health*, **105**(5), 986–993. https://doi.org/10.2105/AJPH.2014.302496

Walsh, C. G., Ribeiro, J. D., & Franklin, J. C. (2017). Predicting risk of suicide attempts over time through machine learning. *Clinical Psychological Science*, **5**(3), 457–469. https://doi.org/10.1177/2167702617691560

Wolitzky-Taylor, K., LeBeau, R. T., Perez, M., Gong-Guy, E., & Fong, T. (2020). Suicide prevention on college campuses: what works and what are the existing gaps? A systematic review and meta-analysis. *Journal of American College Health*, **68**(4), 419–429. https://doi.org/10.1080/07448481.2019.1577861

Wyman, P., Brown, C. H., Inman, J., et al. (2008). Randomized trial of a gatekeeper program for suicide prevention: 1-year impact on secondary school staff. *Journal of Consulting and Clinical Psychology*, **76**(1), 104–115.

Wyman, P. A., Brown, C. H., LoMurray, M., et al. (2010). An outcome evaluation of the sources of strength suicide prevention program delivered by adolescent peer leaders in high schools. *American Journal of Public Health*, **100**(9), 1653–1661. https://doi.org/10.2105/AJPH.2009.190025

Yonemoto, N., Kawashima, Y., Endo, K., & Yamada, M. (2019). Gatekeeper training for suicidal behaviors: a systematic review. *Journal of Affective Disorders*, **246**, 506–514. https://doi.org/10.1016/j.jad.2018.12.052

Zinzow, H. M., Thompson, M. P., Fulmer, C. B., Goree, J., & Evinger, L. (2020). Evaluation of a brief suicide prevention training program for college campuses. *Archives of Suicide Research*, **24**(1), 82–95. https://doi.org/10.1080/13811118.2018.1509749

6

Optimizing Defibrillator Deployment

Timothy C.Y. Chan and Christopher L.F. Sun

Summary of the Problem

The odds of survival following an out-of-hospital cardiac arrest (OHCA) decreases significantly for every minute without treatment, making it one of the deadliest emergency events in the world. Beyond traditional emergency medical service response, effective OHCA treatment can be safely delivered by untrained bystanders through cardiopulmonary resuscitation and automated external defibrillator (AED) use. An AED is a medical device that automatically diagnoses irregular heart rhythms in an OHCA victim and subsequently resuscitates them through defibrillation. Rapid bystander AED use has been shown to reduce the time to treatment and triple the chance of OHCA survival. Accordingly, the strategic placement of AEDs in public areas to facilitate bystander response has been a primary focus of many health organizations. However, despite the tremendous amount of effort dedicated to the dissemination of AEDs, bystander AED use and OHCA survival remain low.

Summary of the Solution

In this chapter, we explore how data-driven modeling can improve the understanding of OHCA risk, help identify the limitations of current AED placement strategies, and guide the development of optimal AED networks to increase the chance of AED use and OHCA survival. More specifically, we frame AED network design and related response efforts as a facility location problem, focusing on the maximum coverage location and p-median problems. We also highlight how novel tools that combine techniques from areas including information theory and machine learning with optimization models can shape the future of OHCA response efforts and AED placement strategies.

Summary of Relevance in a Post-COVID World

The response to COVID-19 precipitated massive shifts in where people live, work, eat, and spend time. Millions of people transitioned to working remotely at home and less frequently visited public areas, where the majority of defibrillators are currently placed. All of these changes necessitate the updated placement of defibrillators to match the new population and cardiac arrest incidence distributions. Methods in this chapter describe how the updated placement can be data-driven and optimized.

6.1 Introduction

6.1.1 Out-of-Hospital Cardiac Arrest

Cardiac arrest is an often-fatal emergency event caused by a malfunction in the heart's electrical system, leading to the sudden loss of heart function and blood flow in the body. For every minute without treatment, cardiac arrest survival decreases by roughly 7% to 17% (Larsen et al. 1993, Valenzuela et al. 1997, Robertson 2000, Stoesser et al. 2018). The rapid delivery of treatment, namely, cardiopulmonary resuscitation (CPR) and defibrillation (an electrical shock that restores the heart's normal rhythm), is critical to improving outcomes following cardiac arrest (Page et al. 2000, Valenzuela et al. 2000, Caffrey et al. 2002, Hallstrom et al. 2004, Kitamura et al. 2010).

Out-of-hospital cardiac arrests (OHCAs), in particular, are a tremendous burden on healthcare systems. Roughly 700,000 OHCA-related deaths occur annually in North America and Europe (Sasson, Rogers et al. 2010, Grasner et al. 2016, Benjamin et al. 2018). Moreover, the overall survival rate of OHCA is less than 8% (Robertson 2000, Nichol et al. 2008, Holmberg et al. 2017, Pollack et al. 2018). As OHCAs occur outside of hospitals and healthcare facilities, the increased length of time between the OHCA victim's collapse and the delivery of treatment is an enormous challenge that emergency medical service (EMS) responders must overcome to improve victim outcomes. To minimize the impact of the delay of initial treatment from traditional EMS response, early bystander response using an automated external defibrillator (AED) has been a major focal point for many initiatives aiming to improve OHCA outcomes.

6.1.2 Automated External Defibrillators

An AED, shown in Figure 6.1, is a portable medical device that can automatically detect the irregular heart rhythm present in an OHCA victim and defibrillate them if the heart rhythm can be reset with an electrical shock. These devices are specifically designed to be easily applied and used on OHCA victims, allowing untrained bystanders to administer lifesaving interventions and play a critical role in the OHCA response (Gundry et al. 1999). Bystander AED use can triple the chance of OHCA survival in patients with shockable heart rhythms due to the reduced time to defibrillation (Valenzuela et al. 2000, Caffrey et al. 2002, Hallstrom et al. 2004, Weisfeldt et al. 2010, Berdowski et al. 2011, Murakami et al. 2014). While several factors contribute to successful bystander-based interventions, including OHCA recognition, high-quality CPR, bystander presence, and bystander willingness to act, the placement of accessible AEDs for bystanders to locate and use is an essential component to facilitating rapid OHCA treatment (Cummins et al. 1991, Marenco et al. 2001, Hallstrom et al. 2004).

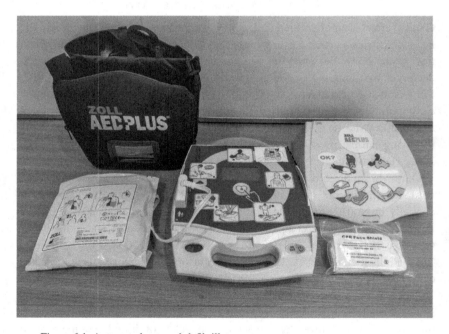

Figure 6.1 Automated external defibrillator.

6.1.3 Current AED Placement Strategies

Health organizations dedicated to improving cardiac health and emergency medicine, including the American Heart Association (AHA) and European Resuscitation Council (ERC), have recognized the importance of AEDs and strive to increase bystander defibrillation rates. One of the many ways they have done this is by creating guidelines for the development of public access AED networks. For example, the 2015 iteration of the AHA and ERC guidelines recommended AED placement in high-traffic public locations with a high likelihood of witnessed OHCA (Kronick et al. 2015, Perkins et al. 2015), as bystanders would likely be present and able to rapidly retrieve accessible AEDs for use in these areas. AED placement recommendations have also focused on targeting location types that have high historical OHCA incidence, such as train stations and casinos (Gratton et al. 1999, Valenzuela et al. 2000, Caffrey et al. 2002, Fedoruk et al. 2002, Davies et al. 2005, Iwami et al. 2006, Reed et al. 2006, Folke et al. 2009, Brooks et al. 2013, Lee et al. 2017, Sun et al. 2017). Government-enacted legislation has also supported bystander AED use by identifying special locations of interest, such has primary schools, to place AEDs in. While schools have low OHCA incidence, the successful resuscitation of young OHCA victims can lead to many quality-adjusted life years saved, and AED placements can also raise awareness of OHCA and AED use from a young age, potentially improving bystander response rates in the future. However, despite the efforts from health organizations and government bodies, AED use and positive patient outcomes remain low (Wissenberg et al. 2013, Hansen et al. 2014, Daya et al. 2015, Hansen et al. 2017, Pollack et al. 2018). More specifically, bystander AED use occurs in approximately 14.2% of all public location OHCAs in North America (Pollack et al. 2018). In Europe, bystander defibrillation (shock delivered from a bystander-applied AED) is approximately 15.3% and 1.3% for public and private location OHCAs, respectively (Hansen et al. 2017).

In the following sections, we will explore the limitations of current placement strategies and demonstrate how data-driven modeling can improve the design of AED networks to increase bystander AED use and OHCA survival rates. Specifically, we will review topics including frameworks to evaluate AED network effectiveness, optimizing the placement and relocation of static AEDs in a city, spatial and spatiotemporal cardiac arrest risk, barriers and facilitators of AED use, approaches to guiding indoor AED placement, and designing drone networks for AED delivery.

6.2 Static AED Placement Optimization Models

6.2.1 Background

Guidelines and strategies for AED network development suggest communities prioritize placement in locations with high historical OHCA incidence. However, there are several challenges when implementing such an approach. While prioritizing placement in obviously high-risk OHCA locations is straightforward, placement decisions become ambiguous for the remaining locations with similar but lower levels of risk. Resources may be ineffectively deployed, since the placement decisions in these guidelines do not consider interactions with existing placements or other stakeholders. Beyond the design of the guidelines themselves, there still may be issues with the adherence and interpretation of their recommendations by communities, which can result in a mismatch between the number of AEDs placed and the level of OHCA risk in certain areas. Even so, should health organizations become centralized decision makers to build AED networks and overcome these challenges, the vast number of possible AED network configurations and combinations of locations for AED placement can be difficult to process.

Data-driven optimization approaches offer a solution to this problem by using historical OHCA data to determine the set of locations for AED placements, out of thousands of possible candidate locations, that maximize the potential for rapid bystander AED use. In this section, we define key concepts and metrics needed to model the AED placement problem, introduce a basic optimization model formulation that improves spatial proximity of AEDs to OHCA events, and examine extensions of the model that incorporate temporal OHCA risk and the relocation of existing AEDs in the design of the AED network.

6.2.2 Key Modeling Concepts to Formulating AED Placement Models

6.2.2.1 Effective AED Range and OHCA Coverage

While bystander AED use is influenced by many factors, including bystander awareness, training, and willingness to use, as well as AED visibility and signage, the bare minimum requirement is that an AED be physically accessible to the bystander and near the OHCA victim during an arrest. Accordingly, this is the foundation that AED placement optimization models are based on.

Let us start by defining the AED's *effective range* as the maximum distance an AED can be from an OHCA victim such that its retrieval and use can significantly increase the victim's chance of survival. Now, consider the ideal scenario where a bystander's response time is dictated by the travel time of the bystander to retrieve an AED and AED setup time only. In this case, by referencing previous AHA guidelines that recommend AED use within 3 minutes of an OHCA victim's collapse (Aufderheide et al. 2006), we can define an AED's *effective range* to be a 100-meter, straight-line distance from the AED. More specifically, 100 m (109 yards) is the maximum round-trip distance an AED could be found and retrieved by a bystander with a brisk walking speed of 8 kilometers per hour (roughly 5 miles per hour), given that it takes approximately 1.5 minutes to set up and apply the AED to the victim (Gundry et al. 1999, Chan et al. 2016).

Next, we define the metric *spatial OHCA coverage* as the number of OHCAs that occur within the *effective range* of an AED placement, the 100-m straight-line distance. We use this easily quantifiable metric to approximate the impact of an AED placement on bystander AED use and OHCA survival. Thinking ahead, more accurate measures of *spatial OHCA coverage* can be obtained by incorporating the effects of additional barriers and facilitators of AED use in our model by reducing or extending an AED's *effective range* (discussed in Section 6.3).

6.2.2.2 Stability of OHCA Incidence

When modeling using historical data, regardless of the area of application, it is essential to ensure that the historical data accurately characterize the future. OHCA incidence has been found to be spatially stable over time, as it is heavily tied to population density, city infrastructure, and activities of individuals (Sasson, Keirns et al. 2010, Chan et al. 2016). Specifically, these two studies found that the intraclass correlation rates, a measure of correlation within groups, of OHCA incidence by census tract over time in North American cities were 0.36 (95% CI: 0.26 to 0.50) and 0.72 (95% CI: 0.66 to 0.78). Therefore, the use of historical OHCA data in analytical approaches, such as these optimization models, is methodologically appropriate.

6.2.3 Spatial-Only AED Optimization

Using the framework described in the previous section, the simplest method to improve bystander AED use is to maximize the *spatial OHCA coverage* provided by an AED network. Accordingly, a spatial-only AED placement optimization model, based on the *maximum covering location problem* (Church and Revelle 1974), was developed to do just that. To validate the spatial-only optimization model, a comparison against a population-guided placement heuristic, which represented a "commonsense" AED placement approach, was conducted in Toronto, Canada (Chan et al. 2013). The two approaches were evaluated based on the *spatial OHCA coverage* provided by each network. The population-guided approach was developed as follows: The daytime population from each census tract in the city was distributed to every building situated in that census tract, according to the number of floors and businesses within each specific building. The buildings with the largest estimated daytime populations were then chosen as locations for AED placements. Optimization provided significantly more *spatial OHCA coverage* compared to the population-guided heuristic, regardless of the number of AEDs placed.

This spatial-only model was also designed to determine optimal AED locations while accounting for the *spatial OHCA coverage* provided by existing AED placements in the setting of interest (Figure 6.2). This highlights how optimization approaches can tailor recommendations to specific sites and supplement the guidelines text, which, by design, provide highly generalized recommendations that do not consider the interactions between new AED placements and existing AED placements.

This spatial-only covering model was later extended to account for varying levels of uncertainty of future OHCA locations. This provided a means to ensure the selected AED locations are robust to potential violations in the

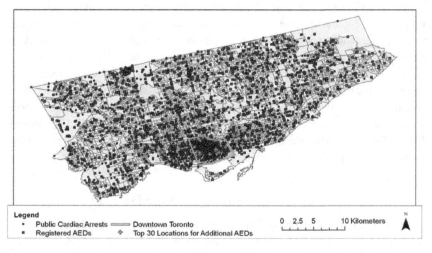

Legend
• Public Cardiac Arrests ══ Downtown Toronto
■ Registered AEDs   ✦ Top 30 Locations for Additional AEDs

0   2.5 5   10 Kilometers

Figure 6.2 Top 30 locations for additional AED placements (uncovered cardiac arrest hot spots) on top of the existing AED network in Toronto as identified by the spatial-only AED optimization model.

Image from: Chan, T. C., Li, H., Lebovic, G., et al. (2013). Identifying locations for public access defibrillators using mathematical optimization. *Circulation*, 127(17), 1801–1809 finding demonstrating the stability of OHCA incidence over time and space. A *distributionally robust* optimization model (Delage and Ye 2010) was developed to do so, determining optimal AED placements using a set of probability distributions that represent future OHCA incidence instead of using the exact locations of historical OHCAs (Chan et al. 2018).

6.2.4 Spatiotemporal AED Optimization

Temporal accessibility is another essential component of improving AED use that has often been overlooked in previous AED placement strategies that focus primarily on spatial accessibility. AEDs are commonly placed indoors and are often only accessible during the building's hours of operation, which vary by time of day and day of week (Figure 6.3). This can be detrimental to patient outcomes, as AEDs may be inaccessible during the time of an OHCA, despite being placed in a nearby location. In fact, previous studies have found over 1 in 5 OHCAs occur near an AED when that AED is inaccessible due to limited temporal availability (Hansen et al. 2013, Sun et al. 2016).

To account for temporal accessibility, let us define *spatiotemporal OHCA coverage* to be the number of OHCAs that occur within an AED's *effective range* when that AED was temporally available. In other words, the AED's *effective range* is set to 0 m when it is not temporally available for use. Also,

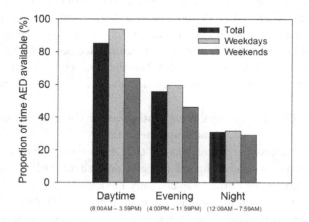

Figure 6.3 Existing automated external defibrillator (AED) availability by time of day and day of week in Toronto, Canada.
Image from: Sun, C. L., Demirtas, D., Brooks, S. C., Morrison, L. J., & Chan, T. C. (2016). Overcoming spatial and temporal barriers to public access defibrillators via optimization. *Journal of the American College of Cardiology*, 68(8), 836–845

we define an AED to be temporally available based on the hours of operations of the building housing the AED.

Given the impact of limited temporal AED availability, spatiotemporal AED placement optimization models were developed to identify locations for placements that maximize *spatiotemporal OHCA coverage*. Intuitively, spatiotemporal optimization models can identify placements that better match the distribution of OHCAs by accounting for temporal information and provide more *spatiotemporal OHCA coverage* compared to spatial-only models. In fact, it was found that spatiotemporal optimization models can reverse the negative effects of limited temporal accessibility stemming from AED placements based on a spatial optimization model (Sun et al. 2016). That is, by properly integrating temporal information in placement decisions and explicitly matching the availability of the buildings housing the AEDs to the times of OHCA incidence through optimization models, decision makers can achieve similar levels of *spatiotemporal OHCA coverage* as when placing AEDs with 24/7 availability while only considering spatial information in placement decisions.

6.2.4.1 The Generalizability of Spatiotemporal Optimization Models

The benefits of spatiotemporal optimization over spatial-only optimization models were also found to be generalizable to different study settings. A spatiotemporal placement model performed similarly in Toronto, Canada, and Copenhagen, Denmark, despite Copenhagen having a different city structure, smaller population, higher population density, fewer individuals of different ethnic origins, larger existing AED network size, and shorter working hours (Sun et al. 2018). Importantly, these differences are all factors that have been shown to influence AED use, OHCA incidence, and victim outcomes (Becker et al. 1993, Reinier et al. 2011, Drennan et al. 2016). This finding is critical to ensuring these models can be used universally as an assistive tool for decision makers.

6.2.4.2 Considerations during Optimization Model Formulation and Implementation

In addition to improving *spatiotemporal OHCA coverage*, the temporal information captured in spatiotemporal models can lead to AED placements at different locations compared to spatial-only models (Tsai et al. 2012, Huang and Wen 2014). When the optimal configurations of 24/7 AED placements based on the two model types were compared, the spatiotemporal model selected locations in dense areas with active populations regardless of time of day, where an available AED could compensate for the increased delays in EMS response that occur during dispatches during the nighttime. In contrast, the spatial-only model prioritized placements in residential areas that were farther away from EMS stations, as an AED could reduce delays in EMS response associated with large travel distances and other spatial barriers. Although the spatiotemporal model provided a relative increase in *spatiotemporal OHCA coverage* of 18.0% to 26.2% over the spatial model, the two different approaches clearly benefit distinct population groups. Stakeholders should be cognizant of these differences and thoroughly understand what type of model to develop, given the historical OHCA risk and existing EMS infrastructure during the development AEDs networks, as well as the implications toward equity of care after implementation.

6.2.5 Static AED Relocation Optimization

It is important to remember that enormous amounts of resources have been spent on existing AED placements that are not well aligned with the distribution of OHCA incidence. While previously mentioned optimization models focus on the design of a new AED network and the placement of additional AEDs in existing networks, the relocation of existing AEDs represents an alternative approach to improving *spatial OHCA coverage* while avoiding the full costs of purchasing and installing new AEDs. The financial benefits of such an approach can be tremendous, as the cost associated with purchasing and installing a new AED was estimated to be approximately 8.5 times greater than the costs associated with relocation (Tierney et al. 2018).

AED placement relocation models aim to maximize *spatial OHCA coverage* by making decisions to add a new AED or relocate an existing AED at their respective costs, under a specified budget. Relocation models have been shown to have relative increases in *spatial OHCA coverage* between 11.5% and 121.9% over fixed location models and can potentially provide savings in the range of millions of dollars when examined in Canton Ticino, Switzerland (Tierney et al. 2018), and Toronto, Canada (Chan et al. 2016).

6.2.5.1 Considerations for AED Relocation Strategies

Compared to traditional placement approaches, relocations models are best suited for centralized bodies with ownership over an AED network, as opposed to cases where existing AEDs are owned by individuals, businesses, or communities that may be reluctant or unwilling to relinquish their AED for relocation. Additionally, efforts must be placed in increasing bystander awareness of any relocated AED, as the location of an AED is often associated with the building that houses it. Relocation may increase the risk of bystanders continually returning to search for an AED in a specific building, even after it has been relocated.

6.3 Modeling Barriers and Facilitators of AED Use

6.3.1 Background

It is often difficult to quantify the interactions within a complex system, and modeling the relationships involved in bystander AED response is no exception. A particularly challenging aspect of optimizing AED placement is quantifying the *effective range* of an AED. As outlined in Section 6.2.2, our current definition of *effective range* of an available AED uses a 100-m radius, which is based on the distance a bystander travels and the setup time of an AED. However, the impact of other barriers and facilitators of AED use can be approximated by changing the definition of an AED's *effective range* and provide a means to improve how well optimization approaches model the real world.

In this section, we examine the sensitivity of *spatial OHCA coverage* and optimal AED network configurations to two alternative approaches to modeling an AED's *effective range*. First, we examine changes in the maximum distance at which an AED is considered to be effective. Second, we redefine the *effective range* of an AED as a probability describing the chance of a bystander successfully locating and retrieving a nearby AED, depending on distance from an OHCA. We will introduce this work as general frameworks and then present the approaches in the context of a specific facilitator of AED use: smartphone applications and notification systems that support bystander response.

6.3.2 Adjusting the *Effective Range* of an AED

Changes in an AED's *effective range* can dramatically alter the level of *spatial OHCA coverage* provided by an AED network (Siddiq et al. 2013). Figure 6.4 highlights this relationship by showing the combination of the number of AEDs placed and distance of an AED's effective range (from 10 m to 300 m) required for an optimal AED network to cover a percentage of all OHCAs in Toronto, Canada. Using this figure, decision makers can explore the impact of placing more AEDs, increasing an AED's *effective range*, or both. For example, to improve coverage from 15% to 20%, an additional 70 AEDs would be required if the *effective range* is 30 m. However, if the *effective range* is 100 m, only 15 additional AEDs would be needed.

Figure 6.4 also shows that if the *effective range* of an AED is too low, enormous amounts of resources are needed to increase *spatial OHCA coverage* through static AED placements. This concept describes one of the limitations of static AED placements, which is explored more in depth in Section 6.5.3.

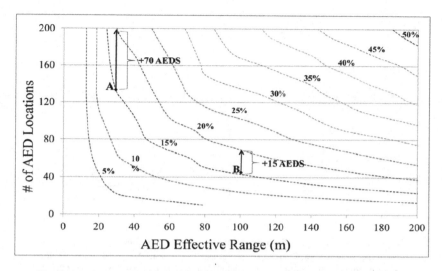

Figure 6.4 Combinations of total AEDs and effective range required to achieve a potential spatial OHCA coverage level between 5% and 50% of all OHCAs in the study setting. Points A and B show 70 and 15 additional AEDs are needed to increase coverage from 15% to 20%, respectively.

Figure from: Siddiq, A. A., Brooks, S. C., & Chan, T. C. (2013). Modeling the impact of public access defibrillator range on public location cardiac arrest coverage. *Resuscitation*, 84(7), 904–909

6.3.3 Probabilistic OHCA Coverage Function

As of now, we have examined two *OHCA coverage* definitions that are each represented as a binary step function (e.g., a value of 1 if covered and 0 otherwise) depending on the spatial or spatiotemporal accessibility of an AED to an OHCA victim. Even when increasing or decreasing the effective range of an AED, these definitions are a simplification of the extremely complex response behaviors that occur in reality. To develop stronger numerical approximations of such interactions, let us consider the scenario where an AED's *effective range* is modeled as a probability of a bystander retrieving an AED that decays exponentially as distance increases from the AED (Chan et al. 2016). Using this probabilistic function (Figure 6.5), more sophisticated model formulations can be developed that accurately reflect reality and consider the different barriers and facilitators of AED use. To demonstrate this, let us explore integrating bystander behavior into AED optimization models.

6.3.3.1 Modeling Bystander and Retrieval Behavior

Beyond the importance of bystander behavior during an OHCA on time to treatment, the actions of responding bystanders can also lead to significantly

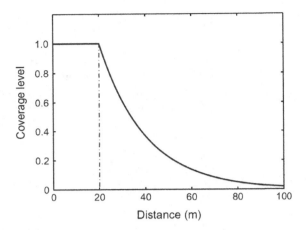

Figure 6.5 An exponentially decreasing OHCA coverage function.
Figure and caption from: Chan, T. C., Demirtas, D., & Kwon, R. H. (2016). Optimizing the deployment of public access defibrillators. *Management Science*, 62(12), 3617–3635

different optimal AED network designs (Chan et al. 2016). To analyze this relationship, three scenarios, each corresponding to a different generalization of bystander behavior during an arrest, were modeled using the probabilistic coverage function in a spatial-only AED placement optimization model framework. The first of the three bystander behavior models characterizes the case in which multiple responders search independently for any covering AED to bring back to the OHCA. This model places AED such that the probability that at least one AED, out of all the AEDs covering an OHCA, is successfully retrieved is maximized for each of the OHCAs in the study setting. The second model examines a worst-case single-responder behavior, where the responding bystander always retrieves the AED within range farthest away from the covered OHCA. This is done by making AED placement decisions based on the minimum probability of AED retrieval, out of all AEDs covering the OHCA, of each OHCA, given that the probability is greater than 0. The last model represents the best-case single-responder scenario, in which the responding bystander retrieves the closest AED to the covered OHCA. This corresponds to AED placement decisions based on the largest probability of AED retrieval, out of all AEDs covering an OHCA, of each OHCA.

The optimal placements from the first (multiple responders) and third (best-case single-responder) models were found to be clustered in OHCA hotspots. This is because for these bystander response behaviors, the probability of retrieval increases when providing overlapping coverage of OHCAs. In contrast, the second model (worst-case single-responder) and the original spatial-only model that uses a binary coverage function do not benefit from overlapping coverage, and places AEDs in a more spread-out manner. Of the three models, the multiple responder case most accurately represents true bystander behavior, as this is typically what is seen in urban areas. The differences in the locations of the optimal placements from each model highlight the sensitivity of optimal spatial-only AED network configurations to different bystander behaviors.

6.3.4 Integrating *Effective Range* Frameworks in AED Placement Optimization Models

Advanced modeling of an AED's *effective range* opens new avenues to integrate additional realistic considerations into AED placement optimization models. The maximum *effective range* of an AED can be set in accordance with the specific characteristics of each potential AED placement to guide decisions. For example, in rural areas, where it is unlikely a bystander will witness the arrest and retrieve an AED, the AED's *effective range* can be set to be a small distance. Similarly, if modeled using a probability function, the chance of successful AED retrieval can be set to have a faster rate of decay for placements in rural areas, compared to those in a dense urban environment. Furthermore, the *effective range* and probability of AED retrieval can be adjusted depending on factors that influence the accessibility of the AED, such as if the AED is locked behind a desk or placed on a floor above the lobby in a multistory building. Tuning modeling parameters, such as an AED's *effective range*, allows for optimization approaches to better reflect reality and improve the translation of analytical results to actual outcomes after implementation.

6.3.4.1 Route Travel Distances and Integrating City Infrastructure into Estimates of an AED's Effective Range

Estimates of an AED's effective range can also be strengthened by using route distances, based on pedestrian streets and a city's infrastructure, that provide more realistic travel distances compared to simplified straight-line distances. In fact, route distances have been found to be approximately 1.5 times longer than straight-line distances (Karlsson et al. 2017). Adjusting for these factors, as well as additional building specific barriers characteristics (such as AED signage and vertical travel times; outlined in Section 6.4) will further improve the performance of AED placement optimization models in practice.

6.3.4.2 Impact on Effective Range of Smartphone Notification Systems to Support Dispatch of Bystander Responders

Numerous smartphone systems have been developed to rapidly notify volunteer bystanders of a nearby OHCA in parallel to traditional EMS response (Ringh et al. 2015, Brooks et al. 2016, Smith et al. 2017). Once an OHCA diagnosis is confirmed by EMS, a text-message alert or notification on a smartphone application is sent to willing bystanders with detailed response instructions. For example, after providing relevant addresses and location information, the notification system may ask the bystander to retrieve an AED from a nearby building and deliver it to the OHCA victim. These systems provide the potential to overcome common barriers to AED use including converting a two-way travel distance to a one-way trip, reducing the amount of time needed to locate an AED, and identifying willing bystanders that are able to respond (Karlsson et al. 2020).

With the knowledge of the techniques covered in the previous section, let us explore the potential changes in an optimization model such that the benefits of smartphone notification systems are accurately captured in its formulation. In these settings, using an effective radius that is larger than the typical 100 m will most accurately reflect the real-life circumstances of response. The exact value of this radius should be determined by the historical response data recorded by the bystander notification system itself. When framing the problem probabilistically, the chance of successful AED retrieval can be modeled as a function of the number of bystanders that are registered with the notification system nearby the AED placement, the response time of traditional EMS that is notified in parallel to the bystanders, as well as the corresponding distances from the bystander to the AED and OHCA.

6.4 Optimal Indoor AED Placement

6.4.1 Background

After optimal locations for AED placement are identified at the city level, additional modeling techniques can be used to determine the specific locations at which an AED should be placed inside a building. At this granular level, new challenges arise that require alternative modeling and data-processing approaches. In particular, cardiac arrest incidence within a single building is usually low and therefore indoor AED optimization models may be unable to use historical incidence to guide placements, as is done at a city level. Furthermore, building characteristics (e.g., the actual paths individuals can travel) and specific barriers of AED accessibility (e.g., the increased time to travel vertically across building floors, AED signage to locate an AED within a building) that were not rigorously considered in city level models need to be accounted for. In this section, we cover methods to overcome these challenges by modeling indoor environments as 3-D networks for optimization, optimizing to minimize distance as opposed to maximizing coverage, and developing a statistical approach to guiding indoor AED placements.

6.4.2 Constructing and Optimizing over 3-D Network Representations of Indoor Environments

A common approach to indoor AED placement optimization is to develop a 3-D network that represents the building in question and accurately captures physical obstacles related to AED retrieval (Figure 6.6). In such a network, the nodes represent components within the building, such as rooms, hallways, and staircases, and the edges connecting the nodes are the corresponding distances or estimated travel times between the components. The nodes can also serve as candidate locations for AED placement in an indoor AED placement optimization model.

A 3-D network representation can also support modeling approaches when limited or no historical OHCA data are available for use. The different components of a building, the nodes, can be used as proxies of historical OHCA incidence and serve as "demand points" to cover. Moreover, the locations of pedestrians within the building can be randomly generated based on the 3-D network and used in place of OHCA incidence (Lee et al. 2019). Further improvements can be made to this approach by generating demand points based on the actual distribution of people in buildings, allowing for stronger model generalizability and impact in practice, while still not requiring historical OHCA data.

Indoor AED optimization models and placement strategies may also benefit from a stronger understanding of bystander behavior when searching for an AED. Incorporating the impact of factors such as AED signage, assistance from building security members, and guidance from bystander response smartphone applications on a bystander's ability to locate indoor AEDs will likely improve estimates of AED retrieval times.

6.4.3 Selecting Appropriate Optimization Formulations

Another challenge to optimizing AEDs indoors is that a single AED alone may be able to cover a large portion of the building, making it difficult to justify a modeling approach that maximizes spatial OHCA coverage. *Spatial OHCA coverage* is a binary metric that does not account for the reduced response time

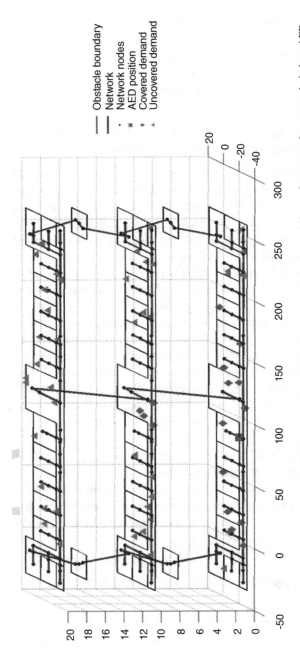

Figure 6.6 A 3-D representation of a building for indoor AED placement optimization and the performance of an example indoor AED placement configuration. The 3-D network's nodes represent components within the building, such as rooms, doorways, and staircases, and the edges connecting the nodes represent the corresponding distances or estimated travel times between the components. In this example, the demand points within the building were randomly generated as no historical OHCA data were available. The figure shows one instance of the example AED placement and performance based on the randomly generated demand points. Generating demand points based on the distribution of people in a building or, when available, the actual historical OHCA incidence, to evaluate indoor placements can improve the model's generalizability and impact in practice.

Figure from: Lee, C. T., Lee, Y. C., & Chen, A. Y. (2019). In-building automated external defibrillator location planning and assessment through building information models. *Automation in Construction*, 106, 102883

126

associated with a smaller distance from the OHCA to an AED when inside an AED's *effective range*. In the indoor setting, a more suitable framework may fall under the *P-Median* problem (Hakimi 1964), where the corresponding optimization model minimizes the total distance between each AED and demand point, given a specified number of AEDs to be placed. The increased precision of minimizing distances between AEDs and OHCAs may improve response times compared to a maximizing *OHCA coverage* approach.

This *P-median* optimization approach has been used in a study that optimizes defibrillator locations in a hospital (Leung et al. 2020). In this setting, there were more historical cardiac arrests than the number of defibrillators to be placed, allowing for the use of historical data to guide placement decisions and evaluate the model's performance. The optimal defibrillator locations decreased the average distance from a defibrillator to a cardiac arrest from 17.1 m to 3.8 m, a relative decrease of 77.8%, compared to existing defibrillator placements.

6.4.4 A Modeling Approach to Informing AED Placement Guidelines in High-Rise Buildings

Modeling approaches can also be used to guide indoor AED placements in unique settings such as high-rise buildings. Buildings like office towers and condominiums represent significant challenges for EMS responders due to the need to travel vertically, which increases response times (Lateef and Anantharaman 2000, Morrison et al. 2005, Silverman et al. 2007, Drennan et al. 2016).

Given this unique setting, a modeling exercise was conducted to compare the hypothetical placement of an AED in a high-rise building's lobby and an AED placed in an elevator that could be activated remotely and sent to the floor of an OHCA (Chan 2017). It was found that in taller buildings with dispersed OHCA risk throughout the building floors, a larger reduction in response time could be achieved if an AED was placed in an elevator. Conversely, in shorter buildings with concentrated OHCA risk in and around the ground floor, which would be the case in buildings with heavy ground floor traffic or connections to underground pedestrian pathways, it was more advantageous to place the AED in the lobby.

6.5 Combining Modeling Techniques to Guide OHCA Response Efforts

6.5.1 Background

Analyzing multidimensional problems to support optimal decision making can benefit tremendously from innovative methodologies. The combination of optimization models with established techniques from areas including information theory to machine learning can lead to the development of novel tools that can shape the future of OHCA response efforts. In this section, we highlight two such tools, the first of which enables the rigorous evaluation of AED placement strategies, and the second guides the implementation of new technologies in traditional EMS systems.

6.5.2 *In Silico* trials: A Novel Approach to Evaluating AED Placement Strategies

6.5.2.1 Motivation

While AED placement optimization models are promising approaches to effective AED network design, they have not been thoroughly validated for clinical use. The gold standard for validation would be to compare optimization approaches to current placement practices through a multiyear, multisite clinical trial. However, this would be tremendously resource intensive and time consuming, as well as difficult to design, experimentally. To overcome these challenges, a two-stage analytical pipeline consisting of an *in silico* trial, a computer-simulated clinical trial using observational data, and a patient outcome prediction model were developed to compare optimal AED placements against existing AED placements over a 9-year study period in Copenhagen, Denmark (Sun et al. 2019).

6.5.2.2 Methods

The *in silico* trial framework used in the first stage of the pipeline was developed to calculate, with a high level of certainty, the *spatiotemporal OHCA coverage* provided by an optimization approach had it actually been implemented. In other words, if we were to go back in time and optimize the placement of AEDs, instead of what was actually done in the past, the *spatiotemporal OHCA coverage* level provided by these optimal AEDs would very likely be equal to the *spatiotemporal OHCA coverage* level calculated when evaluating the same optimization approach in the *in silico* trial framework. In fact, the *spatiotemporal OHCA coverage* provided would be equal with complete certainty under the assumption that AED placements neither cause nor prevent OHCAs from occurring. With this assumption, the hypothetical existence of optimal AED placements in new locations, and the hypothetical absence of the real existing AED placements, would not change the locations or order of the historical OHCA events that are needed to evaluate the optimal AED placements in the *in silico* trial framework.

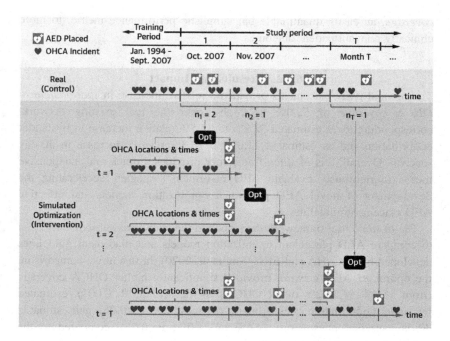

Figure 6.7 An illustration of the optimization approach to determining automated external defibrillator (AED) locations compared with the real AED placements. AED placements are denoted by the boxed logo of the heart with a plus sign. Real placements in each time period are recorded at the time of placement. The optimization models place an equal number of AEDs at the end of the time period. The methodology described in the figure was the same for both intervention arms but with different optimization models, which are represented as the boxes labeled "Opt." In each time period, t, the optimization model considers all out-of-hospital cardiac arrests (OHCAs) prior to the time period as well as any AED placed previously.

Figure and Caption from: Sun, C. L., Karlsson, L., Torp-Pedersen, C., et al. (2019). In Silico Trial of Optimized Versus Actual Public Defibrillator Locations. *Journal of the American College of Cardiology*, 74(12), 1557–1567

By using this framework, we can rigorously compare the *spatiotemporal OHCA coverage* provided by the real existing AED network in a study setting against an equal number of optimized AED placements (Figure 6.7).

In the second stage of the pipeline, the prediction model, a multivariate logistic regression model, was used to estimate patient outcomes based on *spatiotemporal OHCA coverage* as well as patient (e.g., age, gender) and response characteristics (e.g., if a bystander witnessed the arrest, if a bystander applied CPR). This model was the key to translating *spatiotemporal OHCA coverage*, an easily quantifiable but simplistic performance metric, to more clinically relevant patient outcomes.

6.5.2.3 Results and Impact

The optimal AED placements provided a relative increase in *spatiotemporal OHCA coverage* of 52.0% to 95.9% over the real existing network, corresponding to an estimated 52.9% to 83.5% relative increase in bystander defibrillation and an estimated 11.0% to 13.3% relative increase in 30-day survival. Overall, this *in silico* framework provides a quick and inexpensive means to rigorously evaluate AED placement strategies, accelerating the development of novel AED placement optimization models and effective AED placement guidelines.

The *in silico* trial framework developed in the study was subsequently used to compare AED placement optimization models and placement guidelines developed by the AHA and ERC (Sun et al. 2020). In this novel comparison, the optimized AED network provided significantly higher OHCA coverage (from 15.8% to 24.2% of all OHCAs in the setting; $P<0.001$), estimated bystander defibrillation rates (from 15.6% to 18.2%; $P<0.05$), and estimated 30-day survival rates (from 32.6% to 34.0%; $P<0.05$), compared to the guidelines-based placement method.

While these studies demonstrate the advantages of optimized AED networks compared to current AED placements and placement guidelines, the evaluation of AED optimization models in practice is ultimately needed to confirm their potential benefits. With this in mind, it is important to understand that the implementation and success of AED placement optimization models in practice rely on accurate historical OHCA data/databases and central decision makers that can facilitate coordinated AED deployment. Along with this, parallel efforts that aim to improve the public awareness of AEDs and bystander AED use are also crucial in realizing the possible benefits of improved OHCA coverage from using optimization models.

6.5.3 Optimizing Drone AED Delivery: Preparing for Future Technologies

6.5.3.1 Motivation

The value of static AED placements is largest in public urban areas where a single AED can provide coverage to multiple OHCAs and where bystanders are present and willing to act. However, in large and sparsely populated residential or rural settings, where the majority of OHCAs occur, static AED

Figure 6.8 A prototype drone for AED delivery.
Photo from: Drone Delivery Canada

placements are unlikely to be effective (Hansen et al. 2017). Drone technology is a promising intervention for populations in this area, enabling the rapid delivery of an AED to the scene of an OHCA (Figure 6.8), and a potentially transformative advancement in OHCA response in general (Pulver et al. 2016). To help lay the foundation for integrating this technology into existing EMS systems, a two-stage optimization and queuing model approach was developed to determine the configuration of an optimal drone network across eight regions in Ontario, Canada, which cumulatively consists of a population of 7.12 million and spans 26 364 km^2 (Boutilier et al. 2017).

6.5.3.2 Methods
The drone base placement optimization model minimizes the number of drone bases needed to ensure that a specified percentage of all OHCAs is reached within a maximum response time limit. The response time, or time to AED arrival, from drone AED delivery was calculated as a function of the EMS system's average historical dispatch time (from the emergency call to ambulance dispatch), the distance between the OHCA and responding drone base, estimates of the takeoff and landing time of a drone, and the drone's maximum flight speed. This can also be interpreted in the coverage framework described

in Section 6.2.2, where the effective drone response range is the maximum distance a drone can deliver an AED given the specified response time limit. Under this framework, the model identifies the minimum number of locations to establish drone bases, and the locations themselves, in order to cover the specified percentage of all OHCAs.

Following optimization, a queuing model was developed to determine the number of drones stationed at each base such that there is a 99% chance a drone is free in the case that an additional OHCA(s) occurs inside a drone base's coverage area while the drone(s) stationed at that base is currently dispatched and unable to respond. In the queuing model, drone bases were considered a multiserver queue, with a Poisson process modeling OHCA occurrence, and an exponential distribution for out-on-dispatch duration for the drones.

6.5.3.3 Results

Based on an optimal drone network configuration, to achieve a 1-minute reduction from the median 911 response time for all OHCAs, 23 drone bases and 37 drones would be needed across the 8 regions in Ontario. A 2-minute reduction in AED arrival time would require 40 bases and 57 drones and a 3-minute reduction would require 81 bases and 100 drones. Figure 6.9 shows the possible reduction of time to AED arrival from the optimized AED drone network compared to the historical EMS response times in Toronto, a densely populated region, and Muskoka, a large, sparsely populated region in Ontario.

The model also demonstrated that 29.5% fewer bases and 30.0% fewer drones would be needed if the drone network was optimized while considering all eight regions as one aggregated region (integrated network), as opposed to eight individual areas with independent decision makers (region-specific network). However, a trade-off between efficiency and equity was revealed when examining the integrated network, as the model clustered bases in dense urban areas where the majority of OHCAs would occur, neglecting more rural areas.

6.5.3.4 Impact

This optimization and queuing model allows stakeholders to accurately quantify the capabilities of this promising new technology and its requirements for implementation. As an extension of this work, drone AED delivery for EMS response is currently being piloted in EMS systems in North America (Claesson et al. 2017, Cheskes et al. 2019). This study has also helped motivate pilot programs pertaining to the use of drones for emergency events in general, including for search and rescue missions and the delivery of antiepileptic drugs (Homier et al. 2019, Mateen et al. 2020). These drone pilot

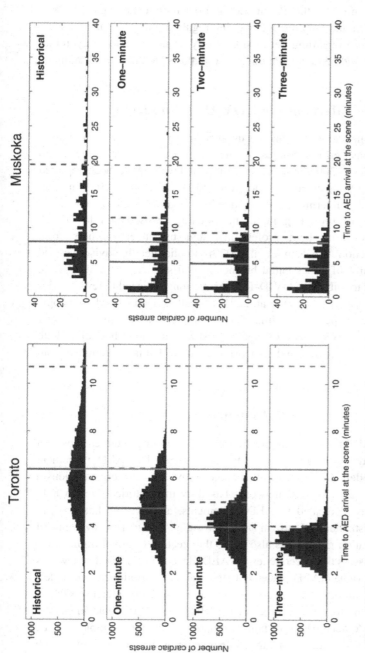

Figure 6.9 Comparison of response time distributions. The first row, labeled Historical, shows the distribution of historical 911 response times in Toronto (a highly urban region in Ontario) and Muskoka (a highly rural region in Ontario). The second row, labeled One-minute, shows the estimated response time distribution corresponding to the drone network configuration designed to improve the historical median response time by 1 minute. The third and fourth rows, labeled Two-minute and Three-minute, show the response time distributions corresponding to the drone network configurations designed to improve the historical median response by 2 and 3 minutes, respectively. The solid line is the median of the distribution, and the dashed line is the 90th percentile. The historical distribution line is extended across all three distributions as a reference.
Figure from: Boutilier, J. J., Brooks, S. C., Janmohamed, A., et al. (2017). Optimizing a drone network to deliver automated external defibrillators. *Circulation*, 135(25), 2454–2465

programs are essential for the global adoption of drone technologies, as they can set a precedent and help resolve ongoing regulatory and technical discussions, such as those regarding permissions to fly drones remotely beyond an operator's line of sight and navigation around airports and high-rise buildings.

6.6 Effects of the COVID-19 Pandemic

The COVID-19 pandemic has had an unprecedented impact on OHCA incidence and response efforts. Surges of OHCA incidence, which range from increases of 30% to 300% relative to historical levels, have been reported worldwide during the pandemic (Baldi et al. 2020, Lai et al. 2020, Sun et al. 2021). Additionally, interim response guidelines were released to balance the competing goals of providing rapid, high-quality resuscitation to OHCA victims and protecting both professional and bystander rescuers from COVID-19 infection (Edelson et al. 2020). Public health advisories and mandatory closures of nonessential businesses and services were also put in place in an effort to mitigate COVID-19 transmissions. This led to fewer AEDs being accessible for use (Leung et al. 2021) as well as a shift in where people live, work, eat, and spend their time. The techniques outlined in this chapter can support the development of updated AED networks that align with changes in OHCA incidence and response guidelines that have stemmed from the pandemic.

6.7 Conclusion

Data-driven modeling has been invaluable in developing interventions that reduce the delays to treatment for OHCA victims. The AED placement optimization models discussed in this chapter provide health organizations a means to design tailored AED networks based on the historical OHCA risk, existing resources dedicated to AED placements, and specific barriers and facilitators of bystander AED use in any given study setting. The development of these optimization models has also led to the creation of novel frameworks that rigorously assess the effectiveness of AED placements. These frameworks can be used to evaluate AED placement strategies, from optimization models or otherwise, to inform healthcare policies and ultimately increase OHCA survival. Furthermore, the principles of modeling static AED placements are generalizable to other OHCA response initiatives and, for example, can be used to develop new models that aim to integrate innovative technologies, such as drones, to traditional EMS systems.

Further Reading

Should readers be interested in learning more about the subject, please refer to Hallstrom et al. 2004, Chan et al. 2013, Smith et al. 2017, Sun et al. 2019, Boutilier et al. 2017 for a deeper understanding of how modeling can impact OHCA response, and Church and Revelle 1974, and Hakimi 1964 for a better understanding of the mathematics behind optimization models.

References

Aufderheide, T., M. F. Hazinski, G. Nichol, et al. (2006). Community lay rescuer automated external defibrillation programs: key state legislative components and implementation strategies: a summary of a decade of experience for healthcare providers, policymakers, legislators, employers, and community leaders from the American Heart Association Emergency Cardiovascular Care Committee, Council on Clinical Cardiology, and Office of State Advocacy. *Circulation* **113**(9): 1260–1270.

Baldi, E., G. M. Sechi, C. Mare, et al. (2020). Out-of-hospital cardiac arrest during the Covid-19 outbreak in Italy. *New England Journal of Medicine* **383**(5): 496–498.

Becker, L. B., B. H. Han, P. M. Meyer, et al. (1993). Racial differences in the incidence of cardiac arrest and subsequent survival. The CPR Chicago Project. *New England Journal of Medicine* **329**(9): 600–606.

Benjamin, E. J., S. S. Virani, C. W. Callaway, et al. (2018). Heart disease and stroke statistics – 2018 update: a report from the American Heart Association. *Circulation* **137**(12): e67–e492.

Berdowski, J., M. T. Blom, A. Bardai, et al. (2011). Impact of onsite or dispatched automated external defibrillator use on survival after out-of-hospital cardiac arrest. *Circulation* **124**(20): 2225–2232.

Boutilier, J. J., S. C. Brooks, A. Janmohamed, et al. (2017). Optimizing a drone network to deliver automated external defibrillators. *Circulation* **135**(25): 2454–2465.

Brooks, S. C., J. H. Hsu, S. K. Tang, R. Jeyakumar and T. C. Chan (2013). Determining risk for out-of-hospital cardiac arrest by location type in a Canadian urban setting to guide future public access defibrillator placement. *Annals of Emergency Medicine* **61**(5): 530–538e532.

Brooks, S. C., G. Simmons, H. Worthington, B. J. Bobrow and L. J. Morrison (2016). The PulsePoint Respond mobile device application to crowdsource basic life support for patients with out-of-hospital cardiac arrest: challenges for optimal implementation. *Resuscitation* **98**: 20–26.

Caffrey, S. L., P. J. Willoughby, P. E. Pepe and L. B. Becker (2002). Public use of automated external defibrillators. *New England Journal of Medicine* **347**(16): 1242–1247.

Chan, T. C., H. Li, G. Lebovic, et al. (2013). Identifying locations for public access defibrillators using mathematical optimization. *Circulation* **127**(17): 1801–1809.

Chan, T. C. Y. (2017). Rise and shock: optimal defibrillator placement in a high-rise building. *Prehospital Emergency Care* **21**(3): 309–314.

Chan, T. C. Y., D. Demirtas and R. H. Kwon (2016). Optimizing the deployment of public access defibrillators. *Management Science* **62**(12): 3617–3635.

Chan, T. C. Y., Z.-J. M. Shen and A. Siddiq (2018). Robust defibrillator deployment under cardiac arrest location uncertainty via row-and-column generation. *Operations Research* **66**(2): 358–379.

Cheskes, S., P. Snobelen, S. McLeod, et al. (2019). AED on the fly: a drone delivery feasibility study for rural and remote out-of-hospital cardiac arrest. *Circulation* **140**(Suppl_2): A147–A147.

Church, R. and C. Revelle (1974). The maximal covering location problem. *Papers of the Regional Science Association* **32**: 101–120.

Claesson, A., A. Backman, M. Ringh, et al. (2017). Time to delivery of an automated external defibrillator using a drone for simulated out-of-hospital cardiac arrests vs emergency medical services. *JAMA* **317**(22): 2332–2334.

Cummins, R. O., J. P. Ornato, W. H. Thies and P. E. Pepe (1991). Improving survival from sudden cardiac arrest: the "chain of survival" concept. A statement for health professionals from the Advanced Cardiac Life Support Subcommittee and the Emergency Cardiac Care Committee, American Heart Association. *Circulation* **83**(5): 1832–1847.

Davies, C. S., M. C. Colquhoun, R. Boyle and D. A. Chamberlain (2005). A national programme for on-site defibrillation by lay people in selected high risk areas: initial results. *Heart* **91**(10): 1299–1302.

Daya, M. R., R. H. Schmicker, D. M. Zive, et al. (2015). Out-of-hospital cardiac arrest survival improving over time: results from the Resuscitation Outcomes Consortium (ROC). *Resuscitation* **91**: 108–115.

Delage, E. and Y. Ye (2010). Distributionally robust optimization under moment uncertainty with application to data-driven problems. *Operations Research* **58** (3): 595–612.

Drennan, I. R., R. P. Strum, A. Byers, et al. (2016). Out-of-hospital cardiac arrest in high-rise buildings: delays to patient care and effect on survival. *CMAJ* **188**(6): 413–419.

Edelson, D. P., C. Sasson, P. S. Chan, et al. (2020). Interim guidance for basic and advanced life support in adults, children, and neonates with suspected or confirmed COVID-19: from the emergency cardiovascular care committee and get with the guidelines-resuscitation adult and pediatric task forces of the American Heart Association. *Circulation* **141**(25): e933–e943.

Fedoruk, J. C., W. L. Currie, M. Gobet, W. L. Currie and M. Gobet (2002). Locations of cardiac arrest: affirmation for community Public Access Defibrillation (PAD) Program. *Prehospital & Disaster Medicine* **17**(4): 202–205.

Folke, F., F. K. Lippert, S. L. Nielsen, et al. (2009). Location of cardiac arrest in a city center: Strategic placement of automated external defibrillators in public locations. *Circulation* **120**(6): 510–517.

Grasner, J. T., R. Lefering, R. W. Koster, et al. (2016). Corrigendum to "EuReCa ONE-27 Nations, ONE Europe, ONE Registry: a prospective one month analysis of out-of-hospital cardiac arrest outcomes in 27 countries in Europe" [Resuscitation 105 (2016) 188-195]. *Resuscitation* **109**: 145–146.

Gratton, M., D. J. Lindholm and J. P. Campbell (1999). Public-access defibrillation: where do we place the AEDs? *Prehospital Emergency Care* 3(4): 303–305.

Gundry, J. W., K. A. Comess, F. A. DeRook, D. Jorgenson and G. H. Bardy (1999). Comparison of naive sixth-grade children with trained professionals in the use of an automated external defibrillator. *Circulation* 100(16): 1703–1707.

Hakimi, S. L. (1964). Optimum locations of switching centers and the absolute centers and medians of a graph. *Operations Research* 12(3): 450–459.

Hallstrom, A. P., J. P. Ornato, M. Weisfeldt, et al. (2004). Public-access defibrillation and survival after out-of-hospital cardiac arrest. *New England Journal of Medicine* 351(7): 637–646.

Hansen, C. M., M. Wissenberg, P. Weeke, et al. (2013). Automated external defibrillators inaccessible to more than half of nearby cardiac arrests in public locations during evening, nighttime, and weekends. *Circulation* 128(20): 2224–2231.

Hansen, C. M., F. K. Lippert, M. Wissenberg, et al. (2014). Temporal trends in coverage of historical cardiac arrests using a volunteer-based network of automated external defibrillators accessible to laypersons and emergency dispatch centers. *Circulation* 130(21): 1859–1867.

Hansen, S. M., C. M. Hansen, F. Folke, et al. (2017). Bystander defibrillation for out-of-hospital cardiac arrest in public vs residential locations." *JAMA Cardiology* 2(5): 507–514.

Holmberg, M. J., M. Vognsen, M. S. Andersen, M. W. Donnino and L. W. Andersen (2017). Bystander automated external defibrillator use and clinical outcomes after out-of-hospital cardiac arrest: A systematic review and meta-analysis. *Resuscitation* 120: 77–87.

Homier, V., F. de Champlain, M. Nolan and R. Fleet (2019). Identification of swimmers in distress using unmanned aerial vehicles: experience at the Mont-Tremblant IRONMAN triathlon. *Prehospital Emergency Care* 24(3): 1–8.

Huang, C. Y. and T. H. Wen (2014). Optimal installation locations for automated external defibrillators in Taipei 7-Eleven Stores: using GIS and a genetic algorithm with a new stirring operator. *Computational and Mathematical Methods in Medicine* 2014: 241435.

Iwami, T., A. Hiraide, N. Nakanishi, et al. (2006). Outcome and characteristics of out-of-hospital cardiac arrest according to location of arrest: a report from a large-scale, population-based study in Osaka, Japan. *Resuscitation* 69(2): 221–228.

Karlsson, L., K. Sondergaard, C. Malta Hansen, et al. (2017). Straight line versus route distance to nearest automated external defibrillator-implications for cardiac arrest coverage. *European Heart Journal* 38(Suppl 1).

Karlsson, L., C. M. Hansen, C. Vourakis, et al. (2020). Improving bystander defibrillation in out-of-hospital cardiac arrests at home. *European Heart Journal: Acute Cardiovascular Care* 9(Suppl 4): S74–S81. 2048872619891675.

Kitamura, T., T. Iwami, T. Kawamura, et al. (2010). Nationwide public-access defibrillation in Japan. *New England Journal of Medicine* 362(11): 994–1004.

Kronick, S. L., M. C. Kurz, S. Lin, et al. (2015). Part 4: systems of care and continuous quality improvement: 2015 American Heart Association guidelines update for cardiopulmonary resuscitation and emergency cardiovascular care. *Circulation* 132(18 Suppl. 2): S397–413.

Lai, P. H., E. A. Lancet, M. D. Weiden, et al. (2020). Characteristics associated with out-of-hospital cardiac arrests and resuscitations during the novel coronavirus disease 2019 pandemic in New York City. *JAMA Cardiology* **5**(10): 1154–1163.

Larsen, M., M. Eisenberg, R. O. Cummins and A. P. Hallstrom (1993). Predicting survival from out-of-hospital cardiac arrest: a graphic model. *Annals of Emergency Medicine* **22**: 1652–1658.

Lateef, F. and V. Anantharaman (2000). Delays in the EMS response to and the evacuation of patients in high-rise buildings in Singapore. *Prehospital Emergency Care* **4**(4): 327–332.

Lee, M., D. Demirtas, J. E. Buick, et al. (2017). Increased cardiac arrest survival and bystander intervention in enclosed pedestrian walkway systems. *Resuscitation* **118**: 1–7.

Lee, C.-T., Y.-C. Lee and A. Y. Chen (2019). In-building automated external defibrillator location planning and assessment through building information models. *Automation in Construction* **106**: 102883.

Leung, K. B., C. L. Sun, M. Yang, et al. (2020). Optimal in-hospital defibrillator placement. *Resuscitation* **151**: 91–98.

Leung, K. H. B., R. Alam, S. C. Brooks and T. C. Y. Chan (2021). Public defibrillator accessibility and mobility trends during the COVID-19 pandemic in Canada. *Resuscitation* **162**: 329–333.

Marenco, J. P., P. J. Wang, M. S. Link, M. K. Homoud and N. A. Estes, 3rd (2001). Improving survival from sudden cardiac arrest: the role of the automated external defibrillator. *JAMA* **285**(9): 1193–1200.

Mateen, F. J., K. B. Leung, A. C. Vogel, A. F. Cissé and T. C. Chan (2020). A drone delivery network for antiepileptic drugs: a framework and modelling case study in a low-income country. *Transactions of The Royal Society of Tropical Medicine and Hygiene* **114**(4): 308–314.

Morrison, L. J., M. P. Angelini, M. J. Vermeulen and B. Schwartz (2005). Measuring the EMS patient access time interval and the impact of responding to high-rise buildings. *Prehospital Emergency Care* **9**(1): 14–18.

Murakami, Y., T. Iwami, T. Kitamura, et al. (2014). Outcomes of out-of-hospital cardiac arrest by public location in the public-access defibrillation era. *Journal of the American Heart Association* **3**(2): e000533.

Nichol, G., E. Thomas and C. W. Callaway (2008). Regional variation in out-of-hospital cardiac arrest incidence and outcome. *JAMA* **300**(12): 1423–1431.

Page, R. L., J. A. Joglar, R. C. Kowal, et al. (2000). Use of automated external defibrillators by a U.S. airline. *New England Journal of Medicine* **343**(17): 1210–1216.

Perkins, G. D., A. J. Handley, R. W. Koster, et al. (2015). European Resuscitation Council Guidelines for Resuscitation 2015: Section 2. Adult basic life support and automated external defibrillation. *Resuscitation* **95**: 81–99.

Pollack, R. A., S. P. Brown, T. Rea, et al. (2018). Impact of bystander automated external defibrillator use on survival and functional outcomes in shockable observed public cardiac arrests. *Circulation* **137**(20): 2104–2113.

Pulver, A., R. Wei and C. Mann (2016). Locating AED enabled medical drones to enhance cardiac arrest response times. *Prehospital Emergency Care* **20**(3): 378–389.

Reed, D. B., A. Birnbaum, L. H. Brown, et al. (2006). Location of cardiac arrests in the Public Access Defibrillation Trial. *Prehospital Emergency Care* **10**(1): 61–67.

Reinier, K., E. Thomas, D. L. Andrusiek, et al. (2011). Socioeconomic status and incidence of sudden cardiac arrest. *CMAJ* **183**(15): 1705–1712.

*Ringh, M., M. Rosenqvist, J. Hollenberg, et al. (2015). Mobile-phone dispatch of laypersons for CPR in out-of-hospital cardiac arrest. *New England Journal of Medicine* **372**(24): 2316–2325.

Robertson, R. M. (2000). Sudden death from cardiac arrest – improving the odds. *New England Journal of Medicine* **343**(17): 1259–1260.

Sasson, C., C. C. Keirns, D. Smith, et al. (2010). Small area variations in out-of-hospital cardiac arrest: does the neighborhood matter? *Annals of Internal Medicine* **153**(1): 19–22.

Sasson, C., M. A. Rogers, J. Dahl and A. L. Kellermann (2010). Predictors of survival from out-of-hospital cardiac arrest: a systematic review and meta-analysis. *Circulation: Cardiovascular Quality and Outcomes* **3**(1): 63–81.

Siddiq, A. A., S. C. Brooks and T. C. Chan (2013). Modeling the impact of public access defibrillator range on public location cardiac arrest coverage. *Resuscitation* **84**(7): 904–909.

Silverman, R. A., S. Galea, S. Blaney, et al. (2007). The "vertical response time": barriers to ambulance response in an urban area. *Academic Emergency Medicine* **14**(9): 772–778.

Smith, C. M., M. H. Wilson, A. Ghorbangholi, et al. (2017). The use of trained volunteers in the response to out-of-hospital cardiac arrest – the GoodSAM experience. *Resuscitation* **121**: 123–126.

Stoesser, C., J. Boutilier, C. L. Sun, et al. (2018). The effect of response time on out-of-hospital cardiac arrest survival varies by patient subpopulation. *Circulation* **138** (Suppl. 2): A249–A249.

Sun, C. L. F., D. Demirtas, S. C. Brooks, L. J. Morrison and T. C. Y. Chan (2016). Overcoming spatial and temporal barriers to public access defibrillators via optimization. *Journal of the American College of Cardiology* **68**(8): 836–845.

Sun, C. L., S. C. Brooks, L. J. Morrison and T. C. Chan (2017). Ranking businesses and municipal locations by spatiotemporal cardiac arrest risk to guide public defibrillator placement. *Circulation* **135**(12): 1104–1119.

Sun, C. L. F., L. Karlsson, C. Torp-Pedersen, et al. (2018). Spatiotemporal AED optimization is generalizable. *Resuscitation* **131**: 101–107.

Sun, C. L., L. Karlsson, C. Torp-Pedersen, et al. (2019). In silico trial of optimized versus actual public defibrillator locations. *Journal of the American College of Cardiology* **74**(12): 1557–1567.

Sun, C. L., L. Karlsson, L. J. Morrison, et al. (2020). Effect of optimized versus guidelines-based automated external defibrillator placement on out-of-hospital cardiac arrest coverage: an in silico trial. *Journal of the American Heart Association* **9**: e016701.

Sun, C., S. Dyer, J. Salvia, L. Segal and R. Levi (2021). Worse cardiac arrest outcomes during the COVID-19 pandemic in Boston can be attributed to patient reluctance to seek care. *Health Affairs (Millwood)* **40**(6): 101377hlthaff202100250.

Tierney, N. J., H. J. Reinhold, A. Mira, et al. (2018). Novel relocation methods for automatic external defibrillator improve out-of-hospital cardiac arrest coverage under limited resources. *Resuscitation* **125**: 83–89.

Tsai, Y. S., P. C. I. Ko, C. Y. Huang and T. H. Wen (2012). Optimizing locations for the installation of automated external defibrillators (AEDs) in urban public streets through the use of spatial and temporal weighting schemes. *Applied Geography* **35** (1-2): 394–404.

Valenzuela, T. D., D. J. Roe, S. Cretin, D. W. Spaite and M. P. Larsen (1997). Estimating effectiveness of cardiac arrest interventions – a logistic regression survival model. *Circulation* **96**(10): 3308–3313.

Valenzuela, T. D., D. J. Roe, G. Nichol, et al. (2000). Outcomes of rapid defibrillation by security officers after cardiac arrest in casinos. *New England Journal of Medicine* **343**(17): 1206–1209.

Weisfeldt, M. L., C. M. Sitlani, J. P. Ornato, et al. (2010). Survival after application of automatic external defibrillators before arrival of the emergency medical system: evaluation in the Resuscitation Outcomes Consortium population of 21 million. *Journal of the American College of Cardiology* **55**(16): 1713–1720.

Wissenberg, M., F. K. Lippert, F. Folke, et al (2013). Association of national initiatives to improve cardiac arrest management with rates of bystander intervention and patient survival after out-of-hospital cardiac arrest. *JAMA* **310**(13): 1377–1384.

7

Optimization of Biomarker-Based Prostate Cancer Screening Policies

Christine L. Barnett and Brian T. Denton

Summary of the Problem

Cancer screening has the potential to improve patient survival and lower the cost of treatment by detecting cancer at an early stage when health outcomes are most favorable for patients. The tests used for cancer screening are imperfect, carry risks, and provide a single result devoid of temporal context. Policies are necessary to optimize the benefits of testing in terms of patient preferences and survival adjusted for the disutility of screening, biopsy, diagnosis, active surveillance, radical prostatectomy, recovery from radical prostatectomy, and metastasis.

Summary of the Solution

Mathematical models may be used to optimize the decision of when to screen for cancer and how invasive a test to use, for example, a biopsy or a biomarker. Partially observable Markov decision process (POMDP) models may be used to optimize screening decisions based on a patient's *belief state*, which is calculated using Bayesian updating and comprises a patient's complete history of biomarker test results. POMDPs can be used to determine how, if at all, biomarkers should be used for cancer screening in order to maximize quality-adjusted life years (QALYs), a population health measure of disease burden that incorporates both the quality and quantity of life.

Summary of Relevance in a Post-COVID World

The methods described in this chapter have the potential to improve decisions about diagnostic tests in many contexts. For example, the recent COVID-19 outbreak requires the careful use of tests with imperfect sensitivity and specificity to control local outbreaks of COVID-19 by efficiently deploying limited testing capacity. The primary considerations, to target the people at sufficiently high risk to merit testing while minimizing the cost and risk associated with testing, are equivalent for many diseases.

7.1 Introduction

Cancer screening has the potential to improve patient survival and lower the cost of treatment by detecting cancer at an early stage when health outcomes are most favorable for patients. However, there are several challenges associated with screening for cancer. For example, the tests used for cancer screening, biomarkers, are imperfect, and there are harms associated with the screening process. Additionally, there are multiple grades of cancer that vary in the risk of adverse health outcomes. While cancer screening could save the life of a patient with high-grade cancer, it is unlikely to benefit patients with low-grade cancer. Moreover, there is uncertainty about progression of cancers over time and uncertainty about the benefits and side effects of treatment. Finally, the benefits of cancer screening depend on all-cause mortality, because patients with a lower expected life span are less likely to receive the full benefits of early cancer detection due to the higher competing risks of mortality from other causes. Due to these issues, crafting cancer screening recommendations is challenging.

Generally, biopsy is the gold-standard test for diagnosing cancer; however, biopsies are painful and can lead to complications, such as sepsis or death. Thus, the goal of cancer screening is to optimize the decision of when to perform a biopsy on a patient based on other, less invasive and less reliable screening tests, such as biomarkers. Many current cancer screening policies are *myopic* in that they make biopsy decisions based solely on a patient's most recent test results, without considering the patient's full medical history. However, benign conditions can cause a sudden spike in a patient's biomarker scores, which motivates the potential to use Bayesian updating to estimate the *belief state* for patients so decisions can be made based on estimates of patient risk of cancer, rather than dichotomous positive/negative interpretation of the biomarker scores. Thus, partially observable Markov decision process (POMDP) models may have a role to play in optimizing screening decisions based on a patient's *belief state*, which is calculated using Bayesian updating and comprises a patient's complete history of biomarker test results in a way that is similar to the model first proposed by Smallwood and Sondik (1973). POMDPs can then be used to determine how, if at all, tests should be used for cancer screening.

Several previous studies have developed POMDPs to optimize cancer screening decisions. The goal of many of these models is to maximize quality-adjusted life years (QALYs). The QALY is a population health measure of disease burden that incorporates both the quality and quantity of life. It ranges from 1 (perfect health) to 0 (death). The QALY measurement incorporates both the benefits of treatment (i.e., increased survival) and the harms (e.g., unpleasant biopsy procedures, treatment side effects). Readers interested in additional information on health-adjusted life years, including QALYs, can see Sanders et al. (2016). Zhang et al. (2012) developed a nonstationary POMDP for prostate biopsy referral decisions that maximizes expected QALYs and found that the decision of when to stop screening is highly dependent on the patient and the disutility of life after treatment. Sufficient conditions for discontinuing prostate-specific antigen (PSA) screening for older patients are presented. Simmons Ivy et al. (2009) developed a simulation model that combines statistical control and a POMDP to quantify the impact of variability and noise on patient outcomes in breast cancer decision making. They found that variability among radiologists in interpreting mammography results has the largest impact on a patient's outcomes. Thus, reducing this variability should be a primary goal to improve women's healthcare. Ayer et al. (2012) developed a POMDP model to determine the optimal personalized mammography screening policies for an individual patient in terms of maximizing the total expected QALYs, incorporating the possibility of self-detection. The authors show that self-detection increases the total expected QALYs while reducing the number of mammograms. Erenay et al. (2014) developed a POMDP to optimize colonoscopy screening policies to maximize expected QALYs. They report that optimal screening policies recommend that women with a history of colorectal cancer be screened via colonoscopy more frequently than men, while women without a history of colorectal cancer should be screened via colonoscopy less frequently than men. Each of these POMDPs was able to provide insights into optimal cancer screening.

Because prostate cancer is asymptomatic at early stages, some physicians screen their patients for prostate cancer using digital rectal examinations (DRE) and the PSA test. If the results of these tests are "suspicious," a biopsy is performed. Prostate cancer can have slow progression, and patients with different grades of prostate cancer have significantly different treatment options and survival outcomes. The risk of developing prostate cancer varies among patients depending on many factors, all of which make balancing the risks and benefits of screening for prostate cancer difficult. Prostate cancer is the ideal context in which to explore these challenging problems (1) because of its societal importance, as prostate cancer is the most common cancer among men in the United States; and (2) there are existing and novel prostate cancer biomarkers, thus how and how often to screen for prostate cancer is currently in question.

Two recent clinical trials to evaluate the effectiveness of PSA screening for preventing prostate cancer death produced contradictory findings. The European Randomized Study of Screening for Prostate Cancer (ERSPC), Schröder et al. (2009, 2012, 2014), randomized 162,387 men to either a screening group or a control group at seven centers in European countries. The relative risk after 11 years of follow-up was a statistically significant 0.79 between the screening and control arms, interpreted as a 20% risk reduction in prostate cancer mortality due to early diagnosis and treatment. The Prostate, Lung, Colorectal, and Ovarian (PLCO) Cancer Screening Trial, Andriole et al. (2009), randomized 76,693 men to either a screening group or a control group at 10 centers in the United States. The relative risk of prostate cancer mortality after 13 years of follow-up was not statistically significantly different between the screening and control arms, suggesting no benefit from early diagnosis and treatment (Andriole et al., 2012). The PLCO trial had a high rate of screening in the control arm, which biased the results, and the duration of follow-up in clinical trials may be insufficient to detect differences in prostate cancer (PCa) mortality. These limitations suggest that randomized control trials are not the ideal way to evaluate screening policies. Because of these conflicting findings, there is disagreement about if and when men should be screened. For example, the American Urological Association (AUA) recommends PSA screening for men from age 55 to 69 at 2-year intervals (Carter et al., 2013) The U.S. Preventive Services Task Force previously recommended against PSA screening due to the overtreatment and unnecessary biopsies that have been attributed to widespread PSA screening (Moyer, 2012), and now recommends patients discuss their options with their physicians to make an informed decision.

In spite of these findings, recent advances in the development of new technologies for the early detection of prostate cancer have the potential to supplement the PSA test and improve patient survival by catching cancer at an early stage when health outcomes are most favorable for patients. For example, the Mi-Prostate Score (MiPS) early detection test combines a patient's serum PSA, urine PCa antigen 3 (PCA3) score, and urine ETS-related gene (ERG) gene fusion (T2:ERG) score into a single multivariate regression model to estimate individualized risk estimates for prostate cancer and high-grade prostate cancer (Tomlins et al., 2016). However, there is little research investigating the long-term health and economic implications of these new technologies. For example, new biomarker tests have been proposed as potential minimally invasive ways to achieve early detection of prostate cancer, but whether and when to use them are unclear due to the high cost and imperfect nature of these tests. Therefore, we have developed a model to investigate how to optimize the use of these new biomarkers to benefit patients' long-term health outcomes.

We extended the model of Barnett et al. (2017) to create a new POMDP model to investigate optimal prostate cancer screening decisions based on a patient's *belief state*, which is calculated using Bayesian updating and comprises a patient's complete history of biomarker test results. This POMDP can be used to determine how, if at all, new biomarker tests should be used for prostate cancer screening. The MiPS early detection test provides a patient's risks for both prostate cancer and high-grade prostate cancer, which we evaluated as two different biomarker tests in Barnett et al. (2017). In this chapter, we present results using high-grade MiPS. We chose the high-grade MiPS biomarker test because it was found to be a good biomarker in Barnett et al. (2017) and because we had access to the data necessary to estimate the probability distribution of MiPS conditional on the patient's cancer status. However, the approach we outline could be applied to other biomarkers and in other disease contexts, especially for other cancers such as bladder, breast, and colorectal cancers, all of which have a breadth of biomarker options available.

7.2 Model

We developed a POMDP model that maximizes total expected QALYs. The QALY measurements account for disutilities of screening, biopsy, diagnosis, active surveillance, radical prostatectomy, recovery from radical prostatectomy, and metastasis; the values of the disutilities with their sources are shown in Table 7.1. The QALY disutility values were all obtained from Heijnsdijk et al. (2012). The disutility for living with metastasis is based on the disutility

Table 7.1. *Quality-adjusted life year parameters*

Parameter	Symbol	Value
Instantaneous QALY disutility for screening	$\delta_{Scr}(a_t)$	0.00019
Instantaneous QALY disutility for a prostate biopsy	$\delta_{Biop}(a_t)$	0.00577
Instantaneous QALY disutility for PCa diagnosis	$\delta_{Dia}(a_t)$	0.01667
Instantaneous QALY disutility for radical prostatectomy	$\delta_{Tre}(a_t)$	0.24667
Annual QALY disutility for 9-year post-radical prostatectomy recovery period	$\delta_{Rec}(a_t)$	0.05
Annual QALY disutility for active surveillance	$\delta_{AS}(a_t)$	0.03
Annual QALY disutility for metastasis	$\delta_{Met}(s_t)$	0.4

PCa = prostate cancer; QALY = quality-adjusted life year.
Source: Heijnsdijk et al. (2012).

of palliative therapy presented in Heijnsdijk et al. (2012). The reward update function for QALYS was

$$
\begin{aligned}
r_t(s_t, a_t) =1 &- \delta_{Scr}(a_t) - \delta_{Biop}(a_t) - \delta_{Dia}(a_t) - \delta_{Tre}(a_t) \\
&- \delta_{Rec}(a_t) - \delta_{AS}(a_t) - \delta_{Met}(s_t),
\end{aligned}
$$

where $r_t(s_t, a_t)$ is the reward a patient receives at age t, which is 1 minus the disutilities associated with screening, biopsy, diagnosis, treatment, or the presence of metastatic cancer, depending on the patient's health status during the year, as defined in Table 7.1. The arguments for the reward are the health state, s_t, that defines the cancer status of the patients and the action, a_t, that defines whether a screening test or biopsy was performed. The total number of QALYs a patient receives in their lifetime is

$$
R = \sum_{t=1}^{T} r_t(s_t, a_t),
$$

where T denotes maximum life span.

The POMDP model optimizes the decision to conduct a biopsy based on the patient's belief state at annual decision epochs. Pretreatment states are not directly observable. Biomarker tests give (imperfect) information about the true state of the patient. The partially observable pretreatment states in the model include:

- no prostate cancer (No PCa)
- undetected organ-confined prostate cancer with Gleason score (GS) less than 7 (GS < 7)
- undetected organ-confined prostate cancer with GS equal to 7 (GS = 7)
- undetected organ-confined prostate cancer with GS greater than 7 (GS > 7)
- extraprostatic or lymph node positive cancer (EPLN)

The EPLN state aggregates these two conditions into one state because they are similarly associated with decreased survival. The partially observable post-treatment states in the model include:

- no recurrence following treatment (NRFT)
- possible recurrence following treatment (PRFT)

The observable states in the model include:

- metastasis (Metastasis)
- death (Death)

In this chapter, to be consistent with the literature on POMDPs we will refer to the patient's underlying health state as the *core state* of the patient. We will

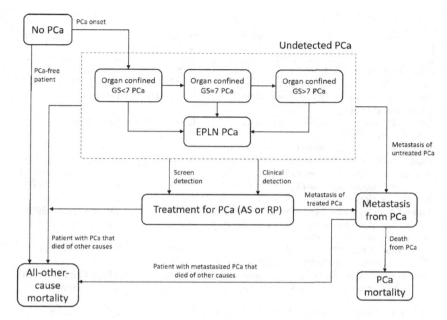

Figure 7.1 State transition diagram. Health states and progression paths in the Markov model are shown, and transitions between states are represented by arrows. Patients who are detected to have prostate cancer (PCa) are treated immediately with radical prostatectomy (RP) or active surveillance (AS). GS = Gleason score; EPLN = extraprostatic or lymph node positive cancer.

refer to the core states as: $S = \{No\ PCa, GS < 7, GS = 7, GS > 7, EPLN,$ $PRFT, NRFT, Metastasis, Death\}$. The states were selected because they distinguish patients on the basis of likely treatment options, outcomes, and survival.

Figure 7.1 displays the health states and possible state transitions for the model. Each year that the screening strategy calls for testing, the following sequence of events in the model occurs: the patient receives one or more biomarker tests according to the specified strategy; the biomarker test results determine whether a biopsy is performed; and the patient transitions to their next health state. As our model focuses on screening of the general population, it only considers the initial screening biopsy decision, and the screening strategy terminates after an initial biopsy. The patient continues to make state transitions in the absence of screening until reaching one of the absorbing states, all-other-cause mortality or prostate cancer mortality. The model makes this assumption because most patients in the general population receive at most a single screening biopsy and the decision-making process around subsequent screening biopsies is more complex and considers additional factors, such as

Table 7.2. *Transition probability parameters*

Parameter	Value(s)	Source
Annual transition rate from No PCa to GS < 7	0.004–0.069	Haas et al. (2007)
Annual other-cause mortality rate	0.002–0.347	Arias (2010)
Annual metastasis rate for patients with undiagnosed PCa	0.002–0.035	Calibrated
Annual PCa-specific mortality rate given metastasized PCa	0.181–0.204	Ries et al. (2007)
Sensitivity of prostate biopsy procedure	0.8	Haas et al. (2007)
Annual transition rate from GS < 7 to GS = 7	0.101	Draisma et al. (2003)
Annual transition rate from GS = 7 to GS > 7	0.087	Draisma et al. (2003)
Annual transition rate from GS < 7 to EPLN	0.029	Draisma et al. (2003)
Annual transition rate from GS = 7 to EPLN	0.081	Draisma et al. (2003)
Annual transition rate from GS > 7 to EPLN	0.097	Draisma et al. (2003)
Probability of no possible recurrence following definitive treatment in state EPLN	0.468	Roehl et al. (2004)
Proportion of patients detected with GS < 7 who undergo active surveillance	0.485	Liu et al. (2015)
Annual metastasis rate for patients with possible recurrence after definitive treatment in EPLN	0.006	Mayo Clinic Radical Prostatectomy Registry

GS = Gleason score; EPLN = extraprostatic or lymph node positive cancer; PCa = prostate cancer.
Source: Heijnsdijk et al. (2012).

the initial biopsy results. The parameters used to calculate the transition probabilities are shown in Table 7.2 and how these parameters were calculated is described in Barnett et al. (2017).

At each decision epoch in the screening interval from $t = 1, \ldots, T$, we assume a high-grade MiPS test is performed. The set of actions is $A = \{Wait, Biopsy\}$, i.e., either wait until the next decision epoch or perform a biopsy. The observations that result from the high-grade MiPS test inform the action. The observation space for the high-grade MiPS test is continuous values between 0 and 1; however, to simplify the problem we discretized these observations into clinically relevant bins. The set of observations is Θ, which includes the MiPS discretized observations in addition to Post-treatment (PT), Metastasis (M), Death (D). The observations for the action "Biopsy" are no prostate cancer (No PCa), organ-confined GS < 7 prostate cancer (GS < 7), organ-confined GS = 7 prostate cancer (GS = 7), and organ-confined GS > 7 prostate cancer (GS > 7). Because only a small amount of tissue is sampled during a biopsy, sampling error can result in a false negative or incorrect grading at diagnosis. Based on the discretization of the MiPS test results, we have developed information matrices by epoch, $Q_t, t = 1, \ldots, T$, where, $t = 1$ corresponds to the initiation of screening, which is age 55 in our study, and T is the age at which screening is discontinued, which is age 69 in our study. The information matrix has rows associated with the core health states and columns associated with the set of possible observations. We denote the components of each information matrix by $q_t(\theta | s_t)$, which defines the probability of observing $\theta \in \Theta$ at age t given the core state of the patient is $s_t \in S$.

7.3 Methods

In the following description of the model, we use notation consistent with the notation used in Smallwood and Sondik (1973). Let $\pi^t = \left[\pi^t_1, \pi^t_2, \ldots, \pi^t_9\right]$ be the belief vector, where π^t_i is the probability that the patient is in state i at decision epoch t and $\sum_i \pi^t_i = 1$. The belief vector is updated via Bayesian updating after the observations at each decision epoch, using the following equation:

$$\pi^{t+1}_j = \frac{\sum_i \pi^t_i P^{Tr}_t(i,j) q_t(\theta|j)}{\sum_{i,j} \pi^t_i P^{Tr}_t(i,j) q_t(\theta|j)},$$

where $q_t(\theta|j)$ denotes the probability of observing θ, given the core state of the patient is j. The numerator calculates the probability of transitioning to state j and observing output θ, and the denominator is the probability of observing output θ. This is an application of Bayes law, and the equation is developed in detail in appendix A of Smallwood and Sondik (1973).

7.3.1 Alpha Vectors

Our model seeks to maximize expected QALYs using the following set of optimality equations:

$$V_t(\pi^t) = \left\{ r(\pi^t, a, \pi^{t+1}) + \sum_{i,j,\theta} \pi^t_i P^{Tr}_t(i,j) q_t(\theta,j) V_{t+1}(j) \right\},$$
$$t = 1, \ldots, T-1,$$
$$V_T(\pi^T) = R(\pi^T),$$

where $r(\pi^t, a, \pi^{t+1})$ is the immediate reward in QALYs and $V_t(j)$ is the maximum expected future QALYs for a patient in state j at age t.

Smallwood and Sondik (1973) presented the first exact method for solving POMDPs, known as the "One-Pass Algorithm." Smallwood and Sondik

(1973) showed that the value function of a POMDP is piecewise linear and convex, and can be written as

$$V_t(\pi^t) = \left\{ \sum_{i=1}^{N} \alpha_i^k(t)\pi_i^t \right\}$$

for some set of vectors $\alpha^k(t) = [\alpha_1^k(t), \alpha_2^k(t), \ldots, \alpha_N^k(t)], k = 1, 2, \ldots$, which are referred to as α-vectors. The terminal reward vector, α^T, consists of the expected QALYs for a patient at age 70 in each core state. Each α-vector has an action associated with it; therefore, we can evaluate each α-vector at a fixed belief state to determine the α-vector that maximizes the value function and the optimal action associated with it. However, there may be many α-vectors in the set that are not needed to define the value function (i.e., they are not a maximum α-vector over the entire belief space). The algorithm described in Smallwood and Sondik (1973) defines regions for an α-vector and searches for a belief where that α-vector is not dominant. The "One-Pass Algorithm" solves a series of linear programs to try to find a minimal α-vector set. However, we must solve a linear program for each α-vector in the set, which is computationally expensive because the set of α-vectors grows exponentially in the size of the set of possible observations.

Cassandra et al. (1994) proposed the "Witness Algorithm," which also defines regions for a vector and looks for a point at which that vector is not dominant. As a result, the "Witness Algorithm" only needs to solve one linear program for each α-vector in the minimal α-vector set, which is an improvement on the "One-Pass Algorithm."

In our approach, we draw on the basic idea of the Witness Algorithm to accelerate the One-Pass Algorithm. Terminal rewards define the α-vector in decision epoch $T + 1$. At each age moving backward, starting from decision epoch T, we use Monahan's algorithm (Monahan, 1982) to calculate the set of α-vectors in decision epoch t using the α-vectors from decision epoch $t + 1$. We use our simulation model and the k-means clustering model to develop a set of grid points that represent the areas of the belief space that our patient population is most likely to be, and we use those grid points to calculate a subset of the *relevant* α-vectors by finding the dominant α-vector associated with each grid point. We then eliminate any α-vectors that do not define the value function at one of the grid points that approximates the belief space, i.e., each grid point acts as a witness point for one α-vector and thus the number of α-vectors is limited to the number of grid points. After we complete this step, we have developed a policy where we determine the (approximated) optimal action at any point in the belief space by selecting the action associated with the α-vector that maximizes the value function, $\alpha^T \pi$.

7.3.2 Defining the Belief Space Grid

The infinite state space of a POMDP makes it difficult to solve. Thus, we have divided the space into a fixed-finite grid, which allows us to approximate the infinite belief space, $B = \{\pi' | \sum_i \pi'_i = 1\}$, with a finite grid of points. By discretizing the belief space, we can associate every sampled belief state with one of the grid points (e.g., based on the closest grid point). Thus, the continuously sampled states are mapped to a finite set of states.

At any given decision epoch, we know that the patient will be in one of three subsets of the state space: $S_1 = \{No\ PCa, GS < 7, GS = 7, GS > 7, EPLN\}$, $S_2 = \{PRFT, NRFT\}$, or $S_3 = \{Metastasis, Death\}$. The set S_1 includes the unobservable pre-diagnosis states, S_2 includes the unobservable post-treatment states, and S_3 includes the observable states. In other words, if a patient has not yet been diagnosed with prostate cancer, we know that they are in one of the five states in S_1; if a patient has been treated for prostate cancer, we know they are in one of the post-treatment states in S_2; and we know the exact state of the patient when they are in the completely observable S_3. Therefore, any grid point in the discretized state space that we generate will have non-zero entries in only one of the three subsets. The grid points in S_3 will consist of $(0, 0, 0, 0, 0, 0, 0, 1, 0)$ and $(0, 0, 0, 0, 0, 0, 0, 0, 1)$, i.e., the states in S_3 are perfectly observable. The state of the patient is referred to as partially observable when in S_1 or S_2 with the belief vector π_t providing the probability distribution based on prior belief and observations.

We utilized a data-driven sampling approach to develop the grid at each age. We denote a sample path to be the stochastic progression of a patient's health states, biomarker test results, biopsy results, and belief states. A patient's sample path depends on the screening strategy being used. For this reason, we generated sample paths using varying policies. The sample paths provided information about not only where patients' beliefs are located in the belief space at each age but also information about where a patient's beliefs are not located in the belief space. Due to the computational burden of having a large number of grid points, we then used these samples to create a smaller grid of points at each age using k-means clustering. The goal of k-means clustering is to divide L points (i.e., the sample belief states) in M dimensions (i.e., the partially observable health states) into k clusters so that within-cluster sum of squares is minimized (Hartigan and Wong, 1979). The centroid of each cluster

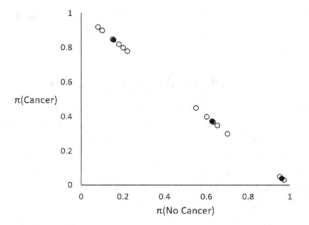

Figure 7.2 An example of k-means for a simple two-dimensional case, where the unfilled points represent the $L = 13$ sample points and the filled points represent the $k = 3$ grid points.

then defines a unique grid point. Algorithm 1 gives a description of the k-means clustering algorithm and an example is given in Figure 7.2.

Algorithm 1. k-means clustering algorithm for grid development.

Inputs: x sample paths through the belief space; number of grid points at each age, k
for $t = 1, \ldots T$ **do**
    Randomly divide the x sample belief states into k clusters.
    Calculate the centroid of each cluster and let that be the mean.
while convergence is not reached **do**
    Cluster each simulated sample belief state with the nearest mean.
    Calculate the centroid of each cluster and let that be the new mean.
    end while
    The k means represent the k grid points for age t.
end for

7.4 Results

To generate results, we used the model described in Barnett et al. (2017). To develop age-dependent grids, we generated 600 randomly sampled patient sample paths through the belief space for 110 different MiPS policies. The 110 policies included every combination of the most well-known previously recommended schedules described in Table 7.3 with the following thresholds: $\{0.05, 0.10, 0.15, 0.20, 0.25, 0.30, 0.35, 0.40, 0.45, 0.50\}$. We then used these samples to create a grid of points at each age using the k-means clustering heuristic in Matlab, where $k = 200$, $L = 66,000$, and $M = 5$. As shown in

Table 7.3. *Screening schedules for the prostate cancer screening policies used to generate sample paths. The screening schedule defines the set of decision epochs during which screening occurs.*

Schedule label	Range of age (yr)	Screening interval (yr)	Source
S1	40–75	5	Ross et al. (2000)
S2	50–75	2	Ross et al. (2000)
S3	50–75	1	Ross et al. (2000)
			Andriole et al. (2009)
S4	40, 45	-	Ross et al. (2000)
	50–75	2	
S5	40, 45	-	Ross et al. (2000)
	50–75	1	
S6	55–69	1	Heijnsdijk et al. (2012)
S7	55–74	1	Heijnsdijk et al. (2012)
S8	55–69	4	Heijnsdijk et al. (2012)
S9	55	-	Heijnsdijk et al. (2012)
S10	60	-	Heijnsdijk et al. (2012)
S11	65	-	Heijnsdijk et al. (2012)

Figure 7.3, we found that at older ages there are more grid points with a higher belief of having prostate cancer, which agrees with the fact that the prevalence of prostate cancer increases at older ages.

Patients were screened at each decision epoch from age 55 to 69. In our experiments, we discretized the continuous observations space of MiPS scores into three observations: $\theta = \{[0, .125), [.125, .375), > .375\}$, which equally divided patients into low-, median-, and high-risk groups. We evaluated two types of POMDP screening policies. The first was based on the policy developed using the data-driven sampling method above to prune α-vectors and create an approximation of the optimal policy subject to error induced by using a finite set of grid points. The second uses a risk-based threshold to trigger a prostate biopsy based on a patient's current belief of having a GS > 7 or extraprostatic or lymph node positive disease (i.e., the belief the patient is in states GS > 7 or EPLN). Under this risk-based POMDP policy with a risk threshold of x, when $\pi_{OCG3} + \pi_{EPLN} > x$, the patient receives a biopsy. We found that a risk threshold of 0.35 maximized expected QALYs for the patient. We evaluated the resulting POMDP policies using our simulation model. We compared the results to the following six myopic screening policies based on commonly used thresholds discussed in the medical literature:

- No screening
- PSA with a threshold of 4 ng/mL

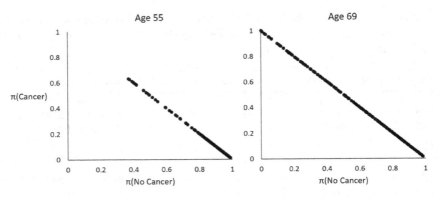

Figure 7.3 The actual grids generated for ages 55 and 69, where the belief of cancer is calculated by adding the belief of each of the four cancer states.

- PSA with a threshold of 2 ng/mL to trigger a PCA3 test with a threshold of 25 (patients with a PSA > 10 ng/mL will automatically receive a biopsy)
- PSA with a threshold of 2 ng/mL to trigger a T2:ERG test with a threshold of 10 (patients with a PSA > 10 ng/mL will automatically receive a biopsy)
- High-grade MiPS test with a threshold of 15
- MiPS test with a threshold of 25

A PSA threshold of 4 is common, the two-stage policies were evaluated in Barnett et al. (2017), and the MiPS and high-grade MiPS thresholds performed well in previous experiments.

We estimated the terminal reward vector using our simulation model of Barnett et al. (2017) with 10,000,000 sample paths starting at age 70 from each core state:

$$\begin{array}{ccccccccc} \text{NC} & \text{OCG1} & \text{OCG2} & \text{OCG3} & \text{EPLN} & \text{NRFT} & \text{PRFT} & \text{M} & \text{D} \end{array}$$
$$\alpha^T = \Big(14.062 \quad 13.887 \quad 13.609 \quad 13.532 \quad 9.826 \quad 14.104 \quad 13.592 \quad 2.823 \quad 0 \Big).$$

Each element of α^T is an estimate of expected remaining life span for the corresponding state.

Figure 7.4 shows the results in terms of QALYs with confidence intervals for 10,000,000 samples. We found that by using the policy generated by our approximated POMDP solution, which accounts for a patient's entire history of their biomarker test results, we can gain 181.7 QALYs per 1,000 men, which significantly outperformed all myopic policies. Thus, we found that it is possible to develop screening policies using our approximated solution technique on a discretized POMDP that result in health benefits for the patient. The

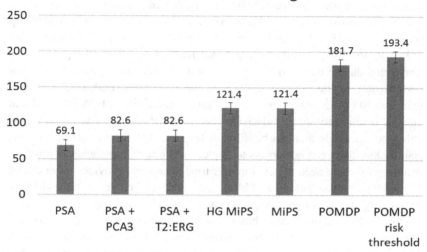

Figure 7.4 Expected increase in quality-adjusted life years (QALYs) per 1000 men compared to no screening for a range of myopic policies compared to two policies based on our partially observable Markov decision process (POMDP) with three high-grade (HG) Mi-Prostate Score (MiPS) observations. The first POMDP policy was generated by our approximated POMDP solution and the second POMDP policy performs a biopsy when a patient's belief of having a Gleason score (GS) > 7 or extraprostatic or lymph node positive cancer (EPLN) is > 0.35.

POMDP policy with a risk threshold of 0.35 gained 193.4 QALYs per 1,000 men. The difference between these POMDP policies was not statistically significant, but the threshold policy may be beneficial for implementation, given that it is easier to interpret. The POMDP-approximated solution depends on the grid selection, while the risk-based POMDP policy does not, suggesting there is potential of increased gains through better grid selection.

7.5 Conclusions

In this chapter, we presented a POMDP model to estimate optimal biopsy screening policies based on a patient's *belief state* rather than their most recent biomarker test results. The underlying health states of the patient are not directly observable; however, their high-grade MiPS results provide some information about their core health state. Patients were screened annually with the high-grade MiPS test from age 55 to 69. Due to the large number of observations and unobservable states, we presented a data-driven approximation method to solve this POMDP. We found that it is possible to develop screening policies using our approximated solution technique on a discretized POMDP, and that it results in significant health benefits for the patient. We also found that an easier-to-implement risk-based threshold policy has similar performance to the optimal solution to the discretized POMDP. However, there would be challenges associated with implementing a POMDP model in clinical practice to support decision making. POMDP models are complex "blackbox" models that can be difficult for clinicians to interpret and understand. Thus, there can be barriers to implementing such approaches in practice, resulting from the need to develop user trust. Chapter 4 provides more details about the potential challenges of blackbox models and two case studies of how to integrate predictive analytics with patient decision making.

Our study has limitations based on assumptions used in the modeling process. First, our study did not consider costs, but rather assumed decision making was based solely on QALYs gained from different screening strategies. Nevertheless, QALYs address what are arguably the most important criteria for physicians and insured patients. Second, active surveillance and radical prostatectomy were assumed to be the only treatment options because radical prostatectomy is the most common curative treatment, and patients undergoing radiation therapy have similar health outcomes (Hamdy et al., 2016). Last, we assumed that each patient receives at most one screening biopsy in his life. About 7% to 12% of men undergoing biopsy have had a previous negative biopsy (Nguyen et al., 2010; Thompson et al., 2006); however, the majority of patients receive a single biopsy, and cancers detected on second biopsy are typically less clinically significant. Since our intent is to measure the public health impact of biomarker screening, we do not believe this assumption significantly influenced our results.

References

Andriole GL, Crawford ED, Grubb RL III, et al. Mortality results from a randomized prostate-cancer screening trial. *New England Journal of Medicine.* 2009 Mar 26;**360**(13):1310–1319.

Andriole GL, Crawford ED, Grubb RL III, et al. Prostate cancer screening in the randomized Prostate, Lung, Colorectal, and Ovarian Cancer Screening Trial: mortality results after 13 years of follow-up. *Journal of the National Cancer Institute.* 2012 Jan 6;**104**(2):125–132.

Arias E. United States life tables 2006. *National Vital Statistics Reports*. 2010;58 (21):1–40.

Ayer, T, Alagz O, Stout NK. A POMDP approach to personalize mammography screening decisions. *Operations Research*. 2012; **60**(5):1019–1034.

Barnett CL, Tomlins SA, Underwood DJ, et al. Two-stage biomarker protocols for improving the precision of early detection of prostate cancer. *Medical Decision Making*. 2017 Oct;**37**(7):815–826.

Carter HB, Albertsen PC, Barry MJ, et al. Early detection of prostate cancer: AUA Guideline. *The Journal of Urology*. 2013 Aug;**190**(2):419–426.

Cassandra AR, Kaelbling LP, Littman ML. Acting optimally in partially observable stochastic domains. Proceedings of the Twelfth National Conference on Artificial Intelligence (AAAI-94), Seattle, WA, 1994: 1023–1028.

Draisma G, Boer R, Otto SJ, et al. Lead times and overdetection due to prostate-specific antigen screening: estimates from the European Randomized Study of Screening for Prostate Cancer. *Journal of the National Cancer Institute*. 2003 Jun 18;**95** (12):868–878.

Erenay, FS, Alagoz O, Said A. Optimizing colonoscopy screening for colorectal cancer prevention and surveillance. *Manufacturing & Service Operations Management*. 2014; **16**(3):381–400.

Haas GP, Delongchamps NB, Jones RF, et al. Needle biopsies on autopsy prostates: sensitivity of cancer detection based on true prevalence. *Journal of the National Cancer Institute*. 2007 Oct 3;**99**(19):1484–1489.

Hamdy FC, Donovan JL, Lane JA, et al. 10-year outcomes after monitoring, surgery, or radiotherapy for localized prostate cancer. *New England Journal of Medicine*. 2016 Oct 13;**375**(15):1415–1424.

Hartigan JA, Wong MA. Algorithm AS 136: a k-means clustering algorithm. *Journal of the Royal Statistical Society. Series C (Applied Statistics)*. 1979 Jan 1;**28**(1):100–108.

Heijnsdijk EA, Wever EM, Auvinen A, et al. Quality-of-life effects of prostate-specific antigen screening. *New England Journal of Medicine*. 2012 Aug 16;**367** (7):595–605.

Liu J, Womble PR, Merdan S, et al Factors influencing selection of active surveillance for localized prostate cancer. *Urology*. 2015 Nov 1;**86**(5):901–905.

Monahan, G. A survey of partially observable Markov decision processes: theory, models, and algorithms. *Management Science*. 1982; **28**(1):1–16.

Moyer, VA. Screening for prostate cancer: US Preventive Services Task Force recommendation statement. *Annals of Internal Medicine*. 2012; **157**(2):120–134.

Nguyen CT, Yu C, Moussa A, Kattan MW, Jones JS. Performance of prostate cancer prevention trial risk calculator in a contemporary cohort screened for prostate cancer and diagnosed by extended prostate biopsy. *The Journal of Urology*. 2010 Feb;**183**(2):529–533.

Ries LA, Young JL Jr, Keel GE, et al. Cancer survival among adults: US SEER program, 1988–2001. *Patient and Tumor Characteristics SEER Survival Monograph Publication*. 2007:07-6215.

Roehl KA, Han M, Ramos CG, Antenor JA, Catalona WJ. Cancer progression and survival rates following anatomical radical retropubic prostatectomy in 3,478 consecutive patients: long-term results. *The Journal of Urology*. 2004 Sep;**172** (3):910–914.

Ross KS, Carter HB, Pearson JD, Guess HA. Comparative efficiency of prostate-specific antigen screening strategies for prostate cancer detection. *JAMA*. 2000 Sep 20;**284**(11):1399–1405.

Sanders GD, Neumann PJ, Basu A, et al. Recommendations for conduct, methodological practices, and reporting of cost-effectiveness analyses: second panel on cost-effectiveness in health and medicine. *JAMA*. 2016 Sep 13;**316** (10):1093–1103.

Schröder FH, Hugosson J, Roobol MJ, et al. Screening and prostate-cancer mortality in a randomized European study. *New England Journal of Medicine*. 2009 Mar 26;**360**(13):1320–1328.

Schröder FH, Hugosson J, Roobol MJ, et al. Prostate-cancer mortality at 11 years of follow-up. *New England Journal of Medicine*. 2012 Mar 15;**366**(11):981–990.

Schröder FH, Hugosson J, Roobol MJ, et al. Screening and prostate cancer mortality: results of the European Randomised Study of Screening for Prostate Cancer (ERSPC) at 13 years of follow-up. *The Lancet*. 2014 Dec 6;**384**(9959):2027–2035.

Simmons Ivy J, Black Nembhard H, Baran K. Quantifying the impact of variability and noise on patient outcomes in breast cancer decision making. *Quality Engineering*. 2009; **21**(3):319–334.

Smallwood RD, Sondik EJ. The optimal control of partially observable Markov processes over a finite horizon. *Operations Research*. 1973 Oct;**21**(5):1071–1088.

Thompson IM, Ankerst DP, Chi C, et al. Assessing prostate cancer risk: results from the Prostate Cancer Prevention Trial. *Journal of the National Cancer Institute*. 2006 Apr 19;**98**(8):529–534.

Tomlins SA, Day JR, Lonigro RJ, et al. Urine TMPRSS2:ERG plus PCA3 for individualized prostate cancer risk assessment. *European Urology*. 2016; **70**(1):45–53.

Zhang, J, Denton BT, Balasubramanian H, Shah ND, Inman BA. Optimization of prostate biopsy referral decisions. *Manufacturing & Service Operations Management*. 2012; **14**(4):529–547.

8

Analytics-Driven Capacity Management

*Principles and Practical Lessons from Projects
at Three Hospitals*

Margaret L. Brandeau and David Scheinker

Summary of the Problem

Hospitals typically have limited resources with which to provide a wide range of services to a patient population with diverse needs. Efficient service provision requires the appropriate level of capacity to deliver high-quality care, satisfy patients, and manage costs. Hospitals must determine the resources that are necessary to satisfy patient demand and determine how to manage the use of these resources. These decisions are challenging because they must be made while accounting for demand variability and numerous interconnections between hospital operations. Moreover, because implementing changes in a hospital is time consuming and expensive, any proposed intervention must be analyzed to estimate its likely impact with a high level of certainty.

Summary of the Solution

Optimization using mathematical programming is a method for identifying the cost-minimizing or profit-maximizing combination of decisions (e.g., resources to acquire or the order in which to schedule procedures) in the presence of constraints and far more combinations than would be possible to evaluate individually. Discrete event simulation is a method for producing a detailed simulation of the operations of a system, thereby allowing one to examine the potential impact of changes to the system. Combining mathematical programming and discrete event simulation allows one to design optimal resource allocation or scheduling policies, for example, and then simulate their impact on the system in the presence of uncertainty or additional factors not captured in the optimization.

Summary of Relevance in a Post-COVID World

COVID-19 has resulted in major challenges in hospital capacity management. In the short term, hospitals have struggled to allocate beds, ventilators, and personal protective equipment to accommodate an influx of COVID-19 patients while minimizing the operational and financial challenges associated with the cancellation of elective procedures. In the longer term, hospitals need to find ways to make permanent the shifts to telemedicine that arose as a result of COVID-19 diminishing in-person visits. This chapter describes how the use of mathematical optimization and discrete event simulation can facilitate hospital capacity and operational planning in response to changing demands.

8.1 Introduction

How does one provide a wide range of hospital services to a diverse patient population in a timely manner with limited resources? To answer this question, one must find the appropriate level of capacity to deliver high-quality care, satisfy patients, and manage costs. This is the goal of hospital capacity management, which involves two interrelated tasks: determining the level and type of resources that are necessary to satisfy patient demand (design) and determining how to manage the use of these resources (operations). For example, when designing the capacity of a surgical suite or a procedural area, the availability of beds, operating rooms, nurses, and surgeons must be considered along with operational hours, scheduling practices, patient preferences, and potential delays associated with other hospital resources. Capacity management decisions are complicated by the fact that patient demands are typically diverse and highly variable, and hospital operations are complex and closely interconnected.

This chapter provides an introduction to analytics-driven hospital capacity management through three projects that employed mathematical programming and discrete event simulation to address common challenges. The first project used mathematical programming to identify the mix of patients at Stanford Hospital that would maximize revenue given the capacity of hospital resources after a planned hospital expansion. The second project used discrete event simulation to plan the physical capacity and operational profile of a new procedural space at a hospital in New England. The third project combined mathematical programming and discrete event simulation to create a tool to schedule surgical procedures at Lucile Packard Children's Hospital Stanford.

In a mathematical program, the goal of the system (e.g., minimize surgical procedure delays due to a lack of recovery beds) is represented with an objective function (e.g., maximize the number of patients assigned to recovery beds at each point in time), and the decisions to be made are represented as variables called decision variables (e.g., the assignment of a given patient to a given bed at a given time) (Hillier and Lieberman, 2004). In a discrete event simulation, all events of interest as well as their interactions and outcomes are simulated using historical or generated data (e.g., if no recovery bed is available and a patient is unable to leave the operating room, then the start time of the next patient's procedure is delayed) (Hillier and Lieberman, 2004). Each of these methods allows for an explicit representation of the system of interest and produces interpretable results. An additional benefit of mathematical programming is that it provides an explicit recommendation for the optimal course of action, that is, the values of the decision variables that yield the best objective function value. Both methods require one to conceptualize and program an explicit mathematical representation, often based on detailed historical data, of the processes of the system.

Queuing models can also be used to support hospital capacity management decisions (Ozcan, 2009). Such models use a relatively simple representation of a service system (e.g., patients being treated in an emergency department), with customer (e.g., patient) arrivals and service durations (e.g., length of procedures) summarized using statistics such as mean and variance, and scheduling represented by a simple rule such as first-come-first-served. Queuing models provide estimates of wait times and system utilization for given values of patient arrival rates, service times, and number of providers and the scheduling rule. These values can be varied to assess the impact of different levels of capacity and different scheduling rules. Queuing models require only simple input data and are easy to implement; many queuing models can be created and run in a spreadsheet. However, such models consider only a simplified version of the system, produce estimates of performance that are accurate primarily at the level of averages, and do not provide explicit recommendations for resource capacity or scheduling. For the three applications we describe in this chapter, we used mathematical programming and discrete event simulation rather than queuing models because we needed a more detailed understanding of the capacity management problems than queuing models can provide.

In the next section, we describe the principles and challenges of hospital capacity management. In the subsequent three sections, we illustrate these ideas in the context of the three hospital capacity management projects. We present healthcare-specific considerations and the basics of the underlying analytical methods, and we describe key lessons learned during the conceptualization, design, and implementation of the projects. We conclude with discussion of future capacity management challenges and opportunities.

8.2 Capacity Management Principles and Challenges

The major steps in healthcare capacity planning are forecasting demand, estimating capacity requirements, measuring effective capacity, estimating gaps between effective capacity and requirements, and determining the appropriate level of capacity. The primary trade-off is between the risk of having insufficient capacity to meet demand and the risk of incurring unsustainable costs. In general, too much capacity leads to unused facilities, wasted money, and reduced profits, while too little capacity can lead to delays, adverse patient outcomes, lost revenue, and a poor competitive position. The challenge, then, is to find the ideal amount of capacity. This decision depends on risk preferences that may be difficult to quantify. Additionally, the decision is complicated by legislation, depends on a variety of interconnected resources, can vary with time, and may be based on difficult-to-measure quality outcomes. Below we describe some of the challenges that arise in finding the ideal level of capacity.

8.2.1 Demand Is Variable and Uncertain

Determining the appropriate level of capacity to satisfy patient demand in a timely fashion is complicated by the variability and uncertainty of patient demand at all scales. For example, new patient populations emerge as a result of disease outbreaks or disappear as a result of new medical treatments; the healthcare needs of a population change based on societal factors such as rates of births, smoking, or obesity; the demand for specific types of admissions changes by season (e.g., more flu in the winter and more heat stroke in the summer); the number and type of patients who come to a hospital differ from day to day; and the time required to diagnose or treat an individual can vary by minutes or hours depending on the complexity of the patient's health condition.

8.2.2 Capacity Is Typically Expensive and Relatively Permanent

Changes to the physical and human capacity of a healthcare system require significant money, time, and effort: new healthcare facilities (or expansions of existing facilities) are expensive; practicing clinicians require years of additional training and licensing to change their specialty; new clinicians take years to train; operating hospitals may not have the option to shut down in order to renovate buildings, upgrade equipment, or build expansions; and new hospitals require years to design and build. Thus, long-term capacity must be robust enough to accommodate changes in demand with relatively little short-term flexibility in available capacity.

8.2.3 Delays Have Adverse Consequences

In a service system with fixed capacity and high variability, periods of high demand result in long wait times. Long wait times are accepted in certain service industries such as coffee shops or airlines. However, long wait times in healthcare (e.g., for trauma surgery, access to medicine, or a cancer screening exam) may lead to worse clinical outcomes and increased mortality rates.

8.2.4 Effective Capacity May Differ from Planned Capacity

Capacity planning decisions are made based on assumptions about how efficiently resources will be used. Depending on how the human and physical resources are managed, effective capacity may differ from planned capacity. Moreover, capacity has inherent variability. For example, the time required for a diagnosis or treatment can vary by minutes or hours depending on the experience and skill of the provider; the capacity of a unit to provide certain specialized procedures can vary from day to day depending on which provider is working; and entire patient pathways or standards of practice may change over years as medical science advances.

8.2.5 Healthcare Operations Are Highly Stochastic, Interdependent Systems

Capacity decisions for a single part of a healthcare process are likely to affect other parts of the process because healthcare operations are often highly stochastic, interdependent systems. The interdependence of resources means that the unavailability or delay of any resource will propagate through the system. For example, for a patient experiencing a heart attack, a delay or detriment in care will occur if any one of the numerous physicians, nurses, technicians, or administrators is unavailable when needed or if the required physical infrastructure (e.g., ambulance, equipment, hospital bed) is unavailable when needed.

8.2.6 Capacity Decisions May Be Constrained by Legislation

The amount of capacity that can be built may be constrained by legislation. For example, certificate-of-need laws in the United States regulate the maximum number of beds for hospitals and nursing facilities and are typically required before a hospital can expand or a new hospital can be built (National Conference of State Legislators, 2016). In some settings, lower limits on capacity are legislated by national performance measures of the form "$x\%$ of patients must be seen within y time units." For example, the Canadian Triage and Acuity Scale (CTAS) specifies compliance percentages and time standards for emergency department patients (Alberta Health Services, 2016).

8.2.7 Capacity Decisions Are Influenced by Difficult-to-Quantify Risk Preferences

As highlighted above, determining the appropriate level of capacity in a healthcare setting involves making a trade-off between the need to contain costs versus the need for timely patient care (and the resulting quality of care). Such decisions, implicitly or explicitly, depend on risk preferences that are difficult to quantify.

8.3 Mathematical Programming Approaches to Capacity Planning

8.3.1 Introduction

Mathematical programming models are well suited for complex capacity planning problems that require decisions about numerous resources that are used in different combinations to meet various types of demand. For example, the mix of patients that maximizes revenue subject to capacity constraints can be formulated as an integer or linear program, and the problem can be solved with different levels of capacity. Once capacity levels have been set, mathematical programming can be useful in managing capacity. For example, the assignment of nurses and physicians to shifts can be formulated as an integer program, as can the assignment of surgeons and surgical procedures to operating rooms.

In this section, we focus on the patient mix model. We describe the model in the following subsection and then we describe the application of such a model for capacity planning at Stanford Hospital.

8.3.2 Patient Mix Model for Capacity Planning

Consider a healthcare provider faced with decisions about how to respond to changes in the mix of patients and what new capacity to invest in. The primary factors influencing this capacity planning decision are the volume of demand for each type of patient, the resources necessary to care for each type of patient, and the revenues and expenses associated with each type of patient. A patient mix model formulated using mathematical programming is well suited for determining the mix of patients that optimizes revenue and understanding how marginal changes in either patient demand or resource availability impact the system.

8.3.2.1 Decision Variables

The decision of interest is to identify, for each type of patient the hospital serves (or could serve), the ideal number to serve each year.

8.3.2.2 Objective Function

Potential objectives for the patient mix problem include maximizing hospital revenue, maximizing patient throughput, minimizing costs, or maximizing resource utilization. In some cases, there may be several relevant objective functions, some of which may be in contradiction with each other, and different stakeholders may have strong preferences for one objective function over another. Some considerations when selecting an appropriate objective function are whether the objective can be expressed as a linear function, whether it approximates another objective (e.g., maximizing throughput and maximizing utilization are similar goals), and whether it could alternatively be incorporated into the model as a constraint (e.g., instead of minimizing costs, costs could be constrained to be within a given budget).

8.3.2.3 Constraints

The constraints of the patient mix problem include the capacity of each resource, limitations on the volume of each type of patient, and budget constraints, among others. For example, operating room capacity is a constraint on the number of surgical patients the hospital can serve, and there may be a lower and upper limit on patient demand for surgical services.

8.3.2.4 Solution

The patient mix model can be formulated as an integer program, with integer numbers of patients of each type. Alternatively, the model can be formulated as a linear program, thereby allowing fractional numbers of patients. After the linear program is solved, the values of the decision variables can be rounded to the nearest integer. The resulting solution is likely very close to the solution that would be obtained from the integer program.

Use of a linear programming formulation for the patient mix model has two advantages. First, linear programs are computationally easier to solve than integer programs. More importantly, linear programs provide shadow prices on the constraints. For the patient mix model, shadow prices on the resource constraints indicate the incremental improvement in the objective function that could be obtained per unit of additional capacity of each resource, and thus the benefit (at the margin) of investing in incremental capacity.

After the patient mix model has been solved, one can compare the resources used with available resources as specified in the model to determine whether excess capacity exists or whether more capacity is needed. If the amount of available resources changes when capacity is expanded, it might be possible – and advantageous – to change the mix of patients that is seen. A patient mix model allows one to answer these intertwined questions: What level of capacity of each resource is appropriate and what patient mix is best for that level of capacity?

8.3.3 Planning for Hospital Capacity Expansion

In the early 1980s, Stanford Hospital was planning to modernize and expand its facilities. A linear programming patient mix model was developed to determine how changes in the mix of patients by intensity level and payer class would affect the hospital's income, expenses, and resource use and – importantly – how increases in the level of different resources (e.g., operating rooms, intensive care beds) would affect net hospital revenue (Brandeau and Hopkins, 1984).

The model was formulated as follows:

$$\max \sum_{j=1}^{n} (r_j - vc_j)x_j \tag{8.1}$$

$$\text{subject to } \sum_{j=1}^{n} a_{ij}x_j \leq b_i \qquad \text{for } i = 1, \ldots, m \tag{8.2}$$

$$d_j^{min} \leq x_j \leq d_j^{max} \qquad \text{for } j = 1, \ldots, n \tag{8.3}$$

$$x_j \geq 0 \qquad \text{for } j = 1, \ldots, n \tag{8.4}$$

In the above formulation,

j = index for classes of patients, $j = 1, \ldots, n$

i = index for resources (departments and services), $i = 1, \ldots, m$

x_j = the number of patients of type j (the decision variable)

r_j = total revenue from a patient of type j

vc_j = total variable cost incurred by a patient of type j

a_{ij} = average number of units of resource i used by type j patient

b_i = amount of resource i available

d_j^{min} = lower bound on number of patients of type j

d_j^{max} = upper bound on number of patients of type j

The objective (Equation 8.1) is to maximize net revenue (contribution to fixed expense), summed over all patient types. Equation (8.2) provides the upper limit on the amount of resource of each type that can be used. Equation (8.3) enforces upper and lower limits on the number of each type of patient j. Note that the lower limit could be zero, and the upper limit could be set large enough so that x_j is essentially unconstrained. Equation (8.4) enforces nonnegativity of the x_j.

Patient categories distinguished patients by case type and intensity level. Since the hospital was reimbursed differently by different insurance entities, patients were also divided by payer type. A total of 14 patient categories were used: medical/surgical patients with high, moderate, or low intensity, reimbursed by MediCal (California's version of Medicaid, for low-income patients), Medicare, or other payers; obstetrics/gynecology patients reimbursed by MediCal, Medicare, or other payers; and pediatric patients, reimbursed by MediCal, or other payers.

The model included 16 categories of resources: beds by type (routine, intensive care unit/critical care unit (ICU/CCU), intermediate ICU, pediatric, and infant ICU), anesthesia, cast room, delivery room, dialysis, electroencephalogram/electrocardiogram/electromyography (EEG/ECG/EMG) testing, laboratory and blood services, operating and recovery rooms, oxygen therapy, physical/occupational therapy, radiology, and supplies and transportation.

For each category of patient, historical patient data were used to estimate average use of each type of resource (a_{ij}), per patient revenue (r_j), and variable cost (vc_j). Lower bounds on the number of each type of patient were set to zero. Upper bounds on the number of each type of patient were obtained from a forecast of future demand, created in a separate study by the hospital.

8.3.3.1 Implementation

The model was used to determine the most profitable patient mix, given existing capacity constraints; the value of adding capacity to different resources; and the revenue effects of different amounts of capacity. The analyses all assumed the same upper limits on the number of patients of each type and focused on how net revenue and the optimal mix of patients would change with different capacity constraints.

When the model was run with the existing level of capacity, the binding constraints were routine beds, dialysis, and operating and recovery rooms. Of these, dialysis had the highest shadow price ($13,593), primarily because it is needed by high-intensity patients who generate significant revenue.

The model was then run with resource levels set to reflect the hospital's planned capacity expansion. With the new resource constraints, a different mix of patients was optimal (fewer medium-intensity medical/surgical patients and more in the high-intensity and low-intensity categories), and the binding resource constraints changed. In this case, the binding constraints were routine beds (shadow price $185), physical/occupational therapy (shadow price $290), and anesthesiology (shadow price $823). The analysis showed that the planned capacity expansion would equip the hospital well to handle more high-intensity medical/surgical patients and would significantly increase monthly net revenue.

We now plan to perform a similar analysis for Lucile Packard Children's Hospital Stanford (LPCH). LPCH, like many hospitals, is seeing a significant shift in procedural volume from the inpatient to the outpatient setting (Robinson et al., 2015). We aim to use the patient mix model analysis to facilitate the simultaneous planning of capacity expansion and plans for serving the hospital's shifting patient mix. Given the richer data now available in the hospital's electronic health record, we plan to expand the model to include significantly more detailed categories of patient types and hospital resources than were considered in the analysis for Stanford Hospital. For example, the electronic health record contains data on the admitting clinical service for each patient, where the patient came from (emergency department, clinic referral, scheduled surgery, transfer from another facility, etc.), and the patient's admission status (scheduled, urgent, emergent, etc.). Similarly, new resource-relevant data include referrals for specialties (doctors, physical therapy, occupational therapy, etc.), medications (date, time, and dosage given), and specific procedures and diagnostics (orthopedic surgery, MRI scan, cardiac catheterization, etc.) for each patient. Use of these new data in the patient mix analysis will allow for a more granular level of planning.

8.4 Simulation-Based Approaches to Capacity Management

8.4.1 Simulation

A shortcoming of capacity planning methods that rely on average levels of demand is that they cannot fully capture impacts of demand variability on system performance (and thus the effects of different levels of capacity).

In practice, healthcare operations are constrained by a number of distinctions that are lost in averaging. For example, the order in which a healthcare provider receives requests for service determines how patient visits are scheduled. The length of procedures determines the difficulty of accommodating them (e.g., 2 surgical suites operating for 10 hours each can accommodate 20 cases that are each 1 hour long, but could accommodate only 4 cases that are 7 hours long). Moreover, service times are variable, so a capacity plan based on average demand will generate an estimate of average utilization but will not indicate the variability of that utilization. Demand may vary significantly from day to day and from season to season. Any analysis that relies only on averages of total demand and total resource availability will fail to account for these factors that affect system utilization. These are but a few examples of the subtlety of stochastic processes that can be captured by a discrete event simulation model but would be obscured by averaging.

8.4.2 Capacity Planning for a New Clinical Laboratory

In this section, we describe the use of a discrete event simulation model to support capacity planning decisions for a new clinical laboratory at a hospital in New England. We show how the model aided a decision process that followed the general capacity planning steps outlined in Section 8.1.

The hospital is a large academic medical center where two clinically similar laboratories, a cardiac catheterization laboratory (Cath Lab) and an electrophysiology laboratory (EP Lab), had been operating separately. Both labs perform minimally invasive cardiac procedures, many of which require only a small incision on the patient's wrist or groin. For example, in the Cath Lab, percutaneous coronary intervention (PCI) is performed, and in the EP Lab, cardiac ablation is performed. To perform these procedures, a specially trained cardiologist accesses the heart by threading a flexible tube (catheter) to the patient's heart with the aid of advanced imaging equipment.

The yearly procedural volume of the Cath Lab had been slowly declining over the past 10 years, as had utilization rates of its procedure rooms. The procedural volume of the EP Lab had remained roughly constant, though other labs in the area had expanded and attracted more volume. The leaders of the EP Lab believed that if they had more procedural space, they could hire an additional provider and significantly increase their volume. The volume decline and growth projections of the two labs aligned with long-term local and regional trends (The Advisory Board Company, 2013; Yeh et al., 2015). In light of these findings, hospital leaders formed a committee to prepare a plan to merge the two labs.

A designated floor of the hospital was to be rebuilt to serve as joint space for the two labs. The new space was intended to achieve four primary goals: (1) improve operational efficiency through shared functions, (2) improve clinical outcomes related to delays in care, (3) improve patient and staff satisfaction, and (4) facilitate advanced procedural techniques. Below we describe the committee's use of a discrete event simulation model to estimate the required procedure and recovery room capacity and determine how use of the space should be operationalized.

8.4.2.1 Required Procedure and Recovery Room Capacity

The committee built a discrete event simulation model to help answer the following questions: How many procedure and recovery rooms in the new joint space are necessary to accommodate demand? What is the optimal level of procedural flexibility in these rooms? What are the optimal inter-day procedure scheduling strategies? During which hours should the recovery rooms operate?

The model used as input a forecast of 12 months of procedures to be performed in the two labs. The range of forecasted future volumes had been developed in a previous modeling effort. For each given forecast, the model was run with a variety of operational constraints. After room availability, the second-most significant constraint on lab capacity was physician availability. The model input included lists of physician shifts and procedures performed in those shifts. Both vary based on which volume scenario is being examined.

The physical and staffing requirements of the two labs were similar, but not identical. Procedure rooms could be staffed and equipped to accommodate only Cath Lab procedures, only EP Lab procedures, certain procedures from each lab, or any procedure from either lab. The model used one of several scheduling algorithms, depending on the degree of procedure sharing between the labs. For each of the 260 weekdays of the year, the model simulated the flow of information available to the labs to assign physician shifts to Cath rooms and EP rooms and to then assign patient procedures to be performed during those shifts. The model provided the following outputs for each day: the schedule of procedure assignments to each room and each lab; room utilization and overtime statistics; and recovery room occupancy at 5-minute intervals.

Hospital decision makers used these outputs to evaluate the performance of the simulated joint lab for all combinations of the following demand and operational variables: the number of procedure rooms of each type; the case volume for the Cath and EP Labs; whether each room could accommodate Cath, EP, or both types of cases; the number of recovery rooms and their operating hours; and which days of the week each physician was assigned to work.

8.4.2.2 Estimate of Available Capacity

The capacity available in each scenario depends on the number and availability of procedure rooms, the policy for sharing procedure rooms, recovery room assumptions, and the policy for scheduling physicians. That each of these settings impacts capacity is clear, with, perhaps, the exception of the recovery room settings. To see why patient recovery times impact available capacity, recall that in this analysis the capacity of a resource was measured by how many patients it could accommodate. If patients have shorter or longer recovery times, then each recovery room has the capacity to accommodate more or fewer patients.

8.4.2.3 Gaps between Available Capacity and Requirements

For each level of demand, the gap between available and required capacity was measured, indirectly, by the number of procedures that could not be accommodated during normal working hours. The output of the model for each scenario was analyzed to determine which procedures were (or were not) successfully scheduled within the allotted time in the available rooms. The procedures that were scheduled but not completed before closing time were identified and quantified. For each scenario, this provided a measure of the gap between available and required capacity.

8.4.2.4 Determining the Appropriate Level of Capacity

The amount of capacity necessary to accommodate all demand can be found by increasing the values of relevant parameters of the model (e.g., number of rooms, operating hours) until the system performance is deemed satisfactory. However, since the simulation model includes days of exceptionally high demand, such an approach would likely lead to a significant amount of unused capacity on the majority of days. Here we describe how the committee used the model to answer the questions they were tasked with answering. In doing so, we call attention to an important distinction that must be drawn between three types of capacity. Physical capacity (e.g., the number of procedure rooms) is often defined by fixed, known parameters. Theoretical operational capacity (e.g., the number of hours per day each procedure room will operate) is often defined by a parameter that may be modified. Operational capacity (e.g., the fraction of operating hours that can effectively be used for procedures) often depends on parameters such as operational efficiency that must be estimated and may be difficult to project.

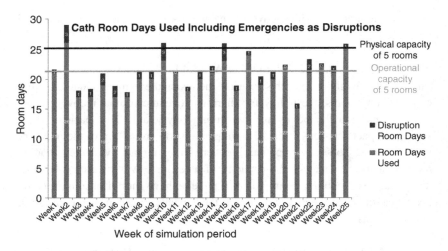

Figure 8.1 Results of a simulation of the number of Cath Lab procedure rooms necessary to accommodate volume during a 25-week simulated period. Time required to accommodate emergency procedure volume, which cannot be scheduled and may disrupt the scheduled cases, is marked in black and denoted "Disruption Room Days."

The results of the simulation model showed that, due to the recent declines in Cath Lab volume, the joint lab would be able to accommodate almost all procedural volume demand with five Cath rooms, as illustrated in Figure 8.1. When the model was run with five Cath rooms and no procedural flexibility (allowing Cath procedures to be performed only in the Cath rooms) only a small percentage of cases could not be completed during current working hours. This finding was supported by historical experience. Approximately one year before the study was conducted, one of the six Cath Lab rooms (in the separate lab) was closed for repairs for almost two months. During this time the Cath Lab was able to accommodate the same procedural volume as when it was operating with all six rooms.

For the EP Lab, the results of the simulation suggested that four procedure rooms would be needed to accommodate the additional volume generated by one or two additional providers, as illustrated in Figure 8.2. Even when the model was run with three EP rooms and a high level of procedural flexibility (allowing less specialized EP procedures to be performed in the Cath procedure rooms when those rooms were available), a large percentage of cases could not be completed during current working hours. This finding was supported by the current state of the hospital in which the EP providers consistently used one of the Cath Lab rooms on Fridays.

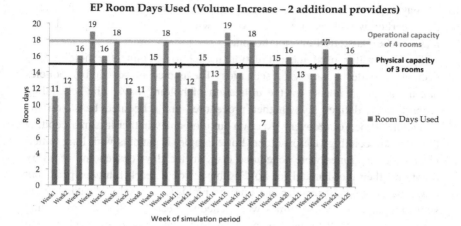

Figure 8.2 Results of a simulation of the number of EP Lab procedure rooms necessary to accommodate volume during a 25-week simulated period.

For both the Cath and EP Labs, the committee tested various inter-day scheduling policies to smooth demand within each week and across weeks. These resulted in minor changes in the numbers of procedures by day of week and across weeks but did not significantly alter the qualitative outcomes of the simulations. The results of the analysis suggested that the space should be designed with five Cath procedure rooms and four EP procedure rooms, and that this would provide enough capacity if policies for room use flexibility and inter-day scheduling were decided based on other operational considerations. Hospital leadership accepted this recommendation and tasked the committee with deciding how the additional available space should be used.

8.4.2.5 Recovery Rooms

Patients are prepared for procedures and then recover in rooms called "holding bays." The decision to revise the architectural plans to include only five Cath procedure rooms (as opposed to six Cath rooms in the original plans) created additional space that could potentially be used for more holding bays. Project leaders asked the committee to evaluate the feasibility of constructing larger, hard-walled holding bays rather than the smaller, curtain-walled holding bays in the current plans.

Too many holding bays would result in low occupancy and the loss of space for other uses. Too few holding bays would result in frequent procedure delays and cancellations. For the chosen number of holding bays, the committee would recommend the time until which the bays would be staffed. Keeping the bays open later would contribute to higher operating costs, while closing them earlier would require that patients who had not yet completed their recovery be transferred into the hospital.

The committee used the simulation model to examine the holding bay occupancy under a variety of scenarios. The choice of scheduling policies had a significant impact on the utilization of holding bays. The scheduling scenarios are defined by whether procedures are scheduled based on the procedure (Proc.) or recovery (Recov.) duration and whether it is in ascending (Asc.) or descending (Desc.) order. For example, if patients with long antici- pated recovery times were scheduled early in the day (descending recovery duration), then the demand for holding bays would reach a higher peak, but fewer patients would recover late into the night. Conversely, if patients with short anticipated recovery times were scheduled early in the day (ascending recovery duration), then the demand for holding bays would not reach as high a peak, but significantly more patients would recover late into the night. Analogously, if the scheduling is based on the procedure duration, then scheduling longer procedures first (descending procedure duration) would delay when patients begin arriving to the recovery bays, while scheduling shorter procedures first (ascending procedure duration) would result in more patients arriving to the holding bays earlier in the morning. The average holding bay occupancy for each of these scenarios is shown in Figure 8.3.

Given the relatively low peak holding bay use in all of the scheduling scenarios, the committee focused on evaluating the performance of the model with the highest peak demand, when procedures were to be scheduled in order of descending recovery time. The analysis of average occupancy showed that 11 holding bays would, on average, be able to accommodate all procedural demand. However, if only 11 bays were built, the lab would face significant delays every time that demand exceeded the capacity of the 11 holding bays. Thus, the relevant operational metric is the maximum, not the average, number of holding bays used at any one time. The committee found that across all scheduling scenarios, the maximum number of occupied holding bays exceeded 11 almost every day, but rarely exceeded 16 bays. For example, peak demand would have exceeded 14, 15, or 16 holding bays during only 4%, 3%, and 2% of all operating hours, respectively. Based on this analysis, the committee concluded that 16 hard-walled holding bay rooms should be built.

To determine the operating hours of the holding bays, the committee examined the additional benefit of keeping the holding bays open later into the evening. They found that closing the holding bays before 8 p.m. would lead to a higher number of hospital admissions and that keeping the holding bays open past 10 p.m. would lead to only small reductions in the number of hospital admissions, as illustrated in Figure 8.4. They recommended that the

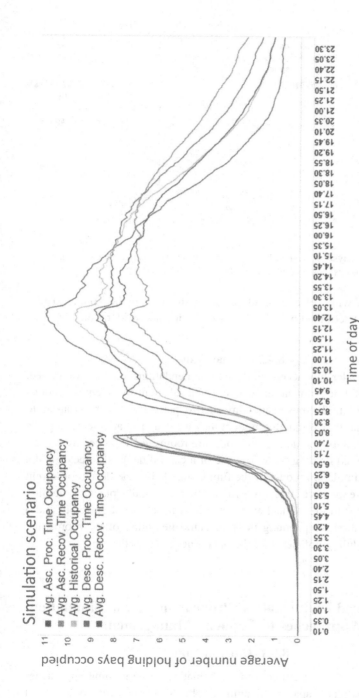

Figure 8.3 Results of a simulation of holding bay occupancy by time of day for different scheduling scenarios over a 50-week simulated period. Procedures are scheduled based on the procedure (Proc.) or recovery (Recov.) duration in ascending (Asc.) or descending (Desc.) order.

175

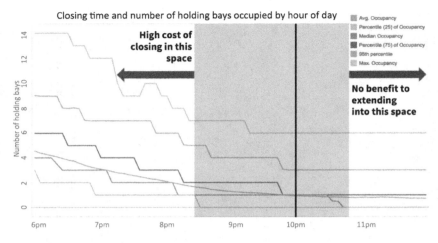

Figure 8.4 Analysis of holding bay occupancy by time of day and the costs and benefits of various closing times.

labs be designed with a planned holding bay closing time in the 8 p.m.–10 p.m. window, to be determined based on other operational considerations.

8.4.2.6 Final Plan

The hospital leadership accepted the recommendations of the committee. Although hospital department leaders are often reluctant to accept reductions in capacity, the simulation results convinced department leaders to agree to less capacity than they originally thought they needed. The architectural plans were thus updated to include 5 Cath procedure rooms, 4 EP procedure rooms, and 16 hard-walled holding bays. The use of a careful demand forecast and a discrete event simulation model of the future state led to the design of a joint lab with fewer expensive procedure rooms than originally planned; holding bays better suited to the clinical and operational needs of the hospital; and a rigorous foundation for planning the procedural flexibility of the rooms, the procedure scheduling policies, and the operating hours of the lab.

8.5 Combined Mathematical Programming and Simulation Approaches to Capacity Management

8.5.1 Introduction

We have described the usefulness of mathematical programming approaches for solving complex capacity planning problems using average levels of demand and simulation models for exploring the operations of a system using detailed data about volume and operations. In this section, we describe a capacity management project at Lucile Packard Children's Hospital Stanford (LPCH) that illustrates how these two methods complement each other in the presence of repeated decision making and uncertainty.

8.5.2 Perioperative Services Capacity Planning

Hospital perioperative services are the services given before, during, and after a surgical procedure. These include, for example, presurgical admission and evaluation, surgery, and then recovery in the hospital before discharge or hospital admission. A key capacity management problem in perioperative services is scheduling operating room procedures, as operating rooms are a key driver of hospital costs and revenues. Operating room scheduling lends itself well to solution using mathematical programming: many procedures must be scheduled, subject to constraints, and the best possible solution typically cannot be determined by inspection. A typical formulation is a binary integer program that has the goal of minimizing the time until all surgeries are completed (or, equivalently, maximizing operating room utilization), subject to constraints on when and in which room surgical procedures can be scheduled. Such a formulation uses deterministic estimates of surgical procedure times.

However, surgical processes are not deterministic. For example, surgical case volume differs significantly from day to day; surgical procedures and patient recoveries frequently take more or less time than expected; scheduled cases may be cancelled; and urgent cases may be added to the schedule with little notice. If a deterministic mathematical programming model is to be used numerous times and in the presence of disruptions not accounted for by the model, the results may not be a reliable estimate of the outcome. One way to address this shortcoming is by using stochastic optimization (Birge and Louveaux, 2011). However, stochastic optimization requires one to estimate probability distributions on input parameters, which can be challenging given the typically large number of parameters, and solving such a model can be computationally difficult. Another approach is to use a simulation model to test the performance of the solution from a deterministic optimization model across a wide range of scenarios and with unexpected disruptions.

8.5.3 Operating Room Scheduling and Capacity Management at a Children's Hospital

At LPCH, approximately 6,600 surgical procedures are performed each year in 20 procedure and operating rooms. Patients who have surgery and receive general anesthesia recover in either the post-anesthesia care unit (PACU) or the intensive care unit (ICU), and from there may be admitted to a general inpatient bed. Pediatric patients from a wide range of surgical, procedural, and diagnostic areas require the use of a PACU bed. When PACU bed demand exceeds bed or nurse capacity, the PACU is put "on hold"; the patient must wait in the operating room until a PACU bed becomes available and scheduled surgical procedures in that operating room are delayed. In the last 6 months of 2016, approximately 20 hours of operating room holds occurred at LPCH due to insufficient capacity in the PACU. Because an acute care operating room in California costs approximately $2,200 per hour to run (Childers and Maggard-Gibbons, 2018), these delays cost the hospital up to $44,000 in wasted operating room time alone.

We carried out a project aimed at scheduling procedures in the operating rooms with the goal of minimizing the daily finishing time in each room while minimizing delays caused by downstream PACU congestion (Fairley et al., 2019). We used integer programming to create the schedule of procedures for each day and then used discrete event simulation to estimate how the schedule would perform in the presence of naturally occurring variability.

8.5.3.1 Optimization Model

To create the daily operating room schedule, we used two sequential integer programs. The integer programs use as input the estimated duration of each procedure in the operating room and the estimated recovery time for each procedure. These values were estimated using machine learning on historical data (Fairley et al., 2019; Zhou et al., 2016). The first integer program schedules procedures to minimize the ending time of each operating room. The solution to this integer program identifies the earliest time by which all scheduled cases in each room could be completed, based on the estimates of procedure durations. The second integer program uses this earliest ending time, with an added amount of allowable extra time in each operating room, as an input to find the schedule of procedures that minimizes the maximum PACU occupancy over the course of the day, based on the estimates of recovery time durations. The output of the second integer program is a proposed case schedule specifying the start time of each procedure in each room.

8.5.3.2 Simulation Model

The integer programs schedule procedures based on expected length of each procedure in the operating room and expected recovery time in the PACU, ignoring variability in procedure length, recovery length, case availability (e.g., cancellations), and other factors. To evaluate the performance of the optimized schedule in the presence of uncertainty, we developed a model to simulate, for each day, operating room and PACU occupancy given deviations from the expected schedule that may occur. For each day, the model simulates the scheduled start of each case, the deviation of procedure and recovery durations from the schedule, and the cancellation or addition of cases.

We used the last 6 months of hospital data to simulate, in the presence of unexpected disruptions, what PACU occupancy would have been had the integer programs been used to set the schedule. We showed that, had the optimized schedule been used, PACU holds would have been reduced by 76% and PACU admission delay time would have been reduced by 80%. Based on these estimated improvements, the decision was made to start using the optimization model, combined with the simulation model, to schedule cases.

8.5.3.3 Implementation

The optimization/simulation tool was implemented as follows: On the morning of the day before the day for which the schedule was being set, the schedulers would start with a default "original schedule" for the order of procedures in each room currently in the system. This schedule is usually based primarily on the order in which cases had been entered into the system rather than on considerations of operational efficiency, except that it was designed to meet the scheduling constraints discussed above. The integer programs were used to produce an optimized schedule, and then the simulation model was used to project PACU occupancy for the original and optimized schedules. If, based on the simulation, the original schedule would not result in PACU holds, then it would be used. If the original but not the optimized schedule would result in PACU holds, then the optimized schedule would be used.

Shortly after the combined tool was implemented, LPCH opened the first of several planned new operating rooms and procedural areas. The use of the tool is now on hold until physical changes to the procedural area are complete and the models can be updated. After the physical changes have been completed, a revised version of the tool will be incorporated as a standard part of each morning's procedure schedule planning.

8.6 Discussion

The goal of hospital capacity management is to provide the appropriate level of capacity and organize its use to best meet patient demands. Too little capacity can lead to long wait times, poor clinical outcomes, and, potentially, lost market share. Too much capacity can lead to high costs and underutilized resources. Moreover, a given amount of capacity may be sufficient to meet patient needs if utilized efficiently or may fall short if poorly organized. The goal is to determine the ideal level of capacity and the best operational model for a given setting.

We have described the use of mathematical programming and discrete event simulation for capacity management in three different hospital settings. We showed that in some cases an optimization model that uses average demand values can be sufficient for capacity planning. In other cases, the use of a simulation model that explores alternate capacity scenarios, without optimization, may suffice. For some capacity management problems, especially those involving repeated use of a deterministic optimization model with important uncertainties not captured in the optimization model, both optimization and simulation may be needed for adequate capacity management.

As we have highlighted, the interconnectedness of different parts of a hospital is often relevant when planning capacity of a particular department or service. Such connection was considered in the patient mix model, where resource use in all departments is affected by the mix of patients. Interconnectedness was particularly important in the operating room scheduling problem, where downstream PACU delays affected the effective capacity of the operating rooms.

Additionally, the effective capacity of a space depends on how it is utilized. Thus, it is often important when planning for the capacity of a space to also determine the appropriate operations for the space. This was relevant in the planning process for the combined clinical laboratory where the solution involved flexibility for less specialized EP procedures to be performed in the Cath procedure rooms. Without this flexibility, more EP procedure rooms would be needed.

The capacity management projects we described were carried out at three different hospitals. In each case, we worked closely with hospital planners to develop and instantiate the models, and then to interpret the findings from the models. This collaborative process allowed hospital planners to have trust in the model results. More generally, we have found that successful analytics-based hospital projects tend to be those that align with the priorities of hospital leadership and that are carried out in close collaboration not only with leaders from the directly affected department(s) but also with individuals whose departments may be indirectly affected (Scheinker and Brandeau, 2020).

Looking to the future, increasing amounts of data are becoming available in hospitals. These include data from electronic medical records, hospital dashboards, sensors and patient monitors, and many other sources. Such data can be exploited by hospitals to improve capacity management in a variety of ways. For example, data from electronic medical records can be used to assess patient needs and predict future trends. Data from hospital dashboards can show where bottlenecks in service are occurring as well as which resources are underutilized. Combined with analytical methods such as those we have described in this chapter, improved hospital data can be used to manage capacity in real time and to develop improved plans for future capacity needs.

References

Alberta Health Services. Canadian Triage and Acuity Scale (CTAS) National Guidelines, 2016. www.calgaryhealthregion.ca/policy/docs/1451/Admission_over-capacity_AppendixA.pdf.

J Birge and F Louveaux. *Introduction to Stochastic Programming*. Springer, New York, 2nd ed., 2011.

ML Brandeau and DSP Hopkins. A patient mix model for hospital financial planning. *Inquiry*, **21** (1):32–44, 1984.

P Childers and M Maggard-Gibbons. Understanding costs of care in the operating room. *JAMA Surgery*, **153** (4):e176233, 2018.

M Fairley, D Scheinker, and M L Brandeau. Improving the efficiency of the operating room environment with an optimization and machine learning model. *Health Care Management Science*, **22** (4): 756–767, 2019.

FS Hillier and GJ Lieberman. *Introduction to Operations Research*. McGraw Hill, New York, 8th ed., 2004.

National Conference of State Legislators. CON – Certificate of Need State Laws, 2016. www.ncsl.org/research/health/con-certificate-of-need-state-laws.aspx.

YA Ozcan. *Quantitative Methods in Health Care Management*. Jossey-Bass, San Francisco, 2nd ed., 2009.

JC Robinson, T Brown, and C Whaley. Reference-based benefit design changes consumers' choices and employers' payments for ambulatory surgery. *Health Affairs (Millwood)*, **34** (3): 415–422, 2015.

D Scheinker and M L Brandeau. Implementing analytics projects in a hospital: successes, failures, and opportunities. *INFORMS Journal on Applied Analytics*, **50** (3):176–189, 2020.

The Advisory Board Company. National Ablation Volume Estimates, 2013. www.advisory.com.

RW Yeh, L Mauri, R Wolf, et al. Population trends in rates of coronary revascularization. *JAMA Internal Medicine*, **175** (3): 454–456, 2015.

Z Zhou, D Miller, N Master, et al. Detecting inaccurate predictions of pediatric surgical durations. In *2016 IEEE International Conference on Data Science and Advanced Analytics (DSAA)*, pages 452–457. IEEE, 2016.

9

Practical Advice for Clinician–Engineer Partnerships for the Use of AI, Optimization, and Analytics for Healthcare Delivery

David Scheinker, Robert A. Harrington, and Fatima Rodriguez

Summary of the Problem

The widespread growth of big data and artificial intelligence in industry offers a preview of their promise and peril in medicine and biomedical research. COVID-19 brought about unprecedented cooperation and data sharing between care providers, public health officials, and engineers. The failures and successes of analytics projects in hospitals offer instructive lessons to those who seek to deploy such technologies in healthcare. This chapter combines a recent viewpoint by the authors [1] with a recent article by the first author [2] and extends them to offer lessons from other industries, promising developments in healthcare, and practical guidance for clinician–engineer partnerships.

Summary of the Solution

Clinicians and engineers have made striking developments in the use of artificial intelligence, optimization, and other analytical methods to help guide clinical decisions across a variety of precision medicine initiatives. Yet, buzz words like "big data" and "artificial intelligence" mystify many clinicians and biomedical researchers. Their widespread use in other industries and initial clinical applications can serve as a guide to a clearer understanding of what they are, what they are not, and how clinicians and engineers can better work together to leverage these technologies.

> ## Chapter Outline
>
> This chapter is organized as follows: Section 9.1 provides guidance on how to establish a shared vocabulary and common understanding between engineers and clinicians of what terms such as AI and ML do and don't mean. Section 9.2 identifies the challenges clinician–engineering partnerships must overcome to deliver sustained value and ways to avoid common causes of failure. Section 9.3 provides specific advice on how to design projects to produce value at a series of stages rather than rely on the success of one ambitious final model. Section 9.4 concludes by drawing on cautionary lessons from healthcare and other industries.

9.1 Communicating across the Clinician–Engineer Divide

Effective cross-discipline communication is essential for successful physician–engineer partnerships. Many common terms mean different things in different contexts. Artificial intelligence (AI) refers to a machine with human capabilities, which may mean anything from Siri looking up nearby restaurants when you say "I'm hungry" to an algorithm making a medical diagnosis based on an image. Machine learning (ML) may refer either to a set of computational and statistical tools for identifying relationships in data or to the use of such tools to make predictions based on data, but as used by non-engineers it is often a catch-all for advanced analytics, even deterministic ones such as mathematical optimization. Deep neural networks (DNNs) are a particular type of ML whose success at tasks such as image recognition has led to them being referred to as AI or Deep Learning and sometimes seen as a cure-all, but which are far less appropriate for a large class of problems than older, simpler methods. Even in engineering communities there is controversy about the appropriate use of these terms.

Developing most AI, ML, and DNN tools requires access to "big data," another concept with multiple meanings. For data scientists, it implies using more data than one computer can handle with significant attendant analytical and computational challenges and opportunities; for clinicians and biomedical researchers, it refers to complex data sets with numerous structured and unstructured data fields such as those typically found in electronic health records (EHRs). Figure 9.1 illustrates the relationship between AI, ML, DNNs, and big data. Reinforcement learning is a notable exception to the use of big data to train AI. It is an approach to building AI tools based only on feedback. For example, DeepMind's program AlphaGo Zero became the most

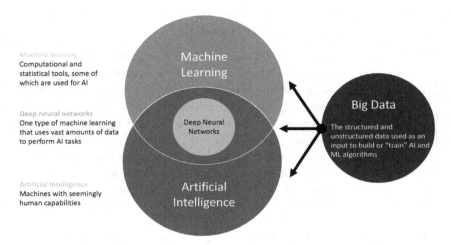

Figure 9.1 Relationship between big data, deep neural networks, artificial intelligence (AI), and machine learning (ML).

powerful Go program in the world solely by playing against itself. Thus far, reinforcement learning in healthcare has been developed using historical data representing decisions and feedback. If (when) AI starts to make and test clinical decisions, algorithms will have the capacity to learn on their own.

The first step to facilitating successful clinician–engineer communication is to establish a clear mutual understanding of the goals, constraints, and resources. If these are not established carefully, a partnership may progress troublingly and surprisingly far with participants on each side harboring misconceptions. A useful strategy is to make an active effort to adopt the mental model of one's partners from the other discipline. An important first step that clinicians and engineers can take is to minimize their use of the technical jargon of their field and instead formulate their perspective in the more general terms of decisions, problems, solutions, inputs, and outputs. Clinicians and engineers will need to develop a common basic understanding of the workings of ML and AI. Just as clinicians and statisticians share a basic statistical literacy essential in interpreting the results of clinical trials and in conducting research, a basic understanding of ML and AI will become necessary for clinicians to evaluate new developments and use the tools they make possible. Concepts new to clinicians will become as frequently used, and abused, as the p-value. These include "training data" and "testing data," which may refer to the best practice of randomly dividing data into distinct subsets, building numerous models on the training data, selecting the best-performing model, and testing only the best-performing model on the not previously seen

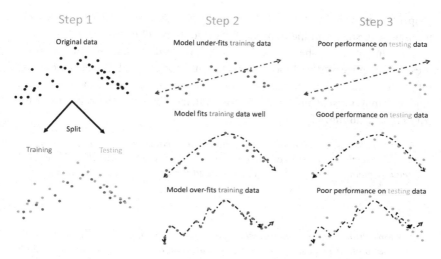

Figure 9.2 Three sequential steps common in the use of a machine learning algorithm to identify a relationship in data. *Left*: An example of how data may be randomly split into a training set and a testing set. *Middle*: An illustration of three variants of a machine learning model. Each variant produces a curve meant to capture the relationship in the data. *Right*: An evaluation on the testing data of the quality of the fit of each curve generated.
Adapted from the work of the authors [1]

testing data. These concepts may be abused by, e.g., cherry-picking testing data on which the model performs exceptionally well or testing numerous models on the testing data and only reporting the best performance. "Supervised learning" refers to models trained on data with labels such as malignant or benign. "Unsupervised learning" describes models that identify previously unknown patterns such as classes of tumors. These and numerous other concepts will inform conversations between clinicians, engineers, computer scientists, and statisticians.

Two closely related concepts address a concern more prominent in ML than traditional statistics: "under-fitting" models that are too simple to adequately describe the training data and "over-fitting" models that are so specific to the training data that they do not generalize well to the testing data. Figure 9.2 illustrates an example of the practice common to ML in which a data set is split randomly into training and testing data; three models are trained with one each that under-fits, fits well, and over-fits the data; and the performance of each of these models is evaluated on the testing data. Unlike traditional statistical models, which are also subject to under-fitting and over-fitting, powerful ML models suffer from an extreme version of this risk. Most ML models, if not properly deployed, can "memorize" training data to produce near zero error on training sets, shown in the bottom of the middle panel of Figure 9.2.

Applying the new, shared vocabulary will present challenges and opportunities. For engineers, it will mean focusing on the high-level inputs and outputs rather than the technical components in between. Consider two ways an engineer may present information to a clinician about an algorithm used for surgical scheduling:

> *A random forest regression model predicting surgical procedure runtime using a vector of relevant features results in lower root mean square error than do decision tree algorithms, support vector machines, and the procedure time averaging algorithms currently in use.*

And

> *The top-performing machine learning model uses patient, provider, and procedure information to predict surgical procedure duration, and it does so more accurately than the algorithm currently in use.*

The second explanation focuses less on technical details and more on the inputs to the model, what the model produces, and how model performance compares to a relevant alternative.

Similarly, consider how a clinician could describe the challenges associated with predicting the risk of a hospital-acquired condition:

> *Oncology patients on active chemotherapy with chronic indwelling lines are at higher risks for central line–associated bloodstream infections as compared with other hospitalized patients (e.g., patients presenting with acute coronary syndromes).*

> *Patients who are frequently hospitalized and with weakened immune systems (as is typical for patients admitted to oncology units) are much more likely to be at risk of hospital-acquired infections.*

The second explanation focuses less on the underlying clinical details and more on the context and a practical way that available data (the unit a patient is on) can be used to categorize patients for the purposes of the analysis.

Striking the ideal balance between the technical or medical details necessary to understand a problem and discipline-independent concepts is an art form. The areas we've seen engineers benefit most from focusing on are high-level, rather than technically specific, descriptions of risk, accuracy, inputs, and outputs. For clinicians, the characteristics of a project most important and challenging to describe to engineers are the relevant patient, procedure, or clinical information categorized not in terms of clinical intuition but in terms of accessible data fields.

9.2 Lessons for Moving beyond Proof-of-Concept

There are numerous proof-of-concept examples of ML in healthcare. It has been applied to clinical risk prediction and to learning from the large volume of data generated by EHRs and other large data sets [1–6]. Notable recent examples include the classification of a picture of a nevus as malignant or benign [3], of a retinal fundus image to predict the risk of cardiovascular disease (CVD) [7], and of using histopathology specimens to predict prognosis in lung cancer [8]. In everyday clinical cardiology, ML has been used for interpreting automated electrocardiogram, determining left ventricular ejection fractions from echocardiography, and scoring coronary artery calcium scans [9]. A form of AI known as computer vision is being developed to prevent clinical errors and improve patient safety [10]. Though relatively few of these methods have been implemented in routine clinical practice, and none on a large scale, they demonstrate the promise of AI in clinical medicine and biomedical research.

The successful deployment of AI in industry stands in contrast to the disappointment many in healthcare feel about how few proof-of-concept projects have been implemented and shown to improve clinical outcomes [11, 12]. Clinician–engineer collaborations are more likely to produce an impact when they start with a problem, idea, or opportunity acutely experienced by a clinician. A project is more likely to lead to an impactful collaboration if the domain experts, e.g., nurses or physicians, define a problem and consult with engineers to determine whether a technical approach may be appropriate. A promising approach occurs when a problem is identified by a clinician as one that she and her colleagues experience frequently and for which they have an intuition that a better approach is possible. A less fruitful but unfortunately common alternative is that of an engineer setting out with a machine learning or optimization algorithm as a "solution in search of a problem" and looking to collaborate with care providers only to the extent necessary to acquire data. The potential problem with an engineering-led approach is that strong technical performance is not sufficient for a model to lead to sustainable improvements. A technically successful model may fail to be implemented if the healthcare institution experiences operational constraints not accounted for during model development, does not prioritize implementation due to competing priorities, or lacks the technical infrastructure to implement the model; or if the potential benefits of the use of the model do not outweigh the costs associated with its implementation and use. In order to increase the chances that a model will be implemented, its intended use should be carefully planned before the model is developed. For example, for a better

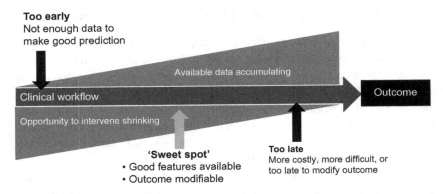

Figure 9.3 Identifying the appropriate use case for a predictive model.
Reproduced with the permission of the author [13]

risk-prediction model to have a chance to eventually benefit patients, it must be designed to accord with a specific decision point in the patient's care path. This may involve significant technical trade-offs such as deploying the model before all relevant data are available but while there is enough time to act on the prediction, visualized in Figure 9.3.

Even if a model is implemented, it may stop being used if it requires significant modification of workflows, it is not tied to feedback and incentives important to those using it, or the benefits associated with its use are not appropriately tracked and quantified. Recent work by DS details numerous examples of engineering projects designed to improve hospital operations that succeed and fail in a variety of stages (Figure 9.4) [2]. The central lesson for developing, deploying, and sustaining a successful model is to focus on a problem important to the institution, choose an approach compatible with the technical and operational infrastructure of the institution, and ensure that the impact of the use of the model is tracked, evaluated, and incentivized.

9.3 Starting Small and Building on Success

A less ambitious and particularly promising area of collaboration is the use of optimization, ML, and AI to automate and simplify tasks too onerous or time consuming for a single person or team to perform. What if we could automate setting efficient staff schedules with the techniques that have been used for decades by other large industries such as aviation [14]? What if we could use voice-recognition software as a medical scribe to allow more doctoring and

Figure 9.4 Steps necessary for a project to succeed and common causes of failure. Reproduced with the permission of the authors [14]

less documenting in patient exam rooms [15]? What if we could aggregate a personalized cohort to ask simple, clinically relevant questions with a few clicks of a mouse? Research teams at Stanford have developed a variety of approaches to leveraging data found in the EHR to help clinicians make decisions based on a patient's unique characteristics. One such approach allows a clinician considering a decision to call for an "informatics consult." This triggers a machine learning algorithm that identifies patients similar to the one being considered and presents their treatments and outcomes [16]. Similar tools could be used to quickly identify patients who meet criteria for entry into randomized clinical trials, dramatically cutting enrollment and recruitment costs. In translational research, ML can efficiently identify candidate molecules for drug development. ML can better risk-stratify populations traditionally underrepresented in our available evidence base and identify patterns and relationships not captured by traditional statistical methods.

When undertaking an ambitious project, a team of clinicians and engineers would do well to identify small, intermediate goals to improve patient health. For most problems, whether prediction, optimization, or disease modeling, the first steps are to quantify the clinical context, acquire data from several sources, and clean and combine the data. These steps usually require a significant amount of work, result in a better quantitative representation of the current state, and can often be used to create value even before the development of a more sophisticated model. For example, DS recently took part in a project to build a model to identify patients at risk for hospital-acquired central line–associated blood stream infections (CLABSIs). Before the development of the risk-prediction model, a careful analysis of central line usage and CLABSI data allowed the institution to build dashboards to monitor and improve adherence to infection prevention best practices and led to insights about the definitions of how CLABSI rates are measured that have implications for defining national guidelines [17]. These two intermediate accomplishments improved the team's understanding of the data and generated significant institutional support for the project. If the final risk-prediction model is implemented and succeeds, it will be in no small part due to these initial successes.

9.4 Cautionary Lessons

With all of this exciting promise, what could possibly go wrong? Among the most feared perils of AI are data misuse and overuse. Will insurance companies use ML algorithms to refuse coverage to patients with a high predicted risk of adverse outcomes? Will these models exacerbate healthcare disparities by inaccurately labeling certain groups as higher risk, nonadherent, etc., based on limited data? Will this result in patient distrust about how their data will impact their clinical care? These unanticipated consequences are common with any new technology and should be considered carefully before implementing such models in larger scales.

It is important to remember that the principles of the scientific method should continue to apply. While AI can yield very accurate predictions, the results are often "blackbox" by obscuring the importance and selection of predictive inputs [18]. As with all observational data, bias will continue to exist and should be dealt with carefully, but the blackbox nature of AI algorithms may make it difficult to prevent algorithms that were trained on biased data from codifying and amplifying that bias. Applications of AI for setting bail, recognizing faces, screening job applicants, and identifying patients at risk of needing a significant amount of care have all been criticized for propagating the racial bias of the data on which they were trained [19,20]. While many of these critiques apply to a particular use of AI, not to the fundamental limitations of AI, they highlight the importance of understanding the mechanism behind predicted associations. For this reason, AI will need to be used in combination with traditional biological, epidemiological, and biostatical tools. Research must remain hypotheses driven, continue to guard against spurious observations based on multiple testing, and carefully consider the construction of the large data sets on which important algorithms will be trained.

Will AI replace doctors and researchers? No, but a clinician who uses AI will replace clinicians who do not. AI will increase efficiency, take over many routine tasks, and provide a first and last set of eyes. Our medical teams will become increasingly multidisciplinary and consist of clinicians, engineers, and data scientists. Imagine twenty years ago someone asking their phone, "What am I doing this afternoon?" If they got a meaningful response with a warning about the traffic, it would have seemed like true AI. It is now so commonplace as to hardly be considered AI at all. We remain optimistic that effective partnerships between care providers and engineers will lead to developments in big data and AI that will improve patient care, reduce costs, and transform our lives as clinicians and researchers. Such partnerships have the potential to reduce the time we spend on cumbersome tasks, warn us about signs of trouble, help catch potential errors, and free us to provide higher-quality, lower-cost care.

References

1. Rodriguez F, Scheinker D and Harrington RA. Promise and perils of big data and artificial intelligence in clinical medicine and biomedical research. *Circulation Research*. 2018;**123**(12):1282–1284.
2. Scheinker D and Brandeau ML. implementing analytics projects in a hospital: successes, failures, and opportunities. *INFORMS Journal on Applied Analytics*. 2020;**50**(3):176–189.
3. Esteva A, Kuprel B, Novoa RA, et al. Dermatologist-level classification of skin cancer with deep neural networks. *Nature*. 2017;**542**:115–118.
4. Monsalve-Torra A, Ruiz-Fernandez D, Marin-Alonso O, et al. Using machine learning methods for predicting inhospital mortality in patients undergoing open repair of abdominal aortic aneurysm. *Journal of Biomedical Informatics*. 2016;**62**:195–201.
5. Vashisht R, Jung K and Shah N. Learning effective treatment pathways for type-2 diabetes from a clinical data warehouse. *AMIA Annual Symposium Proceedings*. 2016;**2016**:2036–2042.
6. Sotiriou C, Neo SY, McShane LM, et al. Breast cancer classification and prognosis based on gene expression profiles from a population-based study. *Proceedings of the National Academy of Sciences U S A*. 2003;**100**:10393–10398.
7. Ryan Poplin AVV, Blumer K, Liu Y. Webster prediction of cardiovascular risk factors from retinal fundus photographs via deep learning. *Nature Biomedical Engineering*. 2018;**2**:158–164.
8. Yu KH, Zhang C, Berry GJ, et al. Predicting non-small cell lung cancer prognosis by fully automated microscopic pathology image features. *Nature Communications*. 2016;**7**:12474.
9. Al'Aref SJ, Anchouche K, Singh G, et al. Clinical applications of machine learning in cardiovascular disease and its relevance to cardiac imaging. *European Heart Journal*. 2018;**40**(24)1975–1986.
10. Yeung S, Downing NL, Fei-Fei L and Milstein A. Bedside computer vision - moving artificial intelligence from driver assistance to patient safety. *New England Journal of Medicine*. 2018;**378**:1271–1273.
11. Emanuel EJ, Wachter RM. Artificial intelligence in health care: will the value match the hype?. *JAMA*. 2019 Jun 18;**321**(23):2281–2282.

12. Shah NH, Milstein A, Bagley SC. Making machine learning models clinically useful. *JAMA*. 2019 Oct 8;**322**(14):1351–1352.
13. Russell, A, Sutherland S, and Scheinker D. *Operationalizing Risk Prediction Algorithms in Healthcare Settings*. INFORMS Healthcare, Cambridge, MA. 2019.
14. Reddy, A and Scheinker, D., 2020. The case for mathematical optimization in health care: building a strong foundation for artificial intelligence. Health Affairs blog.
15. Lin SY, Shanafelt TD and Asch SM. Reimagining clinical documentation with artificial intelligence. *Mayo Clinic Proceedings*. 2018;**93**:563–565.
16. Longhurst CA, Harrington RA and Shah NH. A "green button" for using aggregate patient data at the point of care. *Health Affairs (Millwood)*. 2014;**33**:1229–1235.
17. Scheinker D, Ward A, Shin AY, et al. Differences in central line–associated bloodstream infection rates based on the criteria used to count central line days. *JAMA*. 2020;**323**(2):183–185.
18. Castelvecchi D. Can we open the black box of AI? *Nature*. 2016;**538**:20–23.
19. Zou J and Schiebinger, L. AI can be sexist and racist – it's time to make it fair. *Nature*; 2018;**559**(7714):324–326.
20. Obermeyer Z, Powers B, Vogeli C and Mullainathan S. Dissecting racial bias in an algorithm used to manage the health of populations. *Science*. 2019;**366** (6464):447–453.

Printed in the United States
by Baker & Taylor Publisher Services